Laurence Sterne in France

Continuum Reception Studies

The Reception of Blake in the Orient
Edited by Steve Clark and Masashi Suzuki

The Reception of Jane Austen and Walter Scott
by Annika Bautz

The International Reception of T. S. Eliot
Edited by Elisabeth Däumer and Shyamal Bagchee

Forthcoming volumes include:

The International Reception of Emily Dickinson
Edited by Domhnall Mitchell and Maria Stuart

The International Reception of Samuel Beckett
Edited by Matthew Feldman and Mark Nixon

The Reception of Wordsworth in Nineteenth-Century Germany
by John Williams

Writers Reading Shakespeare
by William Baker

Laurence Sterne
in France

Lana Asfour

Continuum
The Tower Building
11 York Road
London SE1 7NX

80 Maiden Lane, Suite 704
New York
NY 10038

www.continuumbooks.com

© Lana Asfour 2008

All rights reserved. No part of this publication may be reproduced or transmitted in any form or by any means, electronic or mechanical, including photocopying, recording, or any information storage or retrieval system, without prior permission in writing from the publishers.

Lana Asfour has asserted her right under the Copyright, Designs and Patents Act, 1988, to be identified as Author of this work.

British Library Cataloging-in-Publication Data
A catalogue record for this book is available from the British Library.

ISBN: 978-0-8264-9542-6

Library of Congress Cataloging-in-Publication Data
A catalog record for this book is available from the Library of Congress.

Typeset by YHT Ltd, London
Printed and bound in Great Britain by Biddles Ltd, King's Lyn, Norfolk

For Mona
and in memory of Emile

Acknowledgements

Many thanks to Fiona Stafford and Anthony Pilkington for their guidance and encouragement throughout the early stages of my research and writing. I am also indebted to Peter de Voogd, Alain Viala and Elinor Shaffer for their insights and comments on an earlier version of this book and a related essay. To the following people I would like to express special thanks: Matthew Scott read the manuscript and was generous with his time and attention; Will McMorran, Paul Williamson and James Bickford-Smith made helpful comments on individual chapters and Mona Asfour was supportive in innumerable ways. Julia Monkman and the late Kenneth Monkman must be mentioned for their hospitality when I consulted the library of Shandy Hall in Coxwold. Finally, I am grateful to New College and the Faculty of Medieval and Modern Languages at Oxford University for funding several trips to carry out research at the Bibliothèque de l'Arsenal and the Bibliothèque Nationale de France and to the Oxford-Paris programme scholarship, which permitted me to spend a year at the École Normale Supérieure.

Contents

Acknowledgements	vii
List of Abbreviations	xi
Note on Spelling, Grammar and Citations	xiii
Introduction	1

Part I *Criticism*

1	Familiar Categories: Early Reviews of *Tristram Shandy*, 1760–77	11
2	New Critical Expressions: The Later Reviews, 1776–86	29

Part II *Translations*

3	Theories of Translation and the English Novel, 1740–1800	51
4	The Translations of *Tristram Shandy*	63

Part III *Fiction*

5	Sentimental Journeys	87
6	*Tristram Shandy* and *Jacques le fataliste*	109
Appendix	Articles on Sterne in French Periodicals, 1760–1800	127
Notes		133
Bibliography		161
Index		179

List of Abbreviations

AL	*Année littéraire* (1754–76; 1776–91)
DPLP	*La Décade philosophique, littéraire et politique* (1784–1804)
Encyclopédie	*Encyclopédie, ou Dictionnaire raisonné des sciences, des arts et des métiers*, ed. by Diderot and D'Alembert, 17 vols (Paris: Biasson, David, Le Breton, Durand and Neufchâtel: Samuel Faulche, 1751–65)
GLE	*Gazette littéraire de l'Europe* (1764–84)
JA	*Journal anglais* (1775–8)
JE	*Journal encyclopédique* (1756–94)
JF	Denis Diderot, *Jaques le fataliste et son maitre*, ed. by Simone Lecointre and Jean Le Galliot (Geneva: Droz, 1976). 'Jaques' is modernized to 'Jacques' throughout.
JP	*Journal de Paris* (1777–1840)
JPL	*Journal de politique et de littérature* (1774–8)
Letters	Curtis, Lewis Perry, ed., *Letters of Laurence Sterne* (Oxford: Clarendon Press, 1935)
ME	*Magasin encyclopédique* (1792–1816)
MF	*Mercure de France* (1724–78; 1778–91)
SJ	Laurence Sterne, *A Sentimental Journey through France and Italy by Mr. Yorick*, ed. by Gardner D. Stout, Jr (Berkeley: University of California Press, 1967)
Supplément	*Encyclopédie: Supplément*, 4 vols (Paris: Panckoucke, Stoupe, Brunet and Amsterdam: Rey, 1776–7)
TS	*The Life and Opinions of Tristram Shandy, Gentleman* (see below)
Works	*The Florida Edition of the Works of Laurence Sterne*, ed. by Melvyn New and others (Florida: The University Presses of Florida, 1978–). All references give volume and page numbers. In the case of citations from *The Life and Opinions of Tristram Shandy, Gentleman* (Volumes I to III of the Florida edition), the reference will be followed by the abbreviation *TS*, with the volume and chapter numbers of *Tristram Shandy* (any edition). Volumes IV and V contain the *Sermons* and their *Notes*, and Volume VI, *A Sentimental Journey* and *The Brahmine's Journal*.

Note on Spelling, Grammar and Citations

Original spelling has been maintained in all quotations from eighteenth-century texts, even when there are variations, spelling mistakes or typographical errors. I have used *sic* very rarely in order to keep the text as clear as possible.

Dashes and points of suspension in eighteenth-century texts have been standardized in quotations. Wider-spaced suspension points in square brackets are my own and indicate a break in the quotation.

In endnotes, first citations of French translations of English works are listed under the English author's name. Subsequent endnote citations are abbreviated and listed under the translator's name.

For all generalizing usage of 'he', 'him', 'himself', and 'his', please read 'he or she', 'him or her', 'himself or herself', and 'his or her'.

Introduction

A Parisian commuter alighting from the Line 14 train onto the platform of the Bibliothèque Nationale François Mitterand metro station risks stepping on Lawrence [*sic*] Sterne's misspelt name. A quotation from *A Sentimental Journey* translated into French appears on a small round plaque: 'sauf que ses cheveux retombaient épars, alors qu'autrefois ils étaient roulés dans un filet de soie'. Taken from the scene in which he visits Maria, Yorick is comparing her appearance to the description of her by his 'friend' Tristram, who had written of his meeting with Maria in Volume IX of *Tristram Shandy*. The half-sentence, which evokes nothing more than a change in the young woman's hairstyle, suggesting her changed state of mind, appears among other small brass plaques dotted around the floor and walls of the station bearing quotations from writers of all ages and nations, including Dante, Herodotus, Montaigne, Nefer-Seshem-Rê, Walter Benjamin, Jean-Jacques Rousseau, Pasternak, William Burroughs, Paul Valéry, the unknown author of a Homeric hymn to Pan, Gérard de Nerval and Lewis Carroll. If the decision to include Sterne was based on the simple recognition of a writer who has attained the status of a classic both in his country and abroad, it is also testament to his long-standing connection with France.

Since their publication in English and their earliest translations into French, *The Life and Opinions of Tristram Shandy, Gentleman* and *A Sentimental Journey through France and Italy* have been held in special regard in France, indeed close to the nation's cultural heart. Critical interest in self-conscious and fragmentary works of fiction has refocused attention on them, and since the 1970s both have been set texts on the syllabus of the English Language and Literature *agrégation*, the most prestigious of all French examinations. But there is also a long history to the relationship between Sterne's work and French literary culture that can further contribute both to fruitful contemporary readings of Sterne and to Anglo-French literary studies.

This book explores the French reception of *Tristram Shandy* and *A Sentimental Journey* in the period 1760 to 1800. Both crossed the Channel very quickly after publication in Britain and met with a mixed reception: early French readers were far from naïve admirers of Sterne's famously original work, but actively engaged with it, and with each other, in their discussions of it. This engagement took place within the context of contemporary upheaval in France's literary, social and political landscape. During the seventeenth and early eighteenth centuries, French culture had been undisputed in its supremacy. French was spoken in every European court and French literature provided a model of classical elegance and national self-expression. Louis XIV had centralized authority within France, consolidated political power in Europe and acquired colonial territories further afield.[1] From the early to mid-eighteenth century, however, the balance began to tip as Britain was forged as a nation and established as a formidable power through a series of wars with France.[2] Not only were French colonies invaded by British forces, but France herself saw an influx of British tourists, foods, fashions, landscape gardening and English fiction.[3] The rise in British political and economic power was accompanied by a rich and diverse literary culture. Voltaire's *Lettres philosophiques* (1734) and Prévost's journal *Le Pour et contre* (1733–40) fuelled interest in English literature and philosophy, while the taste for novels largely engendered by the theories and practices of Duclos, Marivaux, Prévost and Crébillon fils during the 1730s led, in the mid-century, to some extremely popular translations of English novels, including La Place's *Tom Jones* and Prévost's *Clarisse*.[4]

Among the British writers who were translated into French, Sterne was undoubtedly one of the most interesting and controversial cases, not least because there was little consensus about how to classify his work. This remained true in later periods, and Sterne's well-known reply to his American admirer, Dr John Eustace, on receiving his gift of a Shandean walking stick, has proved apt:

> Your walking stick is in no sense more *shandaic* than in that of its having more handles than one – The parallel breaks only in this, that in using the stick, every one will take the handle which suits his convenience. In *Tristram Shandy*, the handle is taken which suits their passions, their ignorance or sensibility.[5]

Interpretations of Sterne's work since this letter was written have been extremely diverse. Samuel Johnson summarily dismissed *Tristram Shandy* as too odd to last, implying that it was merely fashionable.[6] Coleridge, while censuring Sterne's 'knowingness', nevertheless appreciated Sterne's 'humoristic universality' and declared that his digressiveness was 'the *very form* of his genius'.[7] The German Romantics found irony in Tristram's confrontation with the impossibility of representation.[8] Thackeray expressed Victorian impatience with Sterne's tittering sentimentalism and less than exemplary moral behaviour.[9] Nietzsche saw Sterne as a master of ambiguity,[10] and Virginia Woolf's modernist rehabilitation of *A Sentimental Journey* revealed more about her own stream-of-consciousness style than about Sterne's writing.[11]

Since the turn of the twentieth century, interpretations have broadly tended to fall into two camps. The first, with its origins in Russian formalism, emphasizes Sterne's formal novelistic qualities and regards his work as a subversion of the techniques of realist representation. Viktor Shklovsky's 1921 view of *Tristram Shandy* as 'the most typical novel in world literature' because it 'lays bare' the traditional or familiar devices of realism (in this case, autobiographical novel) brought Sterne into the limelight for critical theory.[12] The work of Mikhail Bakhtin has been immensely important for the study of Sterne's novels. His concepts of dialogism and the carnivalesque have been instrumental in associating Sterne with the subversive nature of modern novelistic discourse, whose origins lie in Menippean satire. For Bakhtin, the legacy of Rabelais, whose carnivalesque narrative constitutes a joyous, corporeal subversion of the dominant ideology, continues into the modern novel, in part through the example and influence of *Tristram Shandy*, with its plurality of voices and discourses.[13]

In Britain, meanwhile, John Traugott emphasized Locke as the main influence and target for *Tristram Shandy*'s philosophical and rhetorical parody. Sterne's extreme scepticism destroyed all philosophical systems, while faith and meaning lay in his sentimentalism. The formalistic appreciation of Sterne sits alongside a reading of his work that examines his literary and intellectual influences. Heralded by Melvyn New's *Laurence Sterne as Satirist*,[14] continued by the meticulous research of several scholars, and exemplified by New's Florida edition, this type of criticism traces Sterne's kinship with earlier comic, satiric and scholastic forms of writing. D. W. Jefferson placed Sterne within a tradition of 'learned wit' which includes Rabelais, Erasmus and Montaigne.[15] Wayne C. Booth compared the use of the self-conscious narrator in Sterne with that of earlier writers of comic fiction,[16] and Michael Seidel considered Sterne within a tradition of satire.[17] J. T. Parnell has focused on Sterne's place in a fideistic tradition alongside Erasmus, Rabelais, Montaigne, Charron, More, Burton, Swift and the Scriblerians: rather than a modernist radical scepticism or a relativism that resembles Bakhtin's carnivalesque, Sterne expresses a conservative Christian scepticism that allies fideism with Menippean form.[18] Most recently, Thomas Keymer has charted a middle ground which acknowledges Sterne's indebtedness to older sources while also identifying his engagement with contemporary narrative fiction, including that of Fielding, Richardson and the popular novels and romances of the 1740s and 1750s.[19] Sterne, according to Keymer, often applied the parodic techniques of older traditions to contemporary concerns with literary fiction, while other novelists such as Richardson and Fielding were, themselves, also experimenting with representation in different ways. Keymer identifies Sterne's playful, parodic and allusive uses of both older and contemporary sources and influences, highlighting the interplay between Sterne's work and the contemporary culture out of which it grew and into which it was received.

These broadly distinguished tendencies overlap with developments in critical debates about the genre of the novel and its origins. If the common Anglo-American idea that the novel was born in eighteenth-century Britain downplays the enormous influence of earlier French and European narrative fiction (with the possible exception of *Don Quixote*) on novelists such as Defoe, Fielding and Richardson,[20] French criticism, on the other hand, has long acknowledged the influence of the English novel in mid-eighteenth-century France, and has placed the French novel within wider contexts and traditions, such as medieval chivalric romance, Italian *novella*, and Spanish *novela* and picaresque.[21] Some Anglophone criticism has begun to do the same by recognizing the influences on the English novel of different cultures and historical periods, including seventeenth-century French romances and comic novels, European, Arab and 'Oriental' narrative forms, and ancient Greek and Roman prose fiction and satire.[22] Such a perspective on the roots and influences of the modern novel also challenges the distinction between 'novel' and 'romance', which reasserts the Anglocentric view of the novel as dissociable from the rise of the eighteenth-century Protestant middle classes. The distinction no longer exists in French; it was made frequently during the 1660s when a new, shorter kind of novel, the *nouvelle*, exemplified by the works of Madame de Lafayette, became more popular than the long *roman*, but this was not a clear or absolute distinction.[23] A less restricted notion of the novel would allow consideration of *Tristram Shandy* and *A Sentimental Journey* as novels that grow out of the contemporary eighteenth-century culture, and as texts whose richness spans earlier periods and very different types of narrative.

Close examination of Sterne's earliest reception in France will show us that it is simplistic to see his work only as a continuation of an older comic-satiric tradition or to claim that his primary concern was the subversion of realistic techniques of representation that had not been established but were in fact experimental and fluid. Early French readers, critics and writers could not have read Sterne through the Romantic, realist, modernist and postmodernist lenses which inevitably influence our interpretations today. Instead, they reveal some of the more immediate concerns within Sterne's writing which are not necessarily considered today, such as his own preoccupation with France and with his French readers. They also both place him within an older 'learned wit' tradition and respond to his sentimental and novelistic qualities. At the same time, French interpretations of Sterne's work in criticism, translations and fiction reveal an engagement with some of the most pressing questions in late eighteenth-century French literary culture, precisely because ideas of national aesthetic taste, theories of translation, attitudes towards genre and the novel, and conceptions of originality and the imagination were in the process of changing.

Sterne's early critical reception in Britain has been the subject of some interest. Alan B. Howes's *Yorick and the Critics: Sterne's Reputation in England, 1760–1868* provides an overview, as does *Sterne: The Critical Heritage*, which also includes some coverage of Sterne's European, Russian and American reception.[24] In a short booklet, *Shandyism and Sentiment*, J. C. T. Oates describes the English imitations of Sterne's work that he collected for Cambridge University Library, and there is a useful series of volumes entitled *Sterneiana*, which contains facsimile reprints of early English imitations, spurious 'continuations' and parodies.[25] On the subject of Sterne's reception in various countries, there have been several articles in *The Shandean*,[26] and two recent full-length studies, Alain Montandon's book on Sterne in Germany and Neil Stewart's on Sterne in Russia.[27] Taking a Bakhtinian approach to Sterne's poetics, Stewart discusses his influence on Pushkin, Gogol, Radishchev and Karamzin among others. In Germany, meanwhile, Sterne influenced some of the major Romantic writers and inspired a popular cult. Montandon looks not only at directly imitative works but also at texts that are more loosely indebted to Sterne, and shows that he influenced German writing during the late eighteenth and early nineteenth centuries, when Germany needed to look externally in its struggle to define a national literature.

These works highlight the lack of a recent book-length study on Sterne's reception in France. While much has been written on the subject of France in Sterne, particularly in relation to *A Sentimental Journey* and Volume VII of *Tristram Shandy*, there has been comparatively little new work on Sterne in France. Francis Brown Barton's 1911 *Etude sur l'influence de Sterne en France au dix-huitième siècle* identified many imitations but his approach is far from satisfactory: Sterne is seen to act upon the French tradition as if it were a stable, fixed and easily described entity, and a biased notion of literary history permeates Barton's argument that Sterne's early French readers liked but misunderstood his work, and produced poor translations and imitations of it.[28] Consequently, he regards *Tristram Shandy* and *A Sentimental Journey* as untouchable, superior originals and does not attempt to examine the reception process itself. These decisions proved influential. Philippe Van Tieghem's *Les Influences étrangères sur la littérature française 1550–1880*,[29] F. C. Green's *Minuet: A Critical Survey of French and English Literary Ideas in the Eighteenth Century*[30] and Harold Wade Streeter's *The Eighteenth-Century English Novel in French Translation: A Bibliographical Study*[31] all contain sections on Sterne in France, but accept Barton's assumptions and conclusions without contributing further insights. Alice Green Fredman's *Sterne and Diderot* looks at similarities between the two writers, but disappointingly attributes them to coincidence, independently similar ideas and 'common readings and sympathies'.[32] There is clearly a need to re-examine the subject, a process which has begun with the publication of *The Reception of Laurence Sterne in Europe*, a collection of essays by a group of international contributors, which includes my own chapter on Sterne's early French reception, and Anne Bandry's more bibliographical chapter on Sterne in nineteenth and twentieth-century France.[33]

While this book takes an empirical approach to Sterne's early reception in France, it is nevertheless also informed by reception theory, and makes use of some of the concepts and terms expounded in Hans Robert Jauss's essay 'Literary History as a Challenge to Literary Theory'.[34] Jauss critiques the 'classical concept of tradition', which is driven by a series of intentioned authors and individual works standing one after the other, unconnected and construed teleologically. He proposes instead a 'dynamic principle of literary evolution', in which literature is considered both aesthetically and historically through the study of its understanding by contemporary and later readers, critics and writers:

the quality and rank of a literary work result neither from the biographical or historical conditions of its origin [*Entstehung*], nor from its place in the sequence of the development of a genre alone, but rather from the criteria of influence, reception, and posthumous fame, criteria that are more difficult to grasp.[35]

Jauss refers to the ways in which a text is judged and gains its status. It is never untouchable and its meaning and quality change over time. Thus the early reception of *Tristram Shandy* and *A Sentimental Journey* in France is part of their history as well as part of the receiving culture's, and offers today's readers a more complete picture that can contribute to the significance and interpretation of the works themselves. There will be frequent discussion of *Tristram Shandy* and *A Sentimental Journey* throughout this book, for purposes of comparison, to point out the ways in which they were read and interpreted in France, and to offer new perspectives on them in light of key interpretations by writers and thinkers as varied as Diderot, Voltaire, Jean-Baptiste Suard and Julie de Lespinasse.

Jauss's notion of the 'horizon of expectations' permits me to take into consideration the vitality of the receiving culture and to identify the different features that were already driving and shaping it. French literary culture during the eighteenth century was far from stable or uniform, and consisted of coexisting, frequently contrasting, tendencies, into which Sterne was partly integrated in a variety of ways, and from which he was also partly rejected. His work presented a challenge to French readers with expectations drawn from their other readings, but some aspects of it were absorbed into existing trends and familiar categories:

The historical context in which a literary work appears is not a factical, independent series of events that exists apart from an observer [...] The coherence of literature as an event is primarily mediated in the horizon of expectations of the literary experience of contemporary and later readers, critics, and authors. Whether it is possible to comprehend and represent the history of literature in its unique historicity depends on whether this horizon of expectations can be objectified [...] An objectifiable system of expectations [...] arises for each work in the historical moment of its appearance, from a pre-understanding of the genre, from the form and themes of already familiar works, and from the opposition between poetic and practical language.[36]

The idea of a 'pre-understanding' is problematic for the novel, which was a developing genre during this period. One can more easily speak of a 'pre-understanding' in reference to older, more established and canonical genres, such as epic or tragedy, for which there were many thematic and formal conventions that had withstood the test of time. While we speak of *Tristram Shandy* and *A Sentimental Journey* as 'novels' today, and while I use the term freely, they were not clearly perceived as such by eighteenth-century readers, for whom there existed many different types of narrative prose. The development of the novel will therefore be a key point of discussion, as will ideas of 'originality', which were also being debated. Although there were many expectations regarding prose fiction, these were mobile, depended on subcategories of prose fiction, and cannot be said to constitute a 'pre-understanding'. Sterne's reception is interesting precisely because there was little unanimity about how to categorize his work.

For Jauss, the horizon of expectations of any given set of readers is identifiable, or 'objectifiable', when the latter brings to its reading of a particular work standards and expectations developed from its reading of other works. Of course, this horizon of expectations can never be fully known or articulated, but it is possible to look at significant points at which Sterne's work was read against standards and expectations held by critics, translators, readers and writers, and derived from forms of writing familiar to them, such as comic, satiric, picaresque and sentimental fiction. From this we can detail the ways in which Sterne's work was absorbed by or excluded from the recipient culture and, consequently, establish how it might have modified expectations and the cultural tradition itself.

The aim of this book is therefore twofold. First, it describes French literary culture between 1760 and 1800 through its responses to and interaction with Sterne and his fiction. This constitutes what may be considered to be an objectification of French readers' horizon of expectations, since the focus is on identifying and analysing the expectations according to which Sterne was interpreted. Second, it reads Sterne in light of early French interpretations. These two processes occur simultaneously in all sections of the book. Part I looks at critical responses, with close readings of articles and reviews of Sterne's work within the context of eighteenth-century critical debates and ideas about genre, originality, the imagination, literary celebrity, Englishness and sentiment. The discussion then moves, in Part II, to the texts themselves – the French translations – which were the primary texts for many French readers. The translators' choices, changes, omissions and substitutions tell us about their aesthetic and moral attitudes towards the English original, and disclose an engagement with contemporary discussions about translation and national aesthetic taste. Finally, in Part III, we turn outwards to look at reception in the widest sense, with readings of fictional texts that are imitative of *A Sentimental Journey* and *Tristram Shandy*. The first focus of attention is on the moral and ideological aspects of sensibility, since *A Sentimental Journey* was frequently exploited for political ends, and its reception merged with popular interpretations of Rousseau's sentimentalism. The second focal point is the relationship between *Tristram Shandy* and Diderot's *Jacques le fataliste et son maître*, now regarded as a great work of French, European and even world literature. The two novels are linked, I will suggest, through their use of self-conscious narrative devices and a playful conception of literary imitation. 1760 is my chosen starting point because it saw the publication of the first French review of *Tristram Shandy*, marking the beginning of a French critical debate about Sterne's work. The terminus of 1800 permits the incorporation of the important translations of *Tristram Shandy* in the 1770s and 1780s, the imitations of *A Sentimental Journey* that appeared during the 1780s and 1790s, and the publication in 1796 of *Jacques le fataliste et son maître*.[37]

Part I

Criticism

Chapter 1

Familiar Categories: Early Reviews of *Tristram Shandy*, 1760–77

J. T. Parnell has rightly warned that we should not view *Tristram Shandy* as a modern subversion of an English Augustan neoclassicism that did not actually exist.[1] He roots it instead within a fideistic scepticism and challenges the idea that Sterne was critiquing the representational methods of the emerging novel genre. Eighteenth-century French culture was no less permeated by the European Christian sceptical tradition to which Parnell linked Sterne and Swift, and we should not interpret early critical responses to Sterne in France simplistically by claiming that his work contributed to the breakdown of a variously defined classicism. The early reviews nevertheless do refer to a classical critical tradition, in some cases even echoing particular ideas of representation, genre and style that had been expressed and codified in the works of seventeenth-century theorists and which continued to be upheld during the eighteenth century. Any work that obtains popular and critical success inevitably challenges and can even redefine expectations. *Tristram Shandy* attracted, fuelled and fed into wider critical debates concerning artistic representation, literary taste and the nature of literary originality during a period of upheaval in ideas about art that we identify today with the shift from Classicism to Romanticism. Whether in art and literature through the 'Querelle des Anciens et des Modernes' and its revisitations throughout the eighteenth century, or in music with the mid-century 'Querelle des Bouffons', questions of representation, taste and beauty were debated by writers, *philosophes* and an increasingly literate public. These public debates have been seen as symptomatic of the rupture with classicism, since they raised questions about the rational foundations of the rules of poetics, and paved the way for a modern conception of art.[2] In such a context, Sterne played a substantial role thanks to the overwhelming perception of *A Sentimental Journey* and *Tristram Shandy* as 'original'. Initially, *Tristram Shandy* was interpreted and judged through familiar and classical categories, which is also the reason why it was immediately placed within a tradition of literary works that satirized and parodied the 'serious' genres.

Sterne's critical reception took place in the periodical press, through which intellectual discussions were eagerly followed by the public. René Wellek has pointed out that for centuries criticism repeated or referred to the views of Aristotle and Horace while literature itself underwent profound revolutions.[3] Criticism nevertheless constitutes a significant mode of literary reception, and since Gerard Genette, previously neglected sources such as articles, reviews, announcements, synopses, extracts and letters have come to be recognized as important 'paratexts'.[4] They reveal the significance of Sterne's work to its readers during the period and, in turn, permit a fuller, contemporary understanding of the work itself. Throughout Part I (Chapters 1 and 2), these texts are read closely and discussed in relation to wider aesthetic concerns that press upon interpretations of Sterne's work. Rather than being subjected to a falsely coherent structure, the articles themselves will provide points of departure to guide my discussion. Clear patterns do, however, emerge, and these will be explored within the various subsections and as they overlap with each other. Chapter 1 addresses classical assumptions about unity and genre, particularly as they relate to comic, satiric and burlesque forms of writing. It focuses on the reviews of the 1760s, which announced the publication of each instalment of *Tristram Shandy* in England, and on Voltaire's 1777 critique of *Tristram Shandy*. Chapter 2 studies articles from 1776 to the mid-1780s, in which interpretations of *Tristram Shandy* and *A Sentimental Journey* were informed by attitudes towards the novel, sentimentalism and ideas of national identity and national literary taste. Both chapters focus on changing conceptions of originality. Before turning to the articles, there follows a brief description of the journals in which they appeared.

The Periodicals

Reviews of Sterne were published in what Jack Censer has called the 'literary-philosophical press' or the 'discussion papers', as opposed to the political press and the *affiches*, or commercial press.[5] This covered a wide range of subjects, including the sciences, philosophy, geography, history, literature, fine art and music. Many periodicals professed a cosmopolitan attitude and a desire to play an important role in the diffusion of foreign, and particularly English, literature. Most of the articles on Sterne focused on *Tristram Shandy*, which inspired more controversy than *A Sentimental Journey*. The latter was also reviewed, though slightly less frequently, and there were a few articles on the *Letters*, the *Journal to Eliza* and the *Sermons*. Sterne's work was announced, reviewed and discussed in some of the most popular and widely distributed periodicals of the eighteenth century, and articles usually appeared in response to recently published translations and new editions.[6]

Of the smaller periodicals, the long-lived *Journal de Paris* (1777–1840) published a review of Sterne's *Sermons* in 1785. The first French daily newspaper, it was founded by a group of *bourgeois* who supported the *philosophes* and *encyclopédistes*. It contained general information and, during the second half of the eighteenth century, more literary than political news. The *Journal anglais* (1775–8), by contrast, was a short-lived, fortnightly periodical which aimed to disseminate political, scientific and literary news about England and her colonies.[7] It printed two articles on Sterne in 1775, the only journal to do so in a year that did not see the publication of any new translations of his work. The first announced the English publication of his letters, and the second was a French translation of the story of Slawkenbergius from *Tristram Shandy*.

Sterne's work was more regularly covered by widely distributed journals, such as the *Mercure de France*, the *Gazette littéraire de l'Europe*, the *Année littéraire* and the *Journal encyclopédique*. The *Mercure de France* (1724–91) was the continuation of the *Mercure galant*, the seventeenth-century newspaper patronized by the government. In 1778, in the middle of a period during which most of its articles on Sterne were printed, it was absorbed into Charles-Joseph Panckoucke's newspaper monopoly. Panckoucke already held government *privilèges* for three other periodicals: the *Journal historique et politique*, a rival to the *Journal encyclopédique*; the *Gazette de France*, which had been the government's official political paper and was also granted by the government to Panckoucke in 1778; and the *Journal de politique et de literature* (also known as the *Journal de Bruxelles*), which published an article by Voltaire on Sterne in 1777 and merged with the *Mercure de France* in 1778. Although it supported the *philosophes*, the *Mercure de France*'s enlightened comments were indirect and cautious rather than polemical. Its readership was varied, mainly bourgeois, with a comparatively high number of women.[8] Its coverage of Sterne was regular: it reviewed Frénais's translation of *A Sentimental Journey* in 1769 and the translations of *Tristram Shandy* in 1777 and 1785 to 1786.

The *Gazette littéraire de l'Europe* (1764–6), which printed an article by Jean-Baptiste Antoine Suard on *Tristram Shandy* in 1765, was the continuation of the *Journal étranger* and, like the latter, sought to diffuse and interpret English literature. An important counterfeit was immediately published in Amsterdam and continued until 1784. The Parisian original was patronized by the foreign affairs minister, the Duc de Praslin, who facilitated the exchange of literary news with England. The French minister in England regularly sent the English *Monthly Review* and *Critical Review* to the editor, the Abbé Arnaud, and travelling diplomats took French journals to England. This diplomatic system explains the rapid translation of Suard's article on *Tristram Shandy* in the *London Chronicle*.[9] It is interesting that the French article should have had so much influence, since French critics neither reprinted English reviews nor slavishly followed their judgements, though they frequently referred to Sterne's reception and celebrity in England.

The mainly literary *Année littéraire* (1754–91) was, along with its rival and ideological enemy the *Journal encyclopédique*, the most widely read periodical. Under the long editorship of Elie-Catherine Fréron, it professed to be the enemy of the *philosophes*, and fiercely criticized them in its characteristically polemical tone. It targeted their cosmopolitanism and their attacks on Christianity.[10] Fréron's own nationalism was manifest in his support for French rather than Italian music in the music debates, and in Chapter 3 we shall see that it was also evident in his ideas of literary translation. Yet despite his criticism of what he perceived to be an unquestioning fashion for foreign literature, the *Année littéraire*'s reviews of Sterne were analytical and generally positive.[11]

In contrast to the *Année littéraire*, the *Journal encyclopédique* (1756–93) propagated its pro-*philosophe*, Enlightenment ideas relatively freely because it was published at Bouillon, an autonomous region at the time.[12] Edited by Pierre Rousseau from 1759, it was self-financing and therefore managed to escape many of the controls imposed on French journals. Although liberal and opposed to clericalism, it did not go as far as expressing anti-religious or materialist ideas.[13] The content was extremely varied and contained a section on 'Nouvelles littéraires' dealing with European publications. During the second half of the eighteenth century, it printed some 82 announcements and book reviews of English fiction – more than any other journal apart from the *Année littéraire*. Most of these, including the articles on Sterne, appeared in the periods 1759 to 1771, and 1784 to 1798, which coincided with increased numbers of French translations of English works.[14] The *Journal encyclopédique* published a greater number of articles on Sterne than any other journal, announcing the English publication of *Tristram Shandy* and discussing all French translations of Sterne's work as they were published. It attempted to be consistent in its approach, though there are marked differences of perspective separating earlier and later articles on Sterne.[15]

While there were political and ideological differences among the periodicals, all the critics dealt with the same issues when writing about Sterne. The different editorial attitudes of each periodical were neither directly related to their aesthetic ideas, nor to individual critics' opinions of particular authors.[16] Critics even referred to each other, creating critical dialogues. Their discussions of Sterne took place around the notion of originality, and all the articles, irrespective of the periodical, identified and remarked upon this quality in his work.

'Le monstre d'Horace': *Tristram Shandy* and French Classicism

René Bray showed that French classicism was not born suddenly in 1660, but that it developed slowly from the humanist rediscovery of Aristotle's *Ars Poetica* in Italy during the early sixteenth century.[17] With Boileau and other theorists of the mid-seventeenth century, classicism was 'formed', in the sense Bray speaks of, as a doctrine: principles were identified through the observation of Greek, Roman and seventeenth-century French masterpieces and these, in turn, became prescriptive rules to guide writers, particularly between 1660 and 1680. The main principle was that of *mimesis*, with theorists recommending the imitation of ancient models and of nature – or rather of *la belle nature*, an idealized and perfected nature. Imitation was governed by the rules of verisimilitude (*la vraisemblance*) and decorum (*les bienséances*). Horace was also an important source; with his belief in unity, propriety and technical perfection, he furnished French classicists, particularly Boileau, with a model for their own conceptions of taste (*goût*) and reasonable elegance. His influence is also apparent in the idea of the moral utility of art, the distinction between genres and the importance of natural genius, which was thought to be essential, but not enough by itself: art and poetry had to conform to reason, and hence to the rational principles and rules of composition.

The tendency to take such rules to an extreme would be criticized throughout the eighteenth century, as we shall see in Chapter 2, and would eventually lead to questions about the principles of imitation itself.[18] Nevertheless, the general tenets of classicism continued to guide eighteenth-century theorists and critics and would even influence the development of the novel.[19] Nearly a century after Boileau, Batteux's frequently reprinted *Les Beaux-Arts réduits à un même principe* (1746) could still assert that the only principle of art was the imitation of *la belle nature*: 'pas le vrai qui est; mais le vrai qui peut être'.[20] Batteux integrated sentiment and the imagination into his conception of artistic composition, but considered them second to reason, insisted that genius should not overstep nature's limits and recommended the imitation of the *anciens*, who understood and correctly interpreted *la belle nature*.[21]

It is to a generalized, yet clearly accepted, classical tradition that the first French article on Sterne refers in its opening passage:

> C'est ici le monstre d'Horace. Des pensées morales, fines, délicates, saillantes, solides, fortes, impies, hazardées, téméraires: voici ce que l'on trouve dans cet Ouvrage. La liberté de penser y est portée à l'excès, & s'y présente avec tout le désordre qui l'accompagne ordinairement. L'Auteur n'a ni plan, ni principes, ni système: il ne veut que parler, et malheureusement on l'écoute avec plaisir. La vivacité de son imagination, le feu de ses portraits, le caractére de ses réfléxions, tout plaît, tout intéresse et tout séduit.[22]

Printed in 1760, it reviews Volumes I and II of the English *Tristram Shandy* and exemplifies the critical dilemma it provoked. The reviewer refers to the beginning of the *Ars Poetica* in which Horace says that if a painter placed a human head on a horse's neck, feathers on various animals' limbs and the top half of a beautiful woman on a fish-tail, one would merely laugh. Through the analogy with painting, Horace argues for unity in poetic works, which otherwise would be 'made up at random like a sick man's dreams'.[23] There are, rather, certain principles of representation, which include consistency, unity and propriety. There are also distinct genres, each of which has its own historical development, rules and sets of proprieties. *Tristram Shandy* is considered by this critic to be a violation of Horatian standards. The adjectives used to describe Sterne's thoughts suggest perplexity in the face of the text's variety and apparent inconsistency: the incongruous mixture of morality, delicacy and solidity with impiety, rashness and daring, must be as untrue to nature as a human head on a horse's body. The text's disorder and the excessive liberty of the author's thought suggest to the critic that it lacks structural principles altogether. Without technique keeping natural genius in check, Horace's poet is unconstrained, even mad: 'He's a man suffering from a nasty itch, or the jaundice, or fanaticism, or Diana's wrath'.[24] Boileau's *Art poétique* (1674), which was modelled on the *Ars poetica*, continued to influence critics during the eighteenth century. In its own poetic themes and structure, Boileau's 'essay' observes the precepts it formulates and recommends, and like his predecessor's, advises writers to follow reason and modify excess. Celebrating poetic genius, he nevertheless repeats that reason and *bon sens* are of prior importance. His own version of Horace's mad poet are those who are 'emportés d'une fougue insensée', and he sides with the Ancients in the belief that following reason meant following models and precedents, and against modern poets who refuse to entertain familiar ideas:

> Ils croiraient s'abaisser, dans leurs vers monstrueux,
> S'ils pensaient ce qu'un autre a pu penser comme eux.
> Evitons ces excès. Laissons à l'Italie
> De tous ces faux brillants l'éclatante folie.[25]

Instead of the *excès* he associates with Italian literature, Boileau recommends balance and proportion, so that each composition is a harmonious whole:

> Il faut que chaque chose y soit mise en son lieu;
> Que le début, la fin répondent au milieu;
> Que d'un art délicat les pièces assorties
> N'y forment qu'un seul tout de diverses parties;
> Que jamais du sujet le discours s'écartant
> N'aille chercher trop loin quelque mot éclatant.[26]

Tristram Shandy was clearly far removed from such a model. With his reference to Horace, Sterne's first French reviewer places himself within an established French classical tradition represented by critics from Boileau to Batteux.[27] As Horace's monster, *Tristram Shandy* embodied all that deviated from the rules: it was a motley mixture, without consistency, order or principles, and did not represent nature truthfully – or appropriately. Apparently a stranger to the classical heritage, *Tristram Shandy* might have been of little interest to a French critic.

Yet while identifying its monstrous excesses, this critic is fascinated by it and even takes pleasure in its very incongruity and lack of structure. The attraction he experiences is somewhat reluctant – 'malheureusement on l'écoute avec plaisir' – but the pleasure is real, and he appears to appreciate Sterne's imagination in a way that suggests a departure from the classical view of the imagination as secondary to reason.[28] Like the 'feu' of his portraits, Sterne's imagination is so vivid, in fact, that it 'seduces' the critic. He likes the text in spite of his reason and better judgement, and in spite of the critical tradition to which he adheres. The idea of excess is applied in particular to the author's voice, which is described as being out of control: 'C'est enfin ici que se trouve plus que partout ailleurs ce bavardage que les Latins expriment par *prurigo loquendi*.'[29] The word 'bavardage' refers to the lack of structure and the informality, in all senses, of the digressive narrative voice. The Latin phrase, meaning 'prurience of speaking', with its suggestion of sexual excess, links moral, thematic and structural transgression. The narrative is morally, as well as aesthetically, dangerous because it seduces the reader away from true structure.[30]

This perceptive critic is a positive, if hesitant, voice that marks the beginning of discussions about Sterne in the French periodical press. *Tristram Shandy* could not be judged by the familiar principles of unity, order and propriety, nor was it subject to clear generic distinctions. The critic has no doubt that Sterne's thoughts are inconsistent and incongruous and that his narrative voice exceeds the rules of decorum. But some aesthetic pleasure is derived from the banter, and the association with seduction offers the suggestion that the pleasure is illicit: Sterne's imagination leads the reader away from the standards normally used to judge a work.

Originalité

The lack of adherence to traditional principles, the excesses, transgressions, lack of restraint and unchecked imagination, are all characteristics of *Tristram Shandy*'s originality. Nearly all the articles comment on this quality, including the announcements of *Tristram Shandy*'s publication during the 1760s, the discussions of the first translation of *A Sentimental Journey* in 1769 and the reviews of the French *Tristram Shandy* in 1776 and 1785 to 1786. The adjective *original* and its related *singulier*, or the nouns *originalité* and *singularité* are used constantly in reference to Sterne's work. The *Journal encyclopédique* is the first periodical to do so:

> Cette nouvelle production [the *Sermons*] ne dement pas le caractere d'esprit & de gaieté, & *d'originalité*, s'il est permis de parler ainsi, qu'on a trouvé dans les autres ouvrages du même Auteur.[31]

The word *originalité* is placed in italics and qualified by the phrase 's'il est permis de parler ainsi', which suggests the novelty and unorthodoxy of its usage. But *original* and *singulier* quickly become inseparable from Sterne. The *Mercure de France* writes: 'il [Sterne] est fort connu par *la vie & les opinions de Tristram Shandy*, ouvrage singulier dont nous n'avons point d'exemple',[32] and the *Journal Anglais*: 'c'est [*Tristram Shandy*] un Roman écrit & conduit de la manière la plus originale'.[33] Later articles reveal that by the 1780s, this originality had become famous. 'Tout le monde connoît [...] l'originalité piquante qui caractérise les ouvrages de Sterne',[34] writes one critic, and another states as a matter of fact that 'l'Auteur du *Voyage Sentimental* est principalement connu par l'originalité de sa manière'.[35] The *Journal de Paris* even qualifies the concept of originality, which suggests that it was evolving. A distinction is made between natural and affected originality with the implication that the former is of higher merit: 'Un grand nombre de nos Lecteurs connoît *Sterne*, le *Rabelais* de l'Angleterre, & son *Voyage Sentimental*, & son *Tristram Shandy*, & son originalité souvent naturelle, par fois affectée'.[36] The term *originalité* is never precisely defined, but it is central to all the critical responses to Sterne's works, and its use, examined within the context of contemporary definitions of the term, is revelatory of the initial hesitation and subsequent popularity with which they were received.

During the seventeenth century, the adjective *original* was used interchangeably with *originel*, borrowed from the Latin *originalis*, that which comes from the origin or source. This was used particularly in religious contexts, as in *le péché originel*. In printing and the arts it could refer neutrally to a source text or to an edition or drawing which is the model from which copies could be made, a sort of prototype. In literary writing, *original* came to be used either as an adjective or a substantive for a source text, the opposite of lesser forms of writing such as literal copying or translation. With the seventeenth-century conception of art as the imitation of classical models such as Homer and Virgil, the *original* signified the imitated model, which was worthy of imitation and had literary value.[37] A work was considered *original* on its own terms if it did not adhere to literary models. This was unambiguously a pejorative use of the term and its synonyms were *bisarre* and *extravagant*. It represented the excess of individuality in a literary or artistic work, and its externality to the established rules of literary composition. However, the seventeenth century also saw a new idea become attached to the adjective *original*. Blaise Pascal is frequently identified as the first writer to use it in a different, more positive way.[38] From the late seventeenth century, it began to be used in the sense of *singulier*, or that which has its own identity, is expressed in its own manner and is derived from nothing else.[39]

But it is only during the eighteenth century that the term acquired its sense of uniqueness and came to represent something of value. At the same time, the derived noun, *originalité*, became more common.[40] During this period, both positive and pejorative meanings of the word *original* coexisted. The 1777 *Dictionnaire de l'Académie française* maintains a conservative understanding of the word. The first entry for *original* tells us that it describes a work of art, a thought, or a style which is not derived from a source or model. As a substantive, an *original* refers either to a work of art or to an official paper which has been copied, or to a person whose portrait has been painted, or, lastly, to an author 'qui excelle en quelque genre, sans être formé sur aucun modèle'. The example cited for the latter definition is 'Les Anciens sont d'excellents originaux'. This usage, as in the seventeenth century, implies the meaning of 'model', gives importance to the model and reasserts both the classical idea that art is the imitation of models, and the view that the ancient writers are superior and the only true originals. The *Encyclopédie*, by contrast, points out that *original* had both positive and negative significances. The first listed definition refers to a drawing that is used as a first copy or model. Under *originaux*, referring to written works, three meanings are listed: first, the authentic manuscripts of an author; second, texts which, though published, are identical to the author's authentic manuscripts; and third, texts that are unique because they have never been copied or reprinted. The word *original* also appears as an adjective in the *Encyclopédie* and refers only to the domain of painting, but this definition does not appear until the mid-eighteenth century:

> *Original* se dit encore d'un dessein, d'un tableau qu'un peintre fait d'imagination, de génie, quoique chacune de leurs parties soient copiées d'après nature. Peinture, tableau *original*, se prend en bonne & en mauvaise part; en bonne, lorsque dans un tableau tout y est grand, singulierement nouveau; & en mauvaise, lorsqu'on n'y rencontre qu'une singularité bisarrement grotesque.[41]

This definition spells out the tension within the concept of originality and its contrasting usages: the positive meaning includes the qualities of grandeur and novelty; the negative consists of the excesses of the positive, when singularity becomes 'bisarrement grotesque'. The *Encyclopédie* thus affirms the coexistence of both good and bad connotations around the middle of the eighteenth century and defines them in terms of degree: when the work of art is excessively original, it becomes bizarre and has no artistic value. The *Encyclopédie* also includes an article on the noun *originalité*, defined in grammatical terms as the manner of expression rather than as the content or subject of an artistic work. It is contrasted with servile copying, but still carries both positive and negative values:

> Originalité, (*Gramm.*) maniere d'exécuter une chose commune, d'une maniere singuliere & distinguée: l'*originalité* est très-rare. La plûpart des hommes ne font en tous genres, que des copies les uns des autres. Le titre d'*original* se donne en bonne & en mauvaise part.[42]

The word's ambiguity forms the basis of, and represents, Sterne's early reception in the French periodical press. On the one hand, originality was important and attractive: associated with novelty and genius, it was contrasted with mediocre works of art and literature that imitated greater works in a servile fashion. On the other hand, excessive originality was bad. The transgression of established standards and principles could lead to a negative judgement by French readers whose taste had been formed within a classical critical tradition. *Tristram Shandy*'s evident originality inevitably led to further questions that both reflected and engaged with wider discussions about the nature of artistic representation. Should originality be considered as an aesthetic value in a work of art? Is it always and necessarily a marginal element? The dilemma embodied in contemporary definitions of the word, which were both positive and negative, was inextricably related to concerns in eighteenth-century criticism that gave rise to modern aesthetics. The classical conception of art as the imitation of nature, or a perfected version of nature, was in the process of being superseded by the view of art as autonomous creation, with an emphasis on the artist's originality and a greater interest in the imagination.[43]

The Burlesque

After the first, ambiguous review of 1760, the *Journal encyclopédique* employed a narrower standard of judgement in a series of articles published from 1761 to 1767. These articles announced the English publication of Volumes III to IX of *Tristram Shandy* and were written before the volumes became available to a wider audience in translation, which may in part account for their conservative stance. While the 1760 critic allowed himself to be seduced, the author (or authors) of these articles retains a more stringent perspective which favours a moderate, elegant style of writing and clear generic distinctions based on recognized models and valued according to a hierarchy. Within such a classical frame of reference, *Tristram Shandy* is identified with the genres and styles of writing traditionally considered to be low: the comic, the satiric and the burlesque. Its originality is regarded with suspicion and the negative similes, *extravagance* and *bisarrerie*, are copiously employed to describe it. The cycle begins in no uncertain terms: 'on ne conçoit pas comment une pareille extravagance a pû avoir un si prodigieux succès.'[44]

The burlesque had lawless tendencies and was characterized by the transgression of the rules of verisimilitude and decorum. It did not even appear to have a moral purpose, like satire, which targeted vice and was at least a distinct genre, though a low one.[45] Seventeenth-century theorists, such as Guez de Balzac, Vaugelas, Pellisson, Chapelain and Boileau, attacked the mid-century vogue for the burlesque which was first inspired by Paul Scarron's *Virgile travesti* (1648). The burlesque encompassed a wide variety of works, both poetry and prose, and included not only works that parodied particular authors, such as Scarron's *Virgile*, d'Associe's *Ovid* and Brébeuf's *Lucain*, but also the more generically parodic *romans comiques* of Scarron, Sorel and Furetière – though Sorel himself distinguished between the comic and satiric on one hand, and the burlesque on the other.[46] From the Italian *burla*, meaning ridicule, mockery or joke, the burlesque in France has been identified variously as a genre or a style of writing. It has been applied very broadly to any work that ridicules its subject and inspires laughter and, more specifically, to writing that applies either a high epic style – whether modelled on a particular precursor or not – to low and ordinary things (often called 'parody' or 'mock-epic'), or a vulgar style to lofty subjects (also called 'travesty').[47] In the case of the *roman comique*, burlesque incongruities exposed the selective representational methods of the long heroic *romans* of Gomberville, La Calprenède, Desmarets, Scudéry and Mademoiselle de Scudéry, with their idealized characters and improbable plots.[48] Within the variety of works to which the term 'burlesque' has been and is applied, the common characteristic is incongruity, usually between style and theme.

The word *extravagance*, so frequently applied to Sterne, was commonly used to describe the burlesque. Boileau advised writers to avoid it. Its popularity indicated to him that Parnassus was being corrupted and he declared that it should be confined to the bouffon comedians of the Pont-Neuf.[49] In fact, he practised his own elevated form of burlesque in the mock-heroic poem *Le Lutrin* (1674–83), which depicted foolish clerical quarrels in heroic verse and inspired Pope's *The Rape of the Lock* (1712–14). Guez de Balzac's systematic attack on the burlesque, meanwhile, focused on its harm to French language and culture. For him, its archaisms, low language and incongruity between style and subject excluded it from the classical ideal: 'Manquant de l'Agreable et du Beau, elle employe l'Estrange et le Monstrueux'.[50]

Tristram Shandy, with its comic incongruities, parodic elements and suggestive language was quickly associated with the burlesque forms and *romans comiques* of the previous century. In the *Journal de politique et de littérature*, Voltaire explicitly linked Sterne with Scarron.[51] The *Journal encyclopédique* articles of the 1760s echo seventeenth-century attacks on the burlesque by dismissing *Tristram Shandy* on both formal and moral grounds, citing its vulgarity and lack of intellectual rigour:

> Parler à tort à travers, entasser bouffonneries sur bouffonneries, saletés sur saletés, répandre sur le tout un tour original et singulier: voilà tout le mérite de cette production.[52]

Its originality is regarded as a mere *tour* attempting to disguise the work's fundamental incoherence and indecency. It has no aesthetic value and is perceived in the negative sense of deviance.

The adjectives *extravagant* and *bisarre* recur in this series of articles: 'On trouve ici [Volumes V and VI] les mêmes allusions indécentes, les mêmes digressions ennuyeuses, les mêmes saillies extravagantes qui distinguent les volumes précédens',[53] while Volume IX is criticized for its 'indécence & [...] trivialité de pensées'.[54] Volumes VII and VIII are received with surprise: 'Nous ne concevons pas comment Mr. Sterne, bénéficier d'Yorck, a pu pousser si loin cette bisarre production',[55] and the burlesque incongruities of *Tristram Shandy* as a whole are noted: 'il [Sterne] mêle presque partout le sacré avec le profane; la Religion n'échappe pas à ses saillies. C'est en un mot, un bouffon très spirituel & très scandaleux'.[56]

Tristram Shandy's originality, characterized by incongruity, indecency and deviance, excluded it from the classical canon, and instead allowed it to become associated with the burlesque. It conformed neither to expectations of satire, which had the clear moral purpose of ridiculing vice within a framework of social criticism, nor to those of allegory, in which *bouffonneries* and aesthetic transgressions might serve the purpose of masking an underlying meaning:

> On avoit d'abord cru qu'il y avoit quelque allégorie; & à la fin du compte on n'y voit qu'un tas de boufonneries, d'extravagances & d'obscénités, qu'on ne passeroit pas à un Grenadier.[57]

Because the attempt to find rational significance behind the digressions, rude jokes and mixture of styles did not work and no clear allegory was discovered, the critic concluded that the text was 'le délire le plus complet de l'imagination', rather like a creation by Horace's mad poet. Jean-Baptiste Suard, one of the most eminent journalists of his day, was also disappointed not to discover a hidden meaning.[58] He even describes Sterne's originality and the serial publication of *Tristram Shandy* as a confidence trick:

> Ces deux Tomes piquerent la curiosité des Lecteurs; on cru y voir une satyre fine et gaie où le sage se cachoit sous le masque de la folie. Le Sage a publié quatre autres Volumes qu'on a lus avec avidité, et on a été surpris de n'y rien comprendre. Les Lecteurs attendoient toujours quelque chose et croyoient que s'ils n'entendoient rien c'étoient leur faute; ceux qui cherchent finesse à tout découvroient un sens profond dans des bouffonneries qui n'en avoient aucun. Enfin, on finit par s'appercevoir que M. Sterne s'étoit diverti aux dépens du Public et que son Ouvrage étoit à peu près une enigme qui n'avoit point de mot.
> Cette aventure ressemble beaucoup à celle de la bouteille de deux pintes dans laquelle un Charlatan Anglois promit, il y a quelques années, qu'il entreroit publiquement sur le Théatre de Haymarket. Le Charlatan emporta l'argent des Spectateurs et leur laissa la bouteille vide sur la table. Elle n'étoit pas plus vide que la vie de *Tristram Shandy*, sur-tout dans les deux Volumes nouveaux que nous annonçons.[59]

Unable to justify a work that seemed not to have an underlying meaning or satiric target, Suard falls into the kind of trap laid in the prologue to *Gargantua*, in which Rabelais playfully instructs the reader to consider his book as a bone containing sacred marrow that needs to be found, only to criticize attempts to find secret meanings behind texts, as in the case of Homer's early allegorical interpreters.[60]

The Comic-Satiric and Menippean Traditions

The attempt to describe and categorize *Tristram Shandy* for the reader led critics to make comparisons with other texts. In addition to Scarron, Sterne was most frequently associated with Rabelais and Swift. *Tristram Shandy* was also compared with the *Satyre ménippée* (1594), a political pamphlet attacking the Spanish and the Catholic League of the 1593 États Généraux.[61] Burlesque and parodic, it was composed of prose and verse in different languages. By linking Sterne's work with other texts, critics suggested that Sterne belonged to a particular tradition or style. This was not clearly defined or analysed, nor did it take on the characteristics of a single literary genre. It was nevertheless familiar enough to be invoked, and critics allude in a general manner to a satiric tradition or style of writing characterized by inconsistency, digression, philosophical wit and ribaldry. For the purposes of this discussion about Sterne's early French critics, I will refer to this very loosely as a comic-satiric tradition, in which European comic prose fiction (with its picaresque, burlesque and romance elements) meets the philosophical and formal 'medley' of Menippean satire, traced from the Greek cynic Menippus (whose works have been lost) via his Greek disciple Lucian, his Roman disciple Varro and the Varronian legacy represented by Petronius and Apuleius, to later ancient, medieval, renaissance and modern forms.[62]

Modern critics have been more detailed than their eighteenth-century counterparts in their attempts to trace Sterne's ancestors. Placing Sterne in a tradition of 'learned wit', D. W. Jefferson explains that this depends on the intellectual materials and habits of a pre-Enlightenment world, such as those found in scholastic and other types of medieval learning, and on the exploitation of rhetoric.[63] Embedded in or inspired by medieval cosmology, medicine, law and religion, learned wit is characterized by speculative freedom, dialectical ingenuity, visualization of the concrete, and an elasticity in movement between the general and particular and between the serious and the flippant. Works of learned wit use wordplay and parody of legal quibbles, rhetorical elaboration and rationalist logic. In Sterne's case, old forms of wit are often applied to more modern ideas, such as those of Descartes, Newton or Locke. W. C. Booth, meanwhile, locates Sterne's ancestry in the device of the self-conscious narrator in comic fiction of the seventeenth and eighteenth centuries; such a narrator 'intrudes into his novel to comment on himself as a writer, and on his book, not simply as a series of events with moral implications, but as a created literary product'.[64] Cervantes is the first important practitioner of this device, followed by Sorel, Furetière and Scarron, then Marivaux, Swift and Fielding. The 1750s saw a proliferation of novels that imitated *Don Quixote* and featured self-conscious narrators, but Sterne took the device to a new level.

Recent work on Menippean satire has also influenced ideas of Sterne's literary heritage. Its definition as a 'genre' is disputed by classical scholars, but Eugene Kirk's identification of a wide variety of European texts up to 1660 as Menippean persuasively affirms the existence of a tradition (rather than a 'genre') which encompasses enormous variation.[65] For Kirk, the chief mark of the Menippean style is unconventional diction, which includes neologisms, macaronics, vulgarity, catalogues, bombast, mixed languages and protracted sentences. In other words, a structural 'medley', which grows out of the original Greek definition of Menippean satire as a mixture of verse and prose, dialogue, tales, songs and curses.[66] It also mixed together prevailing forms of philosophical discourse, such as the dialogue, symposium, epistle, allegorical journey and sophistic oration. The Menippean tradition comes to feature digression, 'outlandish fictions' and 'extreme distortions of arguments', aiming to ridicule fraudulent learning.

Focusing on modern rather than ancient fiction, Northrop Frye developed an influential definition of Menippean satire, or 'anatomy', as a principal genre of prose fiction, along with the novel, confession and romance:

> The Menippean satire deals less with people as such than with mental attitudes. Pedants, bigots, cranks, parvenus, virtuosi, enthusiasts, rapacious and incompetent professional men of all kinds, are handled in terms of their occupational approach to life as distinct from their social behaviour. The Menippean satire thus resembles the confession in its ability to handle abstract ideas and theories, and differs from the novel in its characterization, which is stylized rather than naturalistic, and presents people as mouthpieces of the ideas they represent [...] The novelist sees evil and folly as social diseases, but the Menippean satirist sees them as diseases of the intellect, as a kind of maddened pedantry which the *philosophus gloriosus* at once symbolizes and defines.[67]

For Frye, Menippean satire attacks 'philosophical pedantry' as the 'imposing of over-simplified ideals on experience'. He distinguishes it from romance in that it is concerned with 'intellectual fancy' rather than with exploits of heroes. Thus Petronius, Apuleius, Rabelais, Burton, Swift and Voltaire all wrote works that should be placed in this category. Eventually, it begins to merge with the novel, and *Tristram Shandy* is a successful hybrid, a novel with many Menippean features, including

> the digressing narrative, the catalogues, the stylizing of character along 'humour' lines, the marvellous journey of the great nose, the symposium discussions, and the constant ridicule of philosophers and pedantic critics.[68]

Bakhtin's view of Menippean satire has proved even more influential, although both his and Frye's definitions have been criticized for being too broad.[69] For Bakhtin, Menippean elements are found in different genres and at different times. He charts the rise of the modern, 'polyphonic' novel in relation to Menippean satire, or 'menippea', which is a dialogic and seriocomic form, in contrast to monologic and serious genres such as epic, tragedy, history and the epistle.[70] While insisting that Menippean satire is an open system rather than a strictly defined genre, Bakhtin identifies 14 elements that characterize it, including (to name only five) the importance of the comic; the lack of plausibility, or freedom of plot and philosophical invention; an organic combination of the elevated with the common or low; the use of inserted genres (such as letters, rhetoric speeches, novellas); and a mixture of styles and tones. His Menippean world is the irreverent and inverted world of the carnival which, over a lengthy historical period, has provided a stable, if varied, form through which contradictory ideas could be expressed.

Sterne's early French critics did not attempt intricate definitions of style or genre, but quickly spotted the kinship between *Tristram Shandy* and the *Satyre ménippée*, the *Roman comique* and the works of Swift and Rabelais. The common elements they mention are the disrupted narrative, ribaldry, learned wit, irreverence towards scholasticism and philosophical systems, and excess of all kinds. Suard makes a passing reference to such a tradition when, unable to read *Tristram Shandy* allegorically, he makes connections with other works, claiming that it is written 'dans le goût de' *Pantagruel* and the *Satyre ménippée*. He does not justify the comparison but instead explains his preference for Rabelais over Sterne. Both are comic and indecent, he points out, but Rabelais is more knowledgeable and satirical:

> C'est [*Tristram Shandy*] une espece de Roman bouffon écrit à peu près dans le goût de *Pantagruel* & de la *Satyre Menippée*, l'Auteur n'est cependant ni aussi savant que Rabelais ni aussi satyrique: mais il est aussi gai, & souvent aussi peu décent.[71]

The *Journal encyclopédique* also connects *Tristram Shandy* with *Pantagruel* and the *Satyre ménippée*. The comparison is not in Sterne's favour, however. One article warns that the French works should be distinguished from 'la production monstrueuse de M. Sterne'.[72] Another points out some common characteristics in Rabelais and Sterne, including scholarly theorizations on the arts and sciences, the knowledge of ancient and modern languages and sexual references. For the latter, Rabelais is considered less at fault because his status as a doctor makes his discussion *de ventre inspiciendo* ('concerning the inspection of the womb') more easily acceptable than Sterne's. An affirmation of Rabelais's originality suggests that the unfavourable comparison had more to do with nationalism than prudery: 'L'Auteur de Tristram Shandy, n'est point si original que se l'imaginent les Anglois; Rabelais lui a servi de modèle'.[73] With the not unreasonable contention that Sterne is Rabelais's imitator, the critic nevertheless proves to be a cultural protectionist, affirming Rabelais's place both in a learned comic-satiric tradition and in a French canon, in order to exclude the English imitator from both.

Voltaire and *Tristram Shandy*

Tristram Shandy's place in a comic-satiric tradition and its similarities with other works were not explored in a detailed or systematic way by Sterne's early French critics, but were invoked to give the reader a general idea of his style, or simply to find fault with it. The clearest and most assured discussion of *Tristram Shandy*'s relationship to such a tradition during this period was Voltaire's. Voltaire appreciated Sterne early on, both as a realist and as a writer of sermons, and his article 'Conscience', published in *Questions sur l'Encyclopédie* (1770), pays tribute to the sermon 'On Conscience', which appears in *Tristram Shandy*.[74] His judgement would be repeated in later articles on Sterne and in introductions to French translations of his work:

> Ce qu'on a peut-être jamais dit le mieux sur cette question importante ['de la conscience trompeuse'] se trouve dans le livre comique de *Tristram Shandy*, écrit par un

curé nommé Sterne, le second Rabelais d'Angleterre; il ressemble à ces petits satyres de l'antiquité qui renfermaient des essences précieuses.[75]

Voltaire was nevertheless also very critical of Sterne. In 1777, seven years after the publication of his article 'Conscience', and shortly after the appearance of Frénais's translation of Volumes I to IV of *Tristram Shandy*, Voltaire wrote a substantial review of the latter in the *Journal de politique et de littérature*.[76] Its date categorizes it with articles of the 1776 to 1777 period, which are discussed in the next chapter, but its classical spirit places it with the reviews of the 1760s. Like the earlier critics, Voltaire compares *Tristram Shandy* to other European comic-satiric works and declares that it falls short.

He links *Tristram Shandy* to the commonly recognized influences – Rabelais, Scarron and Swift – and repeats his view of Sterne as the 'second Rabelais D'Angleterre', the first being Swift.[77] Voltaire goes on to identify a learned wit tradition but has his own preferences within it: Swift is superior to Rabelais because Swift's satire upholds the Horatian principles of purity and elegance:

> Aussi gai & aussi plaisant que notre Curé de Meudon, il [Swift] écrivoit dans sa langue avec beaucoup plus de pureté & de finesse que l'Auteur de Gargantua dans la sienne; & nous avons des vers de lui d'une élégance & d'une naïveté dignes d'Horace.

Although he does not offer a precise definition of the tradition he identifies, Voltaire's casual reference to 'ce style' suggests that it was familiar and recognized, and he identifies it by mentioning its common characteristics: 'ce style bouffon & hardi, dans lequel ont écrit Stern [*sic*], Swift & Rabelais'. The mixture of boldness with jest was, for Voltaire, key to the moral and political effectiveness of the texts in question. He traces the roots of this style to the two fifteenth-century German humanists, Reuchlin and Hutten, and explains that the 'lettres *des gens* obscurs' were written in 'latin macaronique', a burlesque mixture of Latin and the authors' native German. For Voltaire, the *Epistolae Obscurorum Virorum* (1516–17) played an important role in the controversy between Johannes Reuchlin and his enemies, the Dominicans of Cologne and Louvain Universities, who were hostile to Reuchlin's development of Hebraic studies and his belief in religious tolerance. The text was a collection of letters by Ulrich von Hutton and Johann Jaeger, but purportedly by the Dominicans and anti-humanist reactionaries in response to a collection of testimonies supporting Reuchlin (the *Epistolae Clarorum Virorum*). The spurious letters use burlesque language and digression to parody the reactionaries.[78]

The publication of these letters, Voltaire writes, was extremely damaging to Rome at a time when the latter's stability was already threatened by the Reformation. Germany was therefore not only attacking Rome with a theological revolution, but also through literature. For Voltaire, the *Epistolae Obscurorum Virorum* had more serious consequences than Rabelais's 'gaieté

Françoise', because it was politically effective: its publication fuelled the Reformation and therefore contributed to the division of the Church. *Tristram Shandy*, however, while containing serious elements, did not have such political motivation or authority. 'Tristram Shandy ne fera point de révolution', Voltaire states flatly. Sterne did not fulfil the serious moral and political function of a comic-satiric writer and, rather than critiquing frivolous novels, preferred simply to make money:

> Il eût été à désirer que le Prédicateur n'eût fait son comique Roman, que pour apprendre aux Anglois à ne se plus laisser duper par la charlatanerie des Romanciers, & qu'il eût pu corriger la Nation qui tombe depuis long-tems, abandonne l'étude des Lokes & des Neutons pour les Ouvrages les plus extravagans & les plus frivoles. Mais ce n'étoit pas-là l'intention de l'Auteur de *Tristram Shandy*. Né pauvre & gai, il vouloit rire aux dépens de l'Angleterre & gagner de l'argent.

It is significant that Voltaire compares Sterne with Shakespeare: 'Il y a chez Stern des éclairs d'une raison supérieure, comme on en voit dans Shakespeare'. An early champion of Shakespeare, Voltaire used the idea of his unpolished, natural genius to attack the rigidity of classical French theatre. But his comparison is instantly qualified: 'Et où n'en trouve-t-on pas! Il y a un ample magasin d'anciens Auteurs, où tout le monde peut puiser à son aise'. With this, he undermines – even while affirming – the 'éclaires d'une raison supérieure' which characterize both English writers, suggesting that their talents reside in plagiarism. It was thanks in great part to Voltaire that Shakespeare became a focus of eighteenth-century literary discussions in France: Shakespeare's lack of *goût* and ignorance of the *unités* of time, place and action were frequently commented upon, and critics debated whether his genius could compensate for such transgressions.[79] Voltaire laid the ground for these discussions in his *Lettres philosophiques*,[80] and in the *Discours sur la tragédie* addressed to Lord Bolingbroke, he maintained that irregularity in tragedy had the advantage of containing great scenes of action, while French tragedy forbade the representation of certain actions on stage and was thus conversational and characterized by a 'délicatesse excessive'.[81]

By 1777, however, the date of his article on Sterne, Voltaire's attitude towards Shakespeare had become more conservative. This change coincides with the publication in 1776 of the first volume of Le Tourneur's translation of Shakespeare with its introductory eulogy of the English playwright, who Le Tourneur considered to be the equal of Corneille, Molière and Racine.[82] This angered Voltaire enough to cause him to write a *Lettre à l'Académie française* (1776) in which he attacked the excesses and extravagances of *anglomanie*, which he believed had led to an unquestioning reverence for Shakespeare above the great French dramatists. His comparison of Sterne with Shakespeare is therefore indicative of an unusually conservative attitude towards both writers precisely at a time when they were becoming increasingly accessible to and popular with a wider French audience.

Chapter 2

New Critical Expressions: The Later Reviews, 1776–86

> C'est en Angleterre, patrie de *Tristram*, et pays des brouillards, des passions sombres et des pensées profondes, que Sterne est le plus bouffon ou le plus gai; c'est en France, où l'on croit entendre tous les grelots de la folie, que Sterne reçoit et qu'il donne le plus d'impressions touchantes. C'est peut-être un art, puisque c'est une surprise; mais c'est peut-être aussi une couleur locale du peintre, et une vérité morale du philosophe.[1]

Between the hesitant or hostile reviews of the 1760s and the eloquent analyses by Romantic critics such as Dominique-Joseph Garat, Madame de Staël and Charles Nodier, there was a change in Sterne's critical reception.[2] The publication of *A Sentimental Journey* in 1768 and of its French translation the following year paved the way for a new perspective on *Tristram Shandy*, which was also eventually translated in 1776 (Volumes I to IV) and in 1785 (Volumes V to IX). With the important exception of Voltaire's article, the reviews of the 1770s and 1780s presented new perspectives that engaged with wider aesthetic and socio-cultural concerns. As Garat's words above suggest, there was a more nuanced critique of Sterne's work that was inextricably linked to ideas of national character and national literary taste. There was also a greater focus on Sterne's humour, imagination, sentimentalism and painterly realism. These 'novelistic' qualities permitted an appreciation of his transgressive mixture of philosophy and *bouffonnerie*, and his work came to be associated with the novel as well as with older comic-satiric writings.

A Sentimental Journey and English Eccentricity

With the publication in 1769 of Joseph-Pierre Frénais's *Voyage sentimental*, Sterne became available in French for the first time.[3] The new work was shorter than *Tristram Shandy*, contained more sentimental episodes and portrayed the French with sympathy. Accessible, humorous and full of sentiment and benevolence, it was an instant success. As Yorick states in the 'Preface in the Desobligeant', his journey was to be different from other British Grand Tour narratives, and it quickly becomes apparent that he is interested neither in describing the sites nor in expressing xenophobic ideas about foreigners.

Smollett's *Travels through France and Italy* (1766), whose splenetic traveller-narrator grumbles his way around France, is a particular target, and Sterne satirizes him as Smelfungus:

> The learned SMELFUNGUS travelled from Boulogne to Paris – from Paris to Rome – and so on – but he set out with the spleen and jaundice, and every object he pass'd by was discoloured or distorted – He wrote an account of them, but 'twas nothing but the account of his miserable feelings.[4]

Given the ambiguity and self-consciousness of Sterne's sentimentalism, a subject that will be explored in Chapter 5, the sincerity and value of Yorick's claim to be undertaking 'a quiet journey of the heart in pursuit of NATURE, and those affections which rise out of her, which make us love each other – and the world, better than we do', has attracted a great deal of discussion.[5] Nevertheless, the ultimate conquest of temptation that characterizes his encounters with various ladies, *filles de chambre* and charming *grissets*, and his willingness to overcome initial prejudice towards the French and their Catholicism, as in the case of father Lorenzo, support the idea that *A Sentimental Journey* was, to some degree at least, Sterne's 'Work of Redemption'.[6]

Smollett had already been reviewed in the *Journal encyclopédique*, which suggests that some readers were aware of the contrast between Sterne's attitude towards the French and Smollett's:

> On diroit que M. Smolett animé contre les François d'une haine implacable, sentiment bien indigne d'un Littérateur, & surtout d'un Historien qui voudroit se piquer d'être Philosophe [...] A quel propos M. Smolett s'obstine-t'il à dénigrer, avec tant de licence, une nation qui lui a fait l'honneur de traduire sa médiocre *Histoire d'Angleterre* [...] Nous l'avons lue sans indignation, quelque grossières que soient les calomnies que M. le Docteur vomit contre les François: ces invectives sont plus méprisable qu'offensantes.[7]

Sterne's evident ability to overcome cultural prejudice was particularly appreciated during a period of war between England and France. The *Journal encyclopédique*, whose criticisms of *Tristram Shandy* during the 1760s had been harsh, now praised the cultural sympathy he expressed. While it had previously attacked his incongruities, it now found that buffoonery did not prevent his work from being moral; on the contrary, gaiety coexisted with humanity and sensibility:

> Ce voyage est une peinture gaye & plaisante des mœurs françoises; mais la bonne humeur de M. Sterne ne l'empêche point d'être touché de tout ce qui blesse l'humanité, & de montrer la sensibilité la plus tendre; c'est ce qui l'a engagé de donner à son ouvrage le titre de *Sentimental.*[8]

Sterne's originality also comes to be associated with benevolence and the finer feelings. No longer a symptom of aesthetic and moral transgression, it lies instead in the expression of the traveller-narrator's feelings: instead of describing the usual sites and buildings in guidebook style, the *Voyage sentimental* reveals nature and the human heart. It is significant that the adjective 'sentimental' did not previously exist in French. Frénais coined the word from the English for his translation, as he explains in the 'Avertissement du traducteur', and his neologism is symbolic of the text's successful integration into French literary culture. The periodical press was unanimous in recommending the *Voyage sentimental*, whose digressiveness was regarded as a harmless, even charming, stylistic feature. The *Mercure de France*, for instance, acknowledges its narrative irregularity but does not see it as excessive or transgressive:

> Il ne faut pas chercher de l'ordre ni de la liaison dans les productions de M. Sterne; il se perd dans des digressions infinies; l'une le conduit à l'autre; il perd de vue son objet principal, & le fait souvent oublier à ses lecteurs qu'il attache par des traits d'une sensibilité tendre & vraie qui leur arrache des larmes.[9]

For this critic, sentimentalism provides the moral structure of the work, holding together an otherwise disordered narrative and compensating for its irregularities.

For French readers, the *Voyage sentimental* also provided a compelling insight into Sterne's life and character. He had already been a familiar figure in the *salons* of Paris during his visits to France. Suffering from pulmonary tuberculosis all of his adult life, Sterne first went to France in January 1762, heading towards the warm climate of the south. As Britain and France were engaged in the Seven Years War, he travelled with the diplomatic party of George Pitt, who was on his way to the court of Turin to take up his post as envoy and participate in the peace negotiations. After a seven-month stay in Paris, his wife and daughter joined him and they travelled south, living first in Toulouse then Montpellier, where they met Smollett, between 1762 and 1764. Leaving his family behind, Sterne returned to Paris on his way back to England in the spring of 1764, when he was asked by Lord Hertford, the British ambassador, to preach in his chapel for the opening of the embassy. Members of Parisian intellectual and social circles, as well as the entire Anglophone community in Paris, were present at the sermon.[10] He passed through Paris again in October 1765 on his way to Italy, and then in May 1766 on his way back, and met some of the most important French writers and thinkers in the *salons*, particularly those of the Baron d'Holbach and Pelletier (president of the Parliament of Paris). D'Holbach, Diderot and their circle of *philosophes*, materialists and atheists gave him a warm welcome.[11] He met Suard,[12] Crébillon fils (whose novel is carried by the *fille de chambre* in *A Sentimental Journey* and with whom he made a literary 'persiflage'),[13] the naturalist Comte de Buffon, the economist Abbé Morellet, and probably the Abbé Raynal, who would become the respected author of the *Histoire des deux Indes* (1770) and, like Sterne, the admirer of Eliza Draper.[14] He also met politicians and princes, including the Prince de Conti (commander of the French armies), the Comte de Bissy (the

Comte de B* who helps Yorick with his passport) and the Duc d'Orléans (the king's cousin). He 'shandied it away' in Paris as he had in London, allowing himself to be identified with Tristram, as he boasts in a letter to David Garrick in 1762:

> [I] have converted many unto Shandeism – for be it known I Shandy it away fifty times more than I was ever wont, talk more nonsense than ever you heard me talk in your days – and to all sorts of people. *Qui le diable est ce homme là* – said Choiseul, t'other day, ce Chevalier Shandy – You'll think me as vain as a devil, was I to tell you the rest of the dialogue.[15]

Anecdotes about Sterne's visits became common in the periodical press and converged with certain episodes from *A Sentimental Journey*, which was not simply regarded as a semi-autobiographical account of his travels; more importantly, it came to be considered as an extension of his personality. Its critical reception was inextricably linked with perceptions of his life and personality, to the extent that by 1820 Garat could write:

> Je ne sais pas, avec assez de certitude, si on avait connu à Paris *Tristram Shandy* et le *Voyage sentimental* avant Sterne, ou Sterne avant *le Voyage sentimental* et *Tristram Shandy*. Mais jamais un auteur et ses ouvrages ne se sont ressemblés davantage: les lire ou le voir et l'entendre, c'était presque la même chose; et cette resemblance parfaite est ce qui rendait plus difficile tout autre parallèle, soit des ouvrages, soit de la personne de l'auteur.[16]

The originality of his work came to be seen as a natural extension of his personality, which made both man and work unique and even beyond comparison. The perception of Sterne as *un original* took shape alongside the critical reception of the *Voyage sentimental*, as anecdotes about him were conflated with episodes in Yorick's travels, and both increased his celebrity.[17]

We saw in the previous chapter that the word *originalité* was defined in relation to works of art and literature. But it was also commonly applied to persons. The *Dictionnaire de l'Académie française* notes this double usage: '*Originalité*. Caractère de ce qui est original. Il se dit des personnes & des choses'.[18] However, while the adjective could be both positive and negative when applied to works of art, it was more clearly pejorative when it pertained to persons. A person described as *original*, or identified as *un original*, was excessive, bizarre, eccentric and ridiculous. Le Roux's definition makes this clear:

> Pour sot, ridicule, qui a des manières affectées et qui est bizarre et extravagant dans tout ce qu'il fait; c'est proprement faire le petit maître [...] original sans copie. Cette manière de parler exprime plus le ridicule d'une personne qu'original seul, c'est comme si on disait: sot, ou cramoisi, le plus ridicule et le plus extravagant de tous les hommes.[19]

A person who does not follow models and conventions, and tries to be completely unique, shows excessive originality. He is bizarre, *extravagant*, affected and arrogant ('c'est proprement faire le petit maître'), and becomes the target of ridicule. Later in the eighteenth century, the Abbé Feraud distinguishes between artistic and personal originality, and reveals that while the former might be valued, the latter is usually viewed negatively. The distinction is manifest in the difference between the adjective and the noun:

> On ne le dit guère substantivement des personnes qu'en mauvaise part, et pour louer on se sert plutôt de l'adjectif:
> – Un auteur original est un homme de genie
> mais
> – un original est un homme bizarre est [sic] singulier.[20]

The *Dictionnaire de l'Académie française* also makes this distinction. While the noun *original* may be used 'figurétivement, d'Un Auteur qui excelle en quelque genre sans être formé sur aucun modèle' (the example given is 'les Ancients sont d'excellents originaux'), another definition is also given:

> On dit par raillerie d'Un homme qui est singulier en quelque chose de ridicule, que (C'est un original, un vrai original, un franc original. Cette femme est un grand original).[21]

Sterne's personal originality was the focus of much attention from 1769. Articles began to include biographical details, information about his place of birth, childhood and schooling, his position in life as a clergyman, and his sudden rise to fame in London. The *Année littéraire* dedicates a quarter of its 1776 article on *Tristram Shandy* to his life,[22] and the *Journal encyclopédique* also provides substantial biographical information in 1777.[23] Incidents that occurred during his visits to Paris are repeated in different articles. Without exception, they serve to illustrate Sterne's personal originality, or eccentricity, and its relationship to his Englishness. In the most frequently recounted anecdote, Sterne uses a coin metaphor to illustrate his view of the difference between the French and the English. The episode is related by Frénais in the introduction to his translation of the *Sentimental Journey*:

> M. Sterne vint à Paris pendant la derniere guerre [the Seven Years War] [...] On lui demandoit s'il n'avoit pas trouvé en France quelque caractere original dont il pût faire usage dans son Roman: Non, dit-il, les hommes y sont comme ces pieces de monnoie, dont l'empreinte est effacée par le frottement.[24]

In the fictionalized version of this anecdote in *A Sentimental Journey*, the conversation takes place between Yorick and the Count de B. When Yorick claims that the French are polite 'to an excess', the Count insists on an explanation, which Yorick delivers:

> I had a few king William's shillings as smooth as glass in my pocket; and forseeing they would be of use in the illustration of my hypothesis, I had got them into my hand, when I had proceeded so far –
>
> See, Monsieur le Count, said I, rising up, and laying them before him upon the table – by jingling and rubbing one against another for seventy years together in one body's pocket or another's, they are become so much alike you can scarce distinguish one shilling from another.
>
> The English, like antient medals, kept more apart, and passing but few peoples hands, preserve the first sharpnesses which the fine hand of nature has given them – they are not so pleasant to feel – but in return, the legend is so visible, that at the first look you see whose image and superscription they bear.[25]

Frénais's version of the story is taken almost word for word from Suard's account, which predates the publication of *A Sentimental Journey*, indicating that the exchange did actually occur between Sterne and a French interlocutor.[26] Suard may have witnessed the exchange, and Sterne enjoyed the effect of the comparison enough to turn it into a scene in his book. The metaphor took on the proportions of an aphorism, every repetition of which contributed to establishing Sterne's reputation as an English eccentric. It is repeated as late as 1786 in an anouncement of a new edition of the *Voyage sentimental*, and in Garat's *Mémoires*.[27] The contemporary interest in national character had already begun with Montesquieu's sociological and anthropological analysis of the subject. His *Ésprit des Lois* (1748) attempted to explain why a nation was inclined towards a certain type of political institution in terms of the interaction between geography, climate and culture.[28] The constitutional monarchy in Britain, with its balance of powers, permitted political liberty but also contributed to the independence, pride and impatience of the people. The British were also afflicted with a 'maladie du climat', leading to an inward-looking and melancholic disgust with everything, including life itself. The association of Englishness and eccentricity was not a new stereotype, but Montesquieu's study provided an intellectual framework for popular French novels filled with pensive and suicidal English characters drawn in contrast with merry and socially polished French characters.[29]

Some articles express particular interest in Sterne's physical appearance as a manifestation of his eccentricity of character. The clergyman's black clothes, his pale complexion and skinny build contributed to his unusual appearance. The *Journal encyclopédique* notes that Sterne's originality extended to his face and clothes, which inspired laughter: 'Sa figure étoit originale, & excitoit le rire. Il s'habilloit d'une maniere particuliere, qui le faisoit encore plus remarquer'.[30] One recurring anecdote encapsulates the double originality of Sterne's physical appearance and personality, while simultaneously focusing attention on his Englishness. It appears in both the *Année littéraire* and the *Journal encyclopédique* and is repeated by Garat:

En passant un jour sur le pont-neuf à Paris, il s'arrêta tout court, & regarda fixement la statue de Henri IV. Il fut presque'aussitôt entouré d'une foule de gens qui le considéroient avec un air de curiosité. *Eh bien! c'est moi,* leur dit-il, & *vous ne me connoissez pas davantage; mais imitez-moi*; & il se mit à genoux devant la statue du roi.[31]

Sterne's physical appearance and posture as he gazes at the statue attracts a curious crowd. He appears to enjoy the attention and addresses the spectators, urging them to imitate him when he makes the dramatic gesture of kneeling at the statue's foot. Such theatrical behaviour may be compared with that of the most famous *original* of the century portrayed in Diderot's *Le Neveu de Rameau* (1761–?). The younger Rameau is a marginal, morally ambiguous and parasitical character who acts roles from which he keeps his inner self distinct, both out of material necessity and in order to mimic the artistic genius he wishes he has.[32] Sterne is also playing a role for his spectators, but he is presented in a more straightforward manner, and it is assumed that his physical gestures are both illustrative of his originality and expressive of his authentic feelings towards the French king. The originality thus stems not only from the oddity of his physical appearance, but also from the meaning and context of his gesture. The homage he pays to a French king proves him to be singular and sympathetic. For Suard (according to Garat), this anecdote illustrated that Sterne was sincere and

toujours et partout le même; jamais détérminé par des projets; et toujours emporté par des impressions; dans nos théâtres; dans nos salons, sur nos ponts, toujours un peu à la merci des objets et des personnes, toujours prêt à être amoureux ou pieux, bouffon ou sublime.[33]

Sterne's popularity in France grew in part thanks to anecdotes such as this, which were repeated in *salon* conversations, memoirs, prefaces and articles in the periodical press. This particular story shows Sterne in a double role: he is both quintessentially English in his eccentricity and, at the same time, unusually sympathetic towards the French. It implies that originality can transcend national difference, and simultaneously creates a link between personal and literary originality in order to suggest that an author's genius might be more important than either conventional behaviour or established forms of literature. Finally, there is an implication that Sterne's originality, despite its transgression of rules, does not necessarily entail a corruption of French taste. His display of respect for Henri IV, a symbol of French patriotism and religious tolerance, was a fitting image – and a self-conscious one on Sterne's part – to indicate that his originality embraced the French tradition, and the anecdote itself reveals that Sterne was welcomed into it.

Realism and Sentiment: *Tristram Shandy* as Novel

The publication of the *Voyage sentimental* and the interest in Sterne's life and character that accompanied it marked a development in attitudes towards his work as a whole. This inevitably led to a reassessment of *Tristram Shandy*, and its translation into French increased its accessibility and appeal. Frénais's translation of Volumes I to IV in 1776 inspired a spate of positive reviews, as did the two different continuations (Volumes V to IX) in 1785 by the Marquis de Bonnay and Griffet de La Beaume respectively. After 1786 there were a few more articles: the *Journal de Paris* reviewed the French edition of the *Sermons* in 1787, and announcements and reviews of new editions and imitations of Sterne's works appeared in several periodicals during the 1790s.[34] Most articles, however, concentrate on *Tristram Shandy* and appeared in the periods 1776 to 1777 and 1785 to 1786.

The connections that had been noted during the 1760s between *Tristram Shandy* and other comic-satiric works continued to be made, but such comparisons became favourable. The *Journal encyclopédique* simply points out that Sterne 'a tant de rapports avec Rabelais & Swift', while the *Année littéraire* pronounces Sterne to be Rabelais's equal: 'M. Stern [...] est regardé comme le Rabelais de l'Angleterre, & ses écrits méritent, en effet, d'être placés, dans les Bibliothèques, sur la même tablette que ceux du jovial Curé de Meudon'.[35] He is even placed in a class of 'inimitable' works and credited with being the inventor of a new genre: 'Sterne est en Angleterre ce que fut l'Arioste en Italie, inventeur d'un genre de plaisanterie presque impossible à traduire ou à imiter'.[36]

These generic connections were not analysed in any detail. Instead, critics described Sterne's originality and narrative structure, with the implicit recognition that these might, after all, possess value and meaning. Reviews now contain plot summaries and extracts, interspersed with critical commentary, and give information about the digressions and lack of chronology. The *Année littéraire* points out that 'le récit n'a pas une marche rapide; il est tellement chargé d'incidens, tellement coupé par des digressions, plus bisarres les unes que les autres, que l'historien n'est encore âgé que d'un jour à la fin de son second volume'.[37] The *Mercure de France* similarly notes that 'l'histoire de quelques minutes occupe fréquemment un grand nombre de pages, & le Héros du Roman ne fait que de naître à la fin du second volume'.[38] The narrator's digressiveness and verbosity are still thought to be extreme, but they do not offend because they include positive features: 'Il est impossible de répandre plus de gaieté & de grâces dans un bavardage poussé jusqu'à la caricature'.[39] For the *Année littéraire*, the comic elements do not constitute a hindrance to intellectual, satirical, philosophical and moral value, which now become the objects of focus:

> Je ne vous citerai pas, Monsieur, toutes les plaisanteries, toutes les scènes bouffonnes, toutes les situations comiques que présente ce roman [...] Il ne faut pas croire cependant que tout l'esprit de l'auteur s'évapore en saillies frivoles: on trouve dans

son ouvrage des allusions fines & ingénieuses, un critique adroite des mœurs & des faux sçavans, des réflexions pleines de justesse & de solidité.[40]

Neither do the irregularities overshadow the work's valuable traits:

Toutes les saillies d'une imagination libre & originale caractérisent, Monsieur, la production facétieuse que je vous annonce; production, qui, malgré ses irrégularités bisarres, éteincèle d'esprit, de gaîté, & de bonne philosophie.[41]

Sterne's legendary originality is no longer perceived to be deviant, and is incorporated instead into a less strictly defined view of what constitutes good writing, which can consist of diversity. The *Journal encyclopédique*, for instance, enjoys 'cet auteur à la foi gai, ingénieux, sentimental, philosophe & profond',[42] while the *Année littéraire* is charmed by the motley mixture of elements to be found in *Tristram Shandy*:

Imaginez-vous un assemblage d'idées folles, agréables & touchantes; quelquefois morales, quelquefois libertines; on rit dans un chapitre, on est attendri dans un autre, on baille dans un troisième.[43]

The *Mercure de France* sees in such an assortment the means by which to observe humanity in all its diversity, an argument that was frequently used in defence of the novel:

On y trouve [in *Tristram Shandy*] des descriptions pittoresques, des réflexions fines & ingénieuses, & sur-tout des caractères singuliers & frappans [...] il deviendra un des livres les plus recherchés par ceux qui veulent s'amuser & observer l'espèce humaine dans une multitude de tableaux variés.[44]

The 'argument du tableau de la vie humaine' is, according to Georges May, one of the four principle defences of the novel, and the most sophisticated.[45] Novels had provoked condemnation since the seventeenth century. In his satiric dialogue *Les Héros de roman* (1665), Boileau was as critical of the long heroic novels and *romans precieux* of Gomberville, La Calprenède, Desmarets, Scudéry and Mademoiselle de Scudéry, as he later would be of the *roman comique* in his *Art poétique* (1674). Although these novelists attempted to formulate neo-Aristotelian rules for their work, Boileau attacked

non seulement leur peu de solidité, mais leur afféterie précieuse de langage, leurs conversations vagues & frivoles, les portraits avantageux faits à chaque bout de champ de personnes de très-médiocre beauté, & quelquefois même laides par excès, & tout ce long verbiage d'Amour qui n'a point de fin.[46]

The Abbé Desfontaines pointed out in 1737 that Boileau's critique had been effective and enduring:

> A l'égard des romans, ce genre si frivole et si nuisible aux mœurs et au progrès des belles letters, il n'y a guère que quinze ans qu'ils sont rentrés en grace. Les grands romans furent entièrement abolis par l'ingénieux dialogue de Despréaux: tel fut le fruit de la critique.[47]

Whether Boileau alone should be credited with the novel's dismissal is questionable, but the genre continued to provoke condemnation well into the eighteenth century on both aesthetic and moral grounds. The lack of ancient ancestry, and hence of solid rules and principles, was frequently criticized. Little consideration was given to the kinds of texts that could have been seen as precursors to the novel, such as those by Apuleius, Lucian and Petronius, which occupied in any case a low position in the hierarchy of genres. For many French critics, the plots in novels were *extravagant* and filled with improbable coincidences and exotic or fantastic settings that flouted the rule of *vraisemblance*. The novel was also morally questionable because it depicted vice, and its thematic preoccupation with love was thought to corrupt the vulnerable, particularly women and the young, by giving their imaginations free reign. Official censorship laws were passed to suppress novels in 1737 to 1738, resulting in what May called a 'dilemma' for the genre and the path it would take between 1715 and 1760 in order to reconcile moral standards with the artistic imperative to depict the world realistically.[48]

The novel survived, of course, and novelists of the 1730s developed new techniques of realism, such as the portrayal of everyday situations, detailed physical descriptions and psychologically complex characters, often from the middle and lower classes.[49] Following Daniel Huet's example, Lenglet-Dufresnoy traced a noble genealogy for the novel by developing the theory that it was descended from epic, but most defences linked it to history.[50] Novelists and some theorists defended it in essays, articles and prefaces, claiming that it followed Horace's precepts by being instructive as well as entertaining (*utile dulci*).[51] It was argued that the depiction of vice provided moral example through warning. Furthermore, in order to be morally effective, the novel had to represent the full spectrum of life in all its detail and should even touch the emotions. In an effort to counter both moral and aesthetic criticism, novelists claimed that their works were truthful by presenting them as authentic autobiography, memoirs or letters, and giving them the titles *histoire, mémoires, lettres* or *vie*. In their prefaces, they distinguished their own works from those which were *extravagant* and *romanesque*. Marivaux, for instance, described *La Vie de Marianne* (1731–7) as a thoughtful and intimate reflection on life and experience, introducing it as a memoir rather than as a *roman*:

> Si vous regardez la Vie de Marianne comme un Roman, vous avez raison, votre critique est juste; il y a trop de Réflexions, et ce n'est pas là la forme ordinaire des Romans, ou des Histoires faites simplement pour divertir. Mais Marianne n'a point songé à faire un Roman non plus. Son Amie lui demande l'Histoire de sa Vie, et elle

l'écrit à sa maniere. Marianne n'a aucune forme d'Ouvrage présente à l'esprit. Ce n'est point un Auteur, c'est une femme qui pense, qui a passé par différens états, qui a beaucoup vû, enfin dont la vie est un tissu d'Évenements qui lui ont donné une certaine connoissance du cœur et du caractere des hommes, & qui, en contant ses Aventures, s'imagine être avec son amie, lui parler, l'entretenir, lui répondre; & dans cet esprit-là, mêle indistinctement les faits qu'elle raconte aux réflexions qui lui viennent à propos de ces faits: voilà sur quel ton le prend Marianne. Ce n'est, si vous voulez, ni celui du Roman, ni celui de l'Histoire, mais c'est le sien: Ne lui en demandez pas d'autre.[52]

Crébillon *fils* also heralded the new realism with the following statement in his preface to *Les Égarements du cœur et de l'esprit* (1736–8): 'On ne pécheroit plus contre les convenances & la raison. Le sentiment ne seroit point outré; l'homme enfin verroit l'homme tel qu'il est; on l'éblouïroit moins, mais on l'instruiroit davantage'.[53] He could justify his dubious portrayal of cynical seducers and fallen women by asserting that the novel should represent 'le tableau de la vie humaine, et qu'on y censurât les vices et les ridicules', an argument developed from defences of comedy in seventeenth-century theatre debates, and which maintained that the truthful portrayal of human society was morally useful.

The *Mercure de France*'s view of *Tristram Shandy* as a portrait of humanity in all its variety reflects a critical interest in its methods of representation that paralleled the on-going debates about realism in the novel. Jacques Mallet du Pan, meanwhile, concentrates on *Tristram Shandy*'s dramatic and painterly qualities, which are explicitly associated with the novel, and Sterne is specifically referred to as an English novelist:

Personne ne narre avec plus de vérité, ne peint avec plus d'âme que Sterne dans ces divers morceaux. Cet Ecrivain est dramatique; on assiste avec lui au lieu de la scène, on en voit les Acteurs, on en reconnoît le langage; jusqu'à l'attitude, au geste, à l'habillement des personnages, tout sert à animer le tableau, à en fortifier l'exposition, à la graver dans l'âme du Lecteur. Pas un coup vague de pinceau, point de recherche ni d'exagération. D'autres Romanciers Anglois se sont appliqués à multiplier les détails minutieux; Sterne les choisit; il les place comme des nuances qui concourent à l'effet total.[54]

In this review, a subtle and emotional realism is seen to provide the unity of the text and permits it to be considered as a novel. The text is made up of 'divers morceaux', but the portrayal of a character's gesture, stance or clothes, and the detailed and dramatic painting of an ordinary situation draw in the reader and allow him to sympathize with the characters in a way that justifies the narrative structure. Each detail contributes to the total effect. Sterne's art – and arguably the novel's during this period – is sentimental: the reader feels intimately present and the scene is 'engraved' in his soul. The *Année littéraire* also speaks of Sterne as a novelist, distinguishing his works from those containing extraordinary and *romanesque* adventures. Although it refers to the

Voyage sentimental, it notes that 'On trouve [...] dans ce *Voyage*, à-peu-près le même caractère que dans les opinions de *Tristram Shandy*'.⁵⁵ Its interest lies precisely in the fine and detailed depiction of ordinary life, which is also distinguished from more 'stilted' and 'affected' French novels:

> Un véritable mérite de cet Ecrivain, c'est de n'avoir point cherché à exciter l'intérêt par ces aventures romanesques & extraordinaires, qui sont presque toujours hors de la nature. Ses tableaux sont puisés dans l'ordre commun de la société, saisis avec finesse, & tracés avec esprit & avec gaieté. Il a enfin le secret, si rare actuellement, de nous intéresser par des peintures & des détails que nous voyons tous les jours, & que nos Auteurs, toujours guindés & précieux, affectent de dédaigner, faute de pouvoir les rendre.⁵⁶

Originality and Imagination: New Critical Expressions

The mid-eighteenth century saw a proliferation of *Poétiques* and *Essais critiques*, including many translations from the English, but Young's *Conjectures on Original Composition* (1759) and its French translation by Pierre Le Tourneur hold particular relevance to a study of Sterne's critical reception in France.⁵⁷ There are two reasons for this: first, the French translation appeared in 1770, only a year after Frénais's *Voyage sentimental*, and second, its focus on originality and use of natural imagery are echoed in critical reviews of Sterne's work from 1776.

The *Conjectures* begins with Young's view of composition as 'a noble Amusement' and 'a sweet refuge' from life's everyday bustle. Whether we write or read the works of others, it rescues us from sloth and sensuality and is a cure for *tedium vitæ* and life's little anxieties. Young spends little time defining originality, specifying only that in composition, originality is that which is not copied or derived from other authors but is new, spontaneous and surprising. Apart from this, he is satisfied with a simple and unequivocal statement about its constitutive value:

> I shall not enter into the curious enquiry of what is, or is not, strictly speaking, *Original*, content with what all must allow, that some Compositions are more so than others; and the more they are so, I say, the better.⁵⁸

Rather than attempting to define it, then, Young distinguishes between originality and imitation through metaphors, gradually refining the distinction and accumulating similes and characteristics for each. Originality is characterized by genius and by the natural, while imitation is associated with acquired learning, knowledge and laboured or mechanical art:

> An *Original* may be said to be of a *vegetable* nature; it rises spontaneously from the vital root of Genius; it *grows*, it is not *made*. *Imitations* are often a sort of Manufacture wrought up by those *Mechanics*, *Art*, and *Labour*, out of pre-existent materials not their own.⁵⁹

Young revisits the debate of the Ancients and Moderns, complaining that there are few modern originals because writers are overwhelmed by their knowledge of the Ancients:

> Let it not be suspected, that I would weakly insinuate any thing in favour of the Moderns, as compared with antient Authors; no, I am lamenting their great Inferiority. But I think it is no *necessary* Inferiority.[60]

Modern writers are too diffident and not ambitious enough, and their own originality is suppressed by that of the Ancients. Transgressing their rules may therefore release them from the chains of imitation:

> Genius can set us right in Composition, without the Rules of the Learned; as Conscience sets us right in Life, without the Laws of the Land: *This*, singly, can make us Good, as Men; *That*, singly, as Writers, can, sometimes, make us Great.[61]

The *Conjectures*, as Roland Mortier points out, initially had small impact on ideas of originality in France, particularly compared with Germany, because the ideal of classical mimesis was fully integrated within the national literature and there was no urgent need to find a distinguishing originality.[62] He maintains, however, that Le Tourneur's translation and presentation of it, more than the English text itself, was the prime force in changing attitudes towards literary originality in France. Le Tourneur criticizes the lack of originality in French *belles-lettres* in his introduction, and presents Young as a refreshing counter to this tendency:

> Si les Anglais s'égarent souvent par trop de licence et de témérité, les Français pourraient bien être accusés quelquefois de lâcheté dans le champ du génie; souvent ils étouffent leur talent à force de goût et de servitude.[63]

Le Tourneur returns to the familiar idea that the English are too free in their writing, but uses this to propose that the French stifle their genius with rules and *goût*. Instead of touching the reader's soul and surprising him, French writing is burdened by cold and imitative forms of expression:

> Au lieu de méditer *soi-même* chaque partie de son sujet, de le féconder en l'échauffant longtemps au feu de *sa propre* imagination, on recueille froidement tout ce que les autres ont écrit qui peut s'y rapporter: on s'environne de cette multitude de lambeaux mal assortis; on offusque, *on masque son âme* sous l'amas de ces décombres. Elle ne sait plus voir *l'original qui est en elle*, et ne se regarde que dans toutes ces images qui ne sont point la sienne. *On n'ose pas écrire un instant seul et libre*: c'est toujours sous les yeux de mille témoins, sous la dictée de tous ces maîtres, dont la présence gêne votre âme et tient l'imagination dans les entraves. L'ouvrage est fini; le style en est pur; il est même élégant: mais vous le saviez par cœur avant de l'avoir lu. Vous n'y trouvez point de ces idées qui interrompent le lecteur, donnent une secousse à l'âme, et l'avertissent de penser, Rien qui vous étonne, rien qui inonde tout à coup votre âme

de lumière, en éclaire un coin nouveau que vous n'aviez pas observé, ou l'affecte d'émotions vives et durables.[64]

Young's principal purpose is to demonstrate to the world the originality of Addison's writing and the virtue of his life and dignified death. Le Tourneur, on the other hand, praises Young for revealing the value of originality in composition and surpasses him in this enterprise. He attempts to explain the idea of originality more clearly, placing greater emphasis on the sincerity of a literary work and its ability to move the reader emotionally. In this respect, Le Tourneur, as Young's interpreter in France, provided impetus for the change in attitudes towards originality. Mortier notes his importance in relation to the wider shift in aesthetic ideas during the period:

> l'analyse que nous propose Le Tourneur rend compte avec une admirable finesse du changement radical qui s'est produit, autour de 1760, dans la perception de l'art et dans la fonction qu'on lui attribue. La beauté n'est plus ressentie comme un équilibre parfait, comme une harmonie qui se laisse contempler, comme une chose entièrement coupée de son créateur et vivant d'une vie autonome, comme un objet de délectation que l'on juge en fonction de canons indiscutés.
> On attend dorénavant de l'art qu'il soit l'expression fidèle – et si possible intégrale – de la singularité de son créateur. La relation de l'homme et de l'œuvre est mise en évidence et son importance est privilégiée. La beauté (au sens de l'esthétique traditionnelle) compte moins que l'effet produit. Puisque l'art devient un dévoilement ('l'imitateur est celui qui 'masque son âme'), une mise à nu de l'original que nous portons en nous, il se doit de procéder de ce qu'il y a en nous de plus intime et de plus individuel. Sa valeur n'est pas liée à des critères formels, mais à la qualité de la relation qui existe entre lui et le vécu, c'est-à-dire à l'authenticité de sa voix.[65]

It is paradoxical that despite Le Tourneur's passionate plea for originality, he is in practice rather conservative. His translation resembles many others of the period in that it corrects elements in the English text which a French reader might have found inappropriate.[66] Le Tourneur frankly admits that 'Mon intention a été de tirer de Young Anglais un Young Français qui pût plaire à ma nation et qu'on pût lire avec intérêt, sans songer s'il est original ou copie'.[67] Nevertheless, his introduction announces a changed attitude towards the irregularities of English writing. It also marks a new kind of literary appreciation that centres on the internal truth of a work, its status as an authentic expression of the author's genius, and the author's ability to speak directly to the reader.

In the reviews of 1785 to 1786, there is an evident interest in Sterne's sincerity, a quality that is seen to enable him to transcend the oppression of established aesthetic rules. A marked difference in style distinguishes these from earlier articles as critics begin to adopt a more natural imagery. This parallels the process by which Sterne himself comes to be seen as natural after previous depictions of his work as unnaturally deviant. At the same time, his originality is allied to the idea of a lack of definition. Because his work cannot be placed entirely within a pre-existent genre or category, its value inheres in its very originality:

> N'attendez pas, Monsieur, une analyse du *Voyage en France. Sterne* est à l'abri de toute analyse; il échappe à toutes les remarques; il ne peut être saisi. C'est un papillon qui voltige d'objets en objets; il moralise, quand on croit qu'il va décrire; il décrit en courant; ses recits sont très-souvent en action; il cause avec son postillon; il interroge une jeune fille qui passe.[68]

This critic's own lack of analysis echoes Young's. Instead of defining, analysing and judging, he presents the reader with the natural image of a butterfly, a symbol of the soul escaping the body, to represent Sterne's freedom from rules. The *Journal encyclopédique* uses the language of liberty to express the idea that Sterne is both sincere and unique:

> Il est des génies souples & faciles que le goût forme en partie, & qui peut-être ne seroient rien sans lui: il en est d'autres au contraire, vraiment originaux, que le goût ne sçauroit épurer, que le joug des regles ne peut asservir, & qui sont d'abord ce qu'ils seront toujours. Tel fut M. Sterne.[69]

While *goût* is viewed as a constraint, and the rules of composition an imprisoning 'yoke', Sterne's originality, by contrast, is natural and 'unpurified' by such rules. The political implications are apparent: originality is made to sound like a triumph over *ancien régime* standards and assumptions.

As the critical reviews begin to incorporate the ideas of authenticity and liberty into their discussion of originality, there is a related emphasis on the imagination. In the first of a pair of articles in the *Journal encyclopédique* which purport to analyse 'l'esprit & les ouvrages de Sterne', both *Tristram Shandy* and *A Sentimental Journey* are considered together as the product of a consistent artistic mind.[70] Sterne is designated 'Enfant de la nature & de l'inspiration', whose works have 'Nul plan, nulles chaînes' because they are inspired, natural and unfettered by structure:

> [Sterne] s'abandonne délicieusement à tous les caprices de son humeur. La libre insouciance de son esprit, la gaieté, la folie, la sublimité, la finesse exquise de ses pensées, son goût, son talent inimitable pour la satyre, y conduisent tour à tour sa plume. Il erre sur tous les sujets, il parcourt sans cesse tous les tons.

The mixture of genres, tones and themes that offended early critics is no longer a hindrance to the harmony of the work as a whole. It is the author's imagination, rather than external rules, that creates the work's unity:

> Son imagination fertile & animée s'élève, s'abaisse, parcourt tous les tons & tous les sujets. Les peintures les plus vives & les plus vraies, les critiques les plus fines & les plus gaies, les richesses de poésie, les séductions de l'éloquence, les plus douces

émanations de la morale & du sentiment, coulent tour à tour sans ordre de sa plume facile, naturelle & à l'abandon.

The critic's imagery and flowing sentence structure imitate the freedom he describes. He slides from one verb of motion to another ('s'éleve', 's'abaisse', 'parcourt', 'coulent') to express the smoothness and facility in the movement of Sterne's imagination, which is represented as a faculty that travels continuously across conventional boundaries between different tones and themes. If his first French reviewer was reluctantly seduced by the 'vivacité de son imagination', this critic's own sinuous language reveals that he has already succumbed to what he sees as Sterne's all-encompassing imagination. No longer associated with the unleashing of mad and dangerous passions, the imagination is set free. This is not quite the fully liberated Romantic imagination, however, as *goût* retains an important guiding role:

Il [Sterne] erre capricieusement & à l'abandon; mais ses vagabondes folies, toujours avouées par le goût, l'esprit & les graces, intéressent souvent le cœur & instruisent quelquefois la raison.

Sterne's characteristic originality, narrative meanderings and textual disorder are nevertheless accepted because ideas of taste have widened enough to encompass them. The critic insists that to appreciate his work, the reading process itself must change: the reader should 'feel' the author and 'penetrate' his genius or the work will appear frivolous, extravagant and childish. It is a sentimental process, for the reader must open himself up to new sensations, pleasures and sources of interest:

Si vous ne sentez pas cet auteur, il vous paroîtra souvent minutieux, frivole, extravagant, puérile; mais pénétrez son génie, & vous trouverez un grand précepteur des hommes.
Il vous montre partout autour de vous ce que vous cherchez au loin si péniblement, de nouvelles sources d'intérêt, de sensations & de jouissances. Il vous apprend à chercher le bonheur dans une douce insouciance, aimant les hommes, égayant vos peines, mettant à la place de vos graves & assujettissantes folies des folies gaies, douces, sentimentales, aussi libres que vos fantaisies.

Sterne Sentimentalized: 'Lettre d'une Femme'

Amélie Suard does exactly what the author of 'Sur l'esprit & les ouvrages de Sterne' advises: she reads Sterne through feeling and turns her experience into a piece of criticism.[71] Her approach constitutes a defence of sentimentalism that is indebted to the theories expressed in Rousseau's *Entretien sur les romans*, the preface to the second edition of *Julie, ou La Nouvelle Héloïse* (1761), which affirms the moral value of his novel's apparently spontaneous epistolary style.[72] In response to a complaint about its exclamatory and simple language,

Rousseau explains that this cannot easily be understood from the perspective of worldly Parisian society. Simple rustic people, in fact, feel all the more deeply because they express themselves without self-consciousness. Society is accustomed to the sophisticated and clever eloquence of novels and romances, which masks a lack of profundity. Only through sensibility can one understand the truth of the feelings behind the simple language: 'ceux qui ne sentent rien, ceux qui n'ont que le jargon paré des passions, ne connaissent point ces sortes de beautés, et les méprisent'.[73] Although elsewhere Rousseau warned against the potential harm of excessive sensibility, he also believed in its virtuous power to enable readers of his novel to draw moral lessons through feeling.[74]

Madame Suard reads *A Sentimental Journey* with Rousseau's recommended naïveté and sensibility. She rejects the wit, or *esprit*, represented by the worldly Mademoiselle de Sommery, whose response to Yorick's pleasure at touching a lady's glove is to faint with laughter, 'pâmer de rire'.[75] Sterne's self-conscious sentimentalism clearly allows for such a comic interpretation, and modern readers are likely to take Mademoiselle de Sommery's side.[76] Madame Suard, however, polarizes sentiment and wit, and consciously chooses to focus on the former, while acknowledging the presence of the latter: 'Sterne pourrait presque se passer d'esprit. Ce ne sont pas les chapitres où il y en a le plus qui intéressent davantage'.[77]

She counters Mademoiselle de Sommery's complaints about the banality of Sterne's subject matter (such as the lamentation of a dead ass, the purchase of a pair of gloves and the employment of a servant) by claiming that these themes stretch the reader's range of thoughts, feelings and pleasure. It is not the subject itself, but its treatment, and the narrator's reflections on it, which are perceptive and profound. For Madame Suard,

> le mérite de Sterne, c'est, ce me semble, d'avoir attaché de l'intérêt à des détails qui n'en ont aucun par eux-mêmes; c'est d'avoir saisi mille impressions légères, milles sentimens fugitifs qui passent par le cœur ou l'imagination d'un homme sensible, et de les avoir rendus par des expressions piquantes, par des images ou des tournures originales.[78]

Originality has little to do with wit or irregular narrative structure, and the term is more accurately applied to the depiction of subtle feelings and fleeting impressions. This leads to a type of morality: 'Souvent, du milieu d'un chapitre dont le fonds n'est rien, on voit sortir des traits d'une morale douce et sublime, et des aperçus profonds sur le cœur, dont il démêle les plus délicats mouvemens'. Sterne's originality is an integral part of his sentimentalism as it lies in the way in which he invests everyday objects and events with feelings, thereby revealing his understanding of the human heart. The result is pleasurable for the reader:

> Quel plaisir on goûte dans cet abandon de son ame, dans cet innocent libertinage de son imagination, sur-tout dans ce sentiment de bonté, d'indulgence, de bienveillance universelle qui l'attache à tous les hommes![79]

Madame Suard's lyrical reading of Sterne recalls the emotional involvement with Richardson's novels that Diderot describes in the *Éloge de Richardson* (1762).[80] He cannot help sympathizing with the characters and plot because Richardson's fictional world is familiar and falls within the reader's experience: 'les passions qu'il peint sont telles que je les éprouve en moi'.[81] He considers Richardson's novels to be deeply moral precisely because the reader engages with them in this direct manner. While a maxim is an abstract rule of conduct which must be applied in practice, Richardson's novels show virtue and vice in action, and lead the reader to experience the sentiments of virtue and vice, which is only a step away from behaving virtuously. Diderot himself responds to Richardson with an immediacy of emotion that allows him to become involved in the fictional world of the novel and leads him in turn to make moral judgements: 'O Richardson! on prend, malgré qu'on en ait, un rôle dans tes ouvrages, on se mêle à la conversation, on approuve, on blâme, on admire, on s'irrite, on s'indigne.'[82]

In a similar manner, when Madame Suard reads Sterne's portrayal of Père Laurent (Father Lorenzo), she 'recognizes' the monk's humble air, 'sees' his movements and looks, and 'hears' his voice speaking against the world's injustices. She has a physical reaction to his momentary embarrassment when Yorick refuses him charity: 'Mes joues, je crois, se colorent aussi lorsqu'un rayon de rougeur traverse les siennes'.[83] Such symptoms are meant to reflect a deep sensibility, and represent a particular way of reading. Rather than judging the text according to recognized standards and expectations which can be discussed and debated, she describes how it makes her feel. She attempts, moreover, to persuade the reader (the 'ami' to whom she addresses her open letter) to feel as she does. In this way she can spread the sentimental effect, and affect, of the work:

> Je voudrais m'étendre, mon ami, sur les chapitres du Voyage Sentimental qui m'ont fait le plus de plaisir: quand vous sentez avec moi, comme moi, vous doublez mon plaisir; vous touchez mon cœur en flattant mon amour-propre.[84]

Madame Suard might have joined Diderot's society of sentimental readers who could weep with him over Richardson:

> Hommes, venez apprendre de lui à vous réconcilier avec les maux de la vie; venez, nous pleurons ensemble sur les personnages malheureux de ses fictions, et nous dirons 'Si le sort nous accable, du moins les honnêtes gens pleureront aussi sur nous'.[85]

But, unlike Madame Suard, the *philosophe* expresses the view that the imaginative sympathy inspired by Richardson's work is likely to lead to virtuous action: 'Qu'est-ce que la vertu? C'est, sous quelque face qu'on la considère, un sacrifice de soi-même. Le sacrifice que l'on fait de soi-même en idée est une disposition préconçue à s'immoler en réalité'.[86] Madame Suard's morality, on the other hand, does not have such a practical side and does not extend beyond the abstract deism that is revealed in her response to Yorick's statement that even in a desert he could find interesting life in a stone or a flower:

> Quelle aimable et douce sensibilité que celle qui s'associe par le sentiment aux êtres muets et inanimés; et n'est-ce pas entrer ainsi dans les vues de la création que de se soumettre avec joie à l'ordre établi par son auteur et à la place qu'il nous a marquée?[87]

Her decision to ignore Sterne's wit constitutes a redefinition of his originality in terms of sentimentalism. Although other critics continue to consider his structural originality and satirical mixture of philosophy and jest, her interpretation remains prevalent throughout the 1780s and 1790s, and is representative of the integration of *A Sentimental Journey* into French culture through the vogue for sentimental fiction, a topic to which I will return in Chapter 5.

Part II

Translations

Chapter 3

Theories of Translation and the English Novel, 1740–1800

André Lefevere speaks of translations as 'rewritings', or strategies of adapting the foreign text to the standards and expectations of the recipient culture:

> Translation is, of course, a rewriting of an original text. All rewritings, whatever their intention, reflect a certain ideology and a poetics and as such manipulate literature to function in a given society in a given way. Rewriting is manipulation, undertaken in the service of power, and in its positive aspect can help in the evolution of a literature and a society. Rewritings can introduce new concepts, new genres, new devices and the history of translation is the history also of literary innovation, of the shaping power of one culture upon another. But rewriting can also repress innovation, distort and contain, and in an age of ever increasing manipulation of all kinds, the study of the manipulation processes of literature as exemplified by translation can help us towards a greater awareness of the world in which we live.[1]

He suggests that translation plays a major role in the development of national cultures and proposes that it should be studied together with other forms of 'rewriting', such as critical reviews, prefaces and introductions, texts that constitute the means by which a foreign work contributes to the shaping of the national culture and aesthetic.[2] The next chapter will examine how *Tristram Shandy* was read and 'rewritten' through translation in eighteenth-century France. By studying the omissions, suppressions and additions of its early French translations, we can better understand the ways in which it was integrated into French literary culture. The present chapter provides a theoretical context for such a discussion by outlining eighteenth-century ideas about translation itself. Translation had been a focus of debate since the Renaissance rediscovery of classical Greek and Latin texts, which led to arguments about the relative inferiority or superiority of antiquity. These took virulent form around the end of the seventeenth and beginning of the eighteenth centuries in the 'Querelle des Anciens et des Modernes' in France and the 'Battle of the Books' in Britain.[3] Discussions about ancient work and translation continued well into the eighteenth century, but the new element to contend with in France was the rapidly increasing body of contemporary foreign, and particularly English, fiction.[4]

Translation in the *Encyclopédie*

Translation was commonly practised during the eighteenth century, and many writers and *philosophes* translated classical and foreign works. As its importance was taken for granted, sophisticated theories developed alongside the intense translation activity. The *Encyclopédie* and *Supplément* contain three articles in which translation is discussed in linguistic and grammatical terms and rooted in the intellectual context of the period, reflecting its most important questions.[5]

While there is no consistent or united view of language and grammar in the *Encyclopédie*, there are certain generalities to which we may refer in order to place ideas about translation within a larger linguistic context. Many of the *encyclopédistes* accepted the fundamental principle of the seventeenth-century Port-Royal grammarians that the goal of language was to express thoughts: 'Toutes les *langues* ont un même but, qui est l'énonciation des pensées'.[6] They also maintained the Cartesian belief in the universality of reason, which argued that all men and women shared common concepts and ideas:

> Toutes les ames humaines, si l'on en croit l'école cartésienne, sont absolument de même espèce, de même nature; elles ont les mêmes facultés au même degré, le germe des mêmes talens, du même esprit, du même génie.

Furthermore, not only did various languages express universal thoughts, but they also obeyed universal rules and could be analysed according to the universal laws of logic and reason, which formed a *grammaire générale* or 'science raisonnée des principes immuables & généraux de la parole prononcée ou écrite dans toutes les langues'.[7] The general science of language was founded upon the very nature of the human mind, which was regarded as logical and rational:

> La construction analytique est celle où les mots sont rangés dans le même ordre que les idées se présentent à l'esprit dans l'analyse de la pensée. Elle appartient à la *Grammaire générale*, & elle est la règle invariable & universelle qui doit servir de base à la construction particulière de quelque langue que ce soit.[8]

Such a rationalist conception of the relationship between thought and language implied the possibility of universal communication and comprehension through 'le lien universel de la communicabilité de toutes les *langues* & du commerce des pensées, qui est l'ame de la société'.[9] This also meant that faithful translation was possible, and this guided the *Encyclopédie*'s view of the translator's duties: 'Le premier & le plus indispensable des devoirs du traducteur est de rendre la pensée'.[10]

Sylvain Auroux calls this view of translation 'l'hypothèse du langage-traduction', which attempted to explain the empirical evidence that expressions of exact equivalence do not always exist in different languages.[11] It was clear to eighteenth-century grammarians that syntax varied greatly between languages, as demonstrated by the frequency in foreign languages of what was termed *inversion*, or syntax which did not conform to the natural and rational order of words. This natural order was subject-verb-object and, unsurprisingly, French conformed to it.[12] Vocabulary in different languages was also considered problematic, as some words or groups of words could only be translated by paraphrase rather than with exact equivalence, particularly as the meaning of words varied with context. Finally, there was a problem of 'semantic arbitrariness', which referred principally to figurative language: each language, for instance, used different metaphors.

The *encyclopédistes* did not see such differences as essential but attempted to explain them. They borrowed from the grammarians of Port-Royal the distinction between *grammaire générale* and *grammaire particulière* in order to assert that the deviations of a particular language from the general and universal structure, for example through *inversions*, *idiotismes*, or figurative expressions particular to each language, were only superficial. The grammarian's role was to analyse these deviations and discover the underlying universal construction and meaning. The basic universality of grammar ensured that local variations and seemingly irreconcilable differences between languages were not fundamental. On the contrary, 'true' translation was attainable, since the inevitable linguistic differences did not affect the deeper, essential meaning, and it was therefore possible to communicate between languages:

> Plutôt que de relier l'arbitraire sémantique à l'idée catastrophique de visions différentes du monde, les Lumières préfèrent en limiter l'effet: l'arbitraire demeure l'accidentel et l'accessoire, contingence irréductible qui, constituant *l'esprit ou le génie* de chaque peuple, exprime pourtant une même raison universelle sous des teintes différentes.[13]

The grammarian Nicolas Beauzée expressed such an optimistic attitude towards translation in his article 'Traduction, Version'. He distinguishes between these two words, which he sees as corresponding to two different types of translation.[14] A *version* is a literal, word for word reproduction of the original undertaken in order to learn the construction of a foreign language. 'True' translation, or *traduction*, is the next stage: the literal and 'servile' translation must be left aside and the particularities or *génie* of the target language should be used to reconstruct faithfully the text's universal and 'primitive' meaning. Literal translation, *version*, exists on a superficial level, concerning itself only with the fine details and local characteristics of a language, while *traduction* deals with universal truths common to all languages, despite initial appearances. This conception of translation suggests a belief not only in effective translation, but also in faithful translation. The differences between languages, remaining contingent and accidental, meant that foreign works did not necessarily threaten the purity of the French language.

Furthermore, French literary models could continue to be considered universal and did not need to be affected by the translation of foreign works.

Some *philosophes*, however, were less optimistic. While the belief in a universal grammar was not fundamentally shaken during the eighteenth century, many spoke about the difficulty of good translation, particularly when the concern was aesthetic rather than linguistic. The problem was located in the attempt to reconcile *fidélité* with *élégance*. Theorists asked whether translators should favour truthfulness to the author at the expense of the translation's overall harmony – conceived according to traditional French models – or whether they should dispense with accuracies if they were not tasteful.[15] D'Alembert articulates this problem in his 'Observations sur l'art de traduire', the preface to his translation of Tacitus:

> Une des grandes difficultés de l'Art d'écrire, & principalement des Traductions, est de savoir jusqu'à quel point on peut sacrifier l'énergie à la noblesse, la correction à la facilité, la justesse rigoureuse à la méchanique du style.[16]

D'Alembert implies that translation is as much an art as writing itself and expresses the need for equilibrium between *énergie* and *noblesse* in both. *Noblesse* refers to the required proprieties of composition, while *énergie* was associated with the vitality of the language. According to the article in the *Encyclopédie*, also by D'Alembert, the word *énergie* 's'applique principalement aux discours qui peignent, & au caractere du style'.[17] Recognizing that exact equivalence of meaning may clash with stylistic requirements, D'Alembert expresses the belief that translation needs to balance 'la justesse rigoureuse', rigorous precision and accuracy, with 'la méchanique du style', the technicalities or poetics of style. He goes on to locate the difficulty of translation in an author's style. While authors characterized more by their *pensée* may be translated satisfactorily, those characterized by their *style* are harder to convey in another language:

> Le caractere des Ecrivains est ou dans la pensée, ou dans le style, ou dans l'un & dans l'autre. Les Ecrivains dont le caractere est dans la pensée, sont ceux qui perdent le moins en passant dans une Langue étrangere [...] Les Ecrivains qui joignent la finesse des idées à celle du style, offrent plus de ressources au Traducteur, que ceux dont l'agrément est dans le style seul. Dans le premier cas, il peut se flatter de faire passer dans la copie le caractere de la pensée, & par conséquent au moins la moitié de l'esprit de l'Auteur; dans le second cas, s'il ne rend pas la diction, il ne rend rien.[18]

D'Alembert does not attribute the difficulty of translating style to the constitutive role of language in meaning, but recognizes that authors distinguished mainly by their style lose most in translation.

Marmontel makes a comparable statement about the difficulty of translation in the *Supplément* to the *Encyclopédie*, expressing a similar belief that works that are full of thoughts are easier to translate:

> les ouvrages qui ne sont que pensées sont aisés à traduire dans toutes les langues. La clarté, la justesse, la précision, la correction, la décence sont alors tout le mérite de la *traduction*, comme du style original [...] jusques-là il n'est pas difficile de réussir, surtout dans notre langue qui est naturellement claire & noble. Un homme médiocre a traduit *l'Essai sur l'entendement humain*, & l'a traduit assez bien pour nous, & au gré de Locke lui-même.[19]

A philosophical work like Locke's *Essay on Human Understanding* can be translated adequately into French because this language has the clarity, accuracy, precision and all the proprieties which permit the straightforward and rational communication of a clear thought or idea. However, a work characterized by *énergie* (Marmontel also uses the words *force* and *vigueur*) is harder to translate:

> Mais si un ouvrage profondément pensé est écrit avec énergie, la difficulté de le bien rendre commence à se faire sentir: on chercheroit inutilement dans la prose si travaillée d'Ablancourt, la force & la vigueur du style de Tacite.

Like D'Alembert, Marmontel proposes a balance between extremes and a 'juste milieu' between two views of translation, though he uses different terms to describe these. The first view is that of the 'gens du monde', who believe that it is impossible to translate perfectly two languages 'dont le génie est différent', and who prefer the translator to cater to the taste of his own nation. This means producing a work which the original author might have written had he employed French, and one that is 'utile ou agréable'. The second view is that of the 'savans', who would like a translation to capture not only the character of the original author, but also the *génie* of the original language and even 'l'air du climat & le goût du terroir' of the author's nation. For Marmontel, both views are justified and the translator must question himself and make his own choice, though he is advised to steer away from extremes and to seek a balanced medium. He thus grants the translator a high degree of artistic responsibility:

> Tout homme qui croit savoir deux langues, se croit en état de traduire; mais savoir deux langues assez bien pour traduire de l'une à l'autre, ce seroit être en état d'en saisir tous les rapports, d'en sentir toutes les finesses, d'en apprécier tous les équivalens; & cela même ne suffit pas: il faut avoir acquis par l'habitude, la facilité de plier à son gré celle dans laquelle on écrit; il faut avoir le don de l'enrichir soi-même, en créant, au besoin, des tours & des expressions nouvelles; il faut avoir sur-tout une sagacité, une force, une chaleur de conception presque égale à celle du génie dont on se pénètre, pour ne faire qu'un avec lui; ensorte que le don de la création soit le seul avantage qui le distingue; & dans la foule innombrable des traducteurs, il y en a

bien peu, il faut l'avouer, qui fussent dignes d'entrer en société de pensée & de sentiment avec un homme de génie.[20]

D'Alembert, who similarly believes in striking the correct balance between *agrément* and *précision*, warns against excessive liberty in translation:

> Quoi qu'il en soit, la différence de caracteres des Langues ne permettant presque jamais les traductions littérales, délivre le Traducteur de l'espece d'écueil dont nous venons de parler, de la nécessité où il se trouveroit quelquefois de sacrifier l'agrément à la précision, ou la précision à l'agrément. Mais l'impossibilité où il se trouve de rendre son original trait pour trait, lui laisse une liberté dangereuse. Ne pouvant donner à la copie une parfaite ressemblance, il doit craindre de ne lui pas donner toute celle qu'elle peut avoir.[21]

To avoid such dangerous extremes, the translator must be very gifted. He must, in fact, rival the author in genius: 'Les hommes de génie ne devroient donc être traduits que par ceux qui leur ressemblent, & qui se rendent leurs imitateurs pouvant être leurs rivaux'.[22] D'Alembert elevates the status of the translator to second place after the creative writer, but also to the position of the writer's rival. Both D'Alembert, in the 'Observations sur l'art de traduire', and Marmontel, in his article 'Traduction', demonstrate more complex views about the possibility of true translation than Beauzée's article 'Traduction, Version'. While Beauzée's conception of translation refers to the universal principles of the *grammaire générale* and the rationalist linguistic ideas expressed in other articles of the *Encyclopédie*, the concerns of Marmontel and D'Alembert are more aesthetic. They seek the correct balance between *fidélité* and *élégance*, between liberty to the point of imitation and the strict literalness that characterizes a school exercise or *version*, and between communication of the style and *énergie* of a work and adherence to the proprieties and rules suitable for a French readership. In this search, the greatest responsibility is placed upon the translator, who is required to have talent and genius equal to the original writer.

Translating the English Novel

Translators of the English novel rarely entered into intricate grammatical or philosophical considerations, but did usually give some justification of their methods. In this respect, there is a large difference between the theories presented in the introductions of Prévost's *Richardson* and La Place's *Fielding* on the one hand, and those in the prefaces of D'Alembert's *Tacitus* and Saint-Simon's *Pope* on the other. The first two, which preface novels, pass over the question of translation fairly briefly, while the second pair contain more complex theories of translation and take into consideration the wider linguistic and philosophical problems examined by the *encyclopédistes*.

Translators of English novels nevertheless still felt the need to engage with contemporary literary debates, particularly those regarding English fiction. As we saw in Part 1, English novels became popular in France during the 1740s. Spurious translations were published, and French novelists frequently used English characters or set their work in England. Some novels and translations carried false imprints, claiming to have been published in London.[23] Reactions to this phenomenon were mixed, for while translation was commonly thought to be enriching, many objected to the excesses of *anglomanie*, which led both to the translation of bad English novels and to the publication of poor quality translations. Criticisms of bad or spurious translations were inextricably linked with the fear of the novel and the view that it was a vulgar genre posing a threat to aesthetic taste and morals, as we can see in Frédéric-Melchior Grimm's letter of 15 August 1754:

> Le démon traducteur nous poursuit ici avec le même acharnement que le démon romancier. Je ne sais si l'on fait aussi des traductions pour les îles; mais tout le petit peuple qui ne fait point de romans, traduit. Trois mois de leçons, chez un maître de langue suffisent pour mettre nos jeunes gens en état de traduire les ouvrages anglais, et sans avoir jamais vécu chez le peuple dont ils osent se faire les interprètes, sans savoir écrire leur propre langue, ils ne laissent pas que d'enrichir notre littérature, tous les deux ou trois mois, de quelque traduction nouvelle.[24]

The English novel was a focal point for debates about the genre as a whole because it was a vehicle for the introduction of a foreign aesthetic standard. French taste was strongly defended against potentially corrupting foreign influences, as the *Année littéraire* makes clear in a comparison of literature with trade:

> Sans doute la littérature étrangère est propre à étendre la sphère de nos idées & à nous enrichir du fruit des travaux & des recherches des autres peuples, de même que le commerce vivifie nécessairement une nation, éveille son industrie, & augmente ses jouissances en lui apportant les productions d'un sol étranger: mais si la littérature étrangère a les mêmes avantages que le commerce, elle a aussi les mêmes inconvéniens. Le commerce avec les fruits des autres climats, nous apporte leurs vices & leurs mœurs; voilà pourquoi *Platon* vouloit l'exclure d'une république bien réglée, comme la source du luxe & de la corruption. De même la littérature étrangère, en nous communiquant les chef-d'œuvres des autres peuples, nous communique aussi leurs défauts & leur mauvais goût, suggère aux écrivains médiocres des innovations dangereuses, & altère le caractère national.[25]

Pride in the cultural tradition was never too far from the anxiety that contemporary literature was decadent compared with the seventeenth-century golden age of French literature, and English novels posed a danger to the national aesthetic taste:

> Une des causes de la décadence de notre théâtre & de notre goût, c'est l'indiscrette imitation des écrivains anglois, dont nous ne prenons que l'enflure, l'extravagance, l'atrocité & l'irrégularité sauvage, sans atteindre à leur génie créateur & à l'énergie de leurs idées. Il seroit à souhaiter, pour les lettres comme pour les mœurs, que la langue & la littérature angloise se fussent moins répandues en France, & que cette connoissance fut restée entre les mains d'un petit nombre d'hommes supérieurs, capables d'en faire un bon usage.[26]

The imperialistic solution recommended by this article is that English fiction should only be translated by the discerning few. Translation entails the selection of the best or most tasteful parts of the work, while those which offend French taste should be eliminated:

> Le goût n'est pas ce qui distingue les écrivains Anglois en général, & le mérite d'un interprète qui fait passer leurs écrits dans notre langue est de les dépouiller de tout ce qui peut blesser notre délicatesse.[27]

Word for word translation was thought to be an easy and worthless occupation. The translator should select and embellish the original work using French models. The resulting composite text would be valuable on its own terms:

> Comme s'il n'était pas plus difficile et plus glorieux d'accommoder un ouvrage anglais à la française, ce qui consiste à lui donner de l'ordre et du goût, que de le laisser avec tous les vices des sa naissance. Rien n'est plus aisé qu'une fidélité scrupuleuse; rien ne l'est moins que le bel art d'*embellir* et de *perfectionner*.[28]

The view that translation must embellish and perfect has its roots in the seventeenth-century notion of the *belles infidèles*, which was instrumental in the creation of a French national literature modelled on Greek and Latin works. It was characterized by the belief that translation was an important literary activity, and the translated text could be unlike the original in many ways as long as it had its own coherence and beauty. Translators such as D'Ablancourt and Guez de Balzac believed in conveying the idea of the original without being slavishly faithful, and aimed to equal or surpass the original to establish a French literary aesthetic.[29]

The translation of English fiction during the eighteenth century also entailed substantial alteration of the original text. Prévost, as translator of Richardson, boldly invokes his right to be creative in order to please the French reader:

> Par le droit suprême de tout Ecrivain qui cherche à plaire dans sa langue naturelle, j'ai changé ou supprimé ce que je n'ai pas jugé conforme à cette vue. Ma crainte n'est pas qu'on m'accusera d'un excès de rigueur. Depuis vingt ans que la Littérature Angloise est connue à Paris, on sait que pour s'y faire naturaliser, elle a souvent besoin de ces petites réparations.[30]

Translators justified their free interpretations by referring to unacceptable elements of English literature, such as vulgar vocabulary and strange metaphors.[31] A frequent criticism of the English novel was that it included unnecessary details that had little to do with the main subject. In reference to his translation of *Sir Charles Grandison*, Prévost felt justified in improving the original text 'par le retranchement des excursions languissantes, des Peintures surchargés, des conversations inutiles & des réflexions déplacées', and in the translation of *Clarissa*, he explains that he shortens 'quelques longueurs, dont il craignoit que l'impatience des lecteurs François ne s'accommodât pas'.[32] La Place similarly believed that the French reader would become impatient with Fielding's digressions, and cleverly suggests that the English author would have made the same changes as La Place himself does, had he written for a French public:

> si M. Fielding [...] avoit écrit pour les François, il eût probablement supprimé un grand nombre de passages très-excellens en eux-mêmes, mais qui leur paroîtroient déplacés. Une fois échauffés par l'intérêt résultant d'une intrigue patétique & adroitement tissuë, ils supportent impatiemment toute espece de digressions, de Dissertations, ou de Traité de Morale, & regardent ces ornemens, quelque beaux qu'ils soient, comme autant d'obstacles au plaisir dont ils sont empressés de jouir. J'ai fait ce que l'Auteur eût fait lui-même.[33]

If Fielding's authorial digressions guide the reader as to what to think of the dramatic events unfolding in *Tom Jones*, the French version seems to prefer a novel based on narrative sequence rather than on moral reflection. Thomas Beebee has shown that Prévost's translation of *Clarissa*, in a comparable fashion, reveals the French novelist's own regard for a pleasing and playful text over a morally didactic one, manifest in his preference for the aristocratic libertine Lovelace over the virtuous, bourgeois Clarissa. Richardson's own distaste for popular novels and his concern to write a new kind of moral novel led him to complain about Prévost's translation:

> This gentleman has left out, a great deal of the book [...] He has given his Reasons for his Omissions, as he went along; one of which is, The Genius of his Countrymen; a strange one to me! He treats the Story as a true one, and says, the English Editor has in many Places, sacrificed it to Moral Instruction, &c.[34]

Like many translators, both Prévost and La Place nevertheless claimed to be faithful to the original authors. Prévost argued that he only changed unimportant elements while retaining the substance of *Clarissa*: 'Les droits d'un Traducteur ne vont pas jusqu'à transformer la substance d'un livre, en lui prêtant un nouveau langage'.[35] La Place maintained that he captured the essence of *Tom Jones*; his Sophia, for instance, was the same as Fielding's, only 'sous un habillement François'.[36] Such statements recall Beauzée's rationalist separation of language and thought in which language is conceived of as a *habillement* which disguises the essential thought of the original author. Of course, the self-justifying preface of the translator is not always to be believed. It frequently hides the extent to which he actually alters the substance of the original for his own creative purposes, as Beebee and Wilcox have amply demonstrated, not least of which was to satisfy the expectations of French readers.[37] Prévost in particular could treat his English model in a cavalier manner because he had his own aims as a novelist and wished to promote the genre of the novel in France by pleasing and instructing French readers.

Towards a New Conception of Translation

At the same time, and increasingly towards the end of the eighteenth century, some theorists criticized the view of the translator as a creative writer, particularly in relation to English fiction. They attacked the methods of Prévost and La Place, which began to be seen as a betrayal or mutilation of the original text, and blamed translators for being overly concerned with the expectations of French readers. Julien-Louis Geoffroy, regular contributor to the *Année littéraire*, teacher of rhetoric, writer and translator of Theocritus's *Idylls*, criticized what he regarded as the constant and limiting reference to French aesthetic standards in the translation of foreign works. In his review of *Galatée* (1783), an imitation of Cervantes's *La Galatea* (1585) by Jean-Pierre Claris de Florian, he disagrees with the latter's disdain for exact and literal translation:

> j'avoue que je fais un gré infini au Traducteur de son exactitude littérale: j'aime à voir les Anglois, les Espagnols, les Italiens dans le costume de leur Pays. Je ne les reconnois plus quand ils sont habillés à la Françoise; cette manie de mutiler & de défigurer les Ouvrages sous prétexte de les ajuster à notre goût & à nos mœurs me paroît extravagante: notre goût & nos mœurs sont-ils donc la règle du beau [...] Quel tort n'a pas fait l'Abbé Prévôt à tous ceux qui ignorent l'Anglois, en retranchant des chefs-d'œuvres de Richardson plusieurs traits admirables, par égard pour notre fausse délicatesse.[38]

Geoffroy's view that a translation should be as close as possible to the original completely refutes the corrective method of Prévost and La Place:

> Je veux voir les Grands Hommes tels qu'il sont, avec la phisionomie qui leur est propre & même avec leurs défauts. Quand on traduit un Ouvrage d'agrément, sans doute, il faut saisir autant qu'il est possible l'esprit de l'Auteur, il faut employer pour rendre ses idées toutes les ressources de la langue dont on fait usage; mais il faut tout rendre; il faut conserver précieusement, les traits de mœurs & même les fautes de goût.

This passionate call for greater fidelity not only affirms that it is possible to have objective knowledge of the original text and the culture which produced it, but also offers a reconceptualization of the translator's role and status, which are now humbled in relation to the original author's:

> N'est-il pas risible que presque tous nos traducteurs modernes aient la manie présomptueuse de vouloir réformer leurs auteurs, & qu'ils s'arrogent un droit absolu de vie & de mort sur leurs pensées, en adoptant les unes & en proscrivant les autres? Qu'ils se persuadent donc, une bonne fois, que ce n'est point leur esprit que nous cherchons dans une version, mais celui des Ecrivains originaux, dont ils se donnent pour les interprêtes; qu'ils sçachent qu'il est utile de connoître jusqu'aux écarts du génie; que nous sommes jaloux d'apprécier par nous-mêmes le mérite littéraire des grands hommes & qu'un lecteur sensé n'aura jamais, ni la fausse délicatesse de ne pouvoir soutenir la vue de quelques taches qui déparent leurs écrits, ni l'injustice de les condamner pour des fautes, abondamment rachetées par des beautés d'un ordre supérieur.

The translator is no longer an artist creating his own work; he may indeed produce a text that stands by itself, but his primary purpose is to provide the reader with a service, even if this means replicating the author's imperfections. This was an important development, marking a change in the translator's task to that of a facilitator aiming at transparency. He was no longer required to be creative in relation to his source material, as another *Année littéraire* article makes clear:

> Le but de la traduction est de suppléer à l'impuissance où je suis de lire un auteur dans une langue morte ou étrangère: si je possédois ces langues originales, je lirois les productions de ces Ecrivains, non refondues & corrigées, mais avec toutes leurs imperfections & telles qu'ils les ont publiées: pourquoi seroi-je plus délicat lorsqu'il s'agit d'une traduction?[39]

Two decades before Geoffroy, Diderot expressed dissatisfaction with Prévost's translation methods. In the *Éloge de Richardson*, he defended Richardson from the accusation that his work was too long and contained unnecessary details that had little to do with the narrative action. The very significance of his novels, Diderot argues, lies in their characteristic length, which permits the reader to experience nature, truth and morality in all their richness and complexity. French readers who complain about it are simply clinging to conservative standards of taste, which prevent them from truly understanding the original work: 'Vous qui n'avez lu les ouvrages de Richardson que dans votre élégante traduction française, et qui croyez les connaître, vous vous trompez'.[40] While English fiction was frequently criticized for corrupting French taste, it was increasingly seen to provide a worthy example for French novelists, who continued to be the target of accusations that their genre was morally and aesthetically flawed. As late as 1755, the Abbé Jaquin wrote in the same vein as the 1735 *Histoire justifée contre les romans*, that the novel was superficial and encouraged a degeneration of morals.[41] Diderot, however, suggested that Richardson's novels represented the best possible manifestation of the genre because they had serious moral intentions as well as aesthetic concerns with psychological and social realism. Rousseau's famous dictum that 'jamais fille chaste n'a lu de romans' epitomized the moral critique of the novel, and *Julie, ou La Nouvelle Héloïse* was his own very successful attempt to write a novel with high moral aims.[42] As Georges May pointed out, English novels with serious intentions, like Richardson's, could provide a solution to the 'dilemma' of the French novel and appeared to reconcile realism with moral edification.[43]

Diderot's presentation of Richardson as an aesthetic and moral model also had consequences for theories of translation. The increasingly widespread idea that a translation should reveal the original text as accurately as possible led to the publication of literal translations of English novels that had already been translated in a 'corrective' manner. Puisieux's translation of *Amelia*, for instance, published in 1763, a year after the *Éloge de Richardson*, promised to be more faithful to Fielding's novel than Madame Riccoboni's 1743 version.[44] Its full title, *Amélie, Histoire angloise. Traduite fidèlement de l'Anglois de M. Fielding*, contrasts with Madame Riccoboni's, *Amélie, roman imité de l'anglais*. In his introduction, Puisieux criticizes her abridgement and adaptation of Fielding's text: 'plus elle a travaillé la portion qu'elle en a conservée, moins on y reconnaîtra le génie Anglois & la touche de l'Auteur original. Il ne fallait donc pas le donner comme une traduction'. He goes on to offer his own translation for the public to judge:

> c'est au public à juger entre nous. Si ce Livre lui plaît dans son entier tel que je le lui présente, & que Mr. Fielding a cru devoir le publier, mon objet est rempli: en tout cas il aura deux Amelies, l'une Françoise, & l'autre dans le goût Anglois: il choisira.[45]

The public did pass judgement and seemed to have preferred Madame Riccoboni's version, for it was reprinted more frequently than Puisieux's. Thus although more literal translations like Puisieux's began to be published, translations in the *belles infidèles* tradition remained popular. An important exception was Prévost's *Clarisse* which, despite its success, was not reprinted after the publication of Le Tourneur's more literal translation in 1785.[46] Some corrective translations remained successful with the reading public, but there was a discernible shift in opinion and practice among theorists, writers and translators towards a more modern view of translation which valued above all the original author.

Chapter 4

The Translations of *Tristram Shandy*

The ideas of translation outlined in the previous chapter emerge in the three French translations of *Tristram Shandy*. The different choices and methods of the translators embody some of the wider aesthetic dilemmas of late eighteenth-century France in its encounter with *Tristram Shandy*. This chapter focuses on *Tristram Shandy* rather than *A Sentimental Journey* precisely because its translation history is more complex. *A Sentimental Journey* was translated relatively faithfully and within a year of its publication in England.[1] The final paragraph is a well-known exception: Frénais could not bear to conclude with Yorick's suggestively outstretched hand, and added a passage to clarify the innocence of the hero's contact with the *fille de chambre*. This should not, however, distract from the fact that the *Voyage sentimental* was closer to the original text than the French *Tristram Shandy*.[2] Chapter 2 looked at some of the reasons for the shorter novel's relatively uncomplicated reception, such as its sympathetic portrayal of the French and the fact that it was read through the familiar structures and expectations of sentimental fiction, a subject that will be explored further in Chapter 5. Its immediate success also accounts in part for why Frénais's was the only translation published until the end of the century. *Tristram Shandy*, by contrast, underwent more significant 'rewriting' in the translation process. It took three different translators and 20 years for all nine volumes to appear in French. Frénais's translation of Volumes I to IV appeared in 1776, and the two different versions of Volumes V to XI, by the Marquis Charles François de Bonnay and Antoine-Gilbert Griffet de La Beaume respectively, were published in 1785.[3] Bonnay and La Beaume took up the challenge of continuing Frénais's translation, each with his own aims, and their achievements contrasted both with their predecessor's and with each other's. *Tristram Shandy* provoked very different responses from its translators and led to the production of three individual French texts.

Frénais

Joseph-Pierre Frénais was born during the early part of the eighteenth century in Fréteval, a town near Vendôme in what is now the Loir-et-Cher department, and died around 1789.[4] During the nineteenth century, he is represented as a local literary celebrity, partly because of his well-known grandsons, Jules-Octave-Frédéric Parisot, a musician and composer, and Valentin Parisot, a writer, translator and professor of foreign literature.[5] A minor literary figure himself, Frénais was a translator of English and German sentimental fiction. In addition to *A Sentimental Journey*, *Tristram Shandy* and Frances Moore Brooke's *The History of Emily Montague* (1769), he is frequently credited with the translation or 'imitation' of works by Susannah Gunning, Charles Johnston and Christophe Martin Wieland,[6] and he is less commonly named as the author or translator of several other anonymous works including, improbably, a treatise on the art of making beer and another on potato bread.[7] The large number of texts attributed to him, published in various cities and by different publishers around 1768 and 1769, makes it highly unlikely that he was responsible for them all. Sterne's novels and Brooke's *Histoire d'Emilie Montague* are the only works in which Frénais's name actually appears on the title page.

In the 'Avertissement' to the *Histoire d'Emilie Montague*, Frénais takes a classical view of translation, defending the right of the translator to be creative with the original text and to think for himself rather than simply to reproduce the author's thoughts:

> Ce roman m'a paru agréable & je l'ai traduit avec la liberté que l'on doit se permettre dans ces sortes d'Ouvrages. Je n'ai pas toujours copié servilement l'Auteur. S'il a pensé pour moi, j'ai cru pouvoir penser aussi, quelquefois, pour lui.

The phrase 'ces sortes d'Ouvrages' is a dismissive one, and the implication is that liberties may be taken with the novel because it is not a particularly serious genre. His belief in the importance of the translator's role is closely tied to a conservative view of English literary language, which is filled with 'ces tournures entortillées, [...] ces inversions pénibles qui déparent si souvent les meilleurs Livres Anglois'.[8] According to Frénais, literal translation is acceptable from French to English, because the French language is stylistically and syntactically more perfect. He thus echoes the seventeenth-century grammarians' view that French conformed to a natural order and embodied the universal rules of grammar.[9] The inverse situation, translation from English to French, calls for a looser type of translation.

He nevertheless also advocates fidelity, partly out of ulterior motives: he claims to be faithful in order to criticize a rival whose own translation of Brooke's novel was published in Amsterdam in the same year:

> la traduction littérale est souvent la meilleure. J'ai, cependant, eu un Concurrent en Hollande qui n'en a pas jugé de même. Me permettra-t-on de comparer, au hazard, quelques-unes de ses manieres avec le texte? L'Auteur dit que rien n'est si favorable à la beauté qu'un bal, qu'un état de repos n'a point de graces, que la nature en mouvement est plus riante. *Les arbres agités par le vent, continue-t-il, un vaisseau sous voile, un cheval dans la course, une belle femme qui danse*, sont des objets ravissans. 'Trees agitated by the wind, a ship under sail, a horse in the course, a fine woman dancing'. Mais le Traducteur de Hollande s'est imaginé que ces expressions rapides & vraies n'étoient pas celles qu'il lui prête. 'Un arbre agité par un vent doux & frais, un

vaisseau que les voiles enflées précipitent au milieu des flots, un coursier qui fait voler la poussiere, une belle qui danse'.[10]

Frénais gives three more examples of mistranslation by his rival, Jean Baptiste René Robinet, expressing increasing antipathy towards him and criticizing his unnecessary elaborations. Although he defends the translator's right to be free with the original, Frénais's overall approach to translation is somewhat complicated by this attempt to dismiss his rival. He believes that the translator should improve and 'beautify' the original, but simultaneously warns against putting too many words in the author's mouth:

> Il est permis, sans doute, en traduisant un Ouvrage d'agrément, d'ajouter, de retrancher, & de faire des changemens: mais ce n'est que pour embellir, s'il est possible, l'Ouvrage que l'on traduit, qu'on doit se permettre cette licence. Il faut se garder, surtout, en mettant du sien, de faire dire des sottises à l'Auteur.[11]

His own approach remains classical and mostly entails shortening and making more concise Brooke's lengthier sentences. This loose method is indicated by the subtitle, which describes the work as '*imitée* de l'anglois'. Robinet's text, on the other hand, is 'traduit de l'anglois', though Frénais insists it is less faithful than his own because it is more verbose.

When confronted with *Tristram Shandy*, however, Frénais's confidence wilts. His translation did not appear until 1776, seven years after his popular *Voyage sentimental*, and in the 'Avertissement', he expresses some doubt that it would be as successful as the shorter novel. The ideas he articulates in the 'Avertissement' tend to be contradictory and are less precise than those expounded in the preface to *Histoire d'Émilie Montague*. He begins by introducing *Tristram Shandy* as one of the most famous books in England and affirms its value by quoting Voltaire's authoritative praise of Sterne.[12] Frénais is careful to add that Sterne did not imitate Rabelais's licentiousness, despite Voltaire's epithet for him as the English Rabelais: 'C'est toujours avec décence qu'il peint les objets, et il est difficile d'y mettre plus d'esprit, plus de finesse'. Frénais's principal reason for translating *Tristram Shandy* is, he assures the reader, its 'gaieté', which he hopes to revive after its disappearance from French literature thanks to the translation of Young's melancholy *Nights* in 1769.[13] He continues nevertheless to voice doubts about its reception in France:

> Ces deux volumes-ci ne font guere que le tiers du tout. M. Stern [*sic*] ne le donnoit que par deux parties à la fois, et je l'ai imité. Il se seroit arrêté, si celles qu'il avoit publiées n'eussent pas plu; et je m'arrêterai tout de même, si ces deux volumes ne font pas desirer la suite. Je ne vois pas pourquoi un Traducteur perdroit haleine pour risquer d'ennuyer ses Lecteurs.

Following Sterne's example, Frénais publishes only two volumes at a time, roughly corresponding to Volumes I to IV in Sterne, preferring to wait for the public's response rather than 'waste his breath' translating it all without knowing whether it would be well received. Frénais's diffidence is caused by his belief that *Tristram Shandy* is 'un des ouvrages les plus difficiles qui aient jamais été écrits en Anglois'. He suggests that the mere attempt to translate it is an achievement that places him among 'les Gens de Lettres'. Yet he has enough confidence in his methods, if not in Sterne's text, to be quite free with it:

> a fallu que je retranchasse beaucoup de l'original, et suppléer à ce que je retranchois: je ne dirois que la vérité. Les plaisanteries de M. Stern ne m'ont pas en effet paru toujours fort bonnes. Je les ai laissées où je les ai trouvées, et j'y en ai substitué d'autres. Je crois que l'on peut se permettre cette liberté dans la traduction d'un ouvrage de pur agrément. Il faut seulement faire son possible pour n'être pas reconnu, et je me trouverai fort heureux si l'on ne m'apperçoit pas.[14]

Such a clear expression of the translator's right to exercise freedom and creativity with the original indicates that Frénais's classical attitude towards translation was not fundamentally shaken. But throughout the 'Avertissement', he is ambiguous about the very decision to translate *Tristram Shandy*. Although he praises the novel's originality and humour, he admits its difficulty and expresses doubt that it will be successful in France. His compromise is to exercise liberty as long as any alterations he makes blend in with the author's style and are not recognizably his own. A reader who is unfamiliar with the original might not recognize Frénais's changes, but some of them are substantial and constitute an attempt to persuade the text to conform to readers' expectations. This was a doomed enterprise given *Tristram Shandy*'s originality, and Frénais's translation, like his 'Avertissement', is contradictory.

Tidying *Tristram Shandy*

There is some paraphrase and very loose translation throughout Frénais's translation, as well as several minor additions, omissions and substitutions. Extensive alterations are more rare, and it should be borne in mind that the first French *Tristram Shandy* is still recognizably *Tristram Shandy*. Frénais's changes on the whole exhibit two opposing tendencies: he modifies some original elements, such as narrative disorder and suggestive ambiguities, while highlighting or exaggerating others.

One of Frénais's most obvious changes is his censorship of bawdy jokes. Suggestive language is repressed, and polite or innocent words substituted for rude ones. For instance, 'she [Mrs Shandy] knew no more than her backside what my father meant', becomes '[Ma mère] ne comprit pas plus que sa chaise ce que mon pere vouloit dire'.[15] Whenever Tristram offers two options, Frénais chooses the innocent meaning. The 'whim wham', which Didius wishes to place in the licence of practising midwives, can mean either a 'fantastic notion' or 'odd fancy' or, according to seventeenth-century slang, 'penis'.[16] The sexual meaning is missing in the French text, which opts for a neutral expression and an inoffensive contextual sentence. Where the English reads, '[he] coax'd many of the old licensed matrons in the neighbourhood, to open their faculties afresh, in order to have this whim-wham of his inserted', the French has: 'il vouloit obliger toutes les matrones du voisinage à faire ajouter à leurs brevets son idée capricieuse'.[17] Frénais also adds moral observations that have little to do with the events in the text. Tristram's description of the midwife's importance in her small village, for example, is used as an opportunity to complain about the vanity of poets:

> Un Poëte maussadement tragique, mais qui n'en est pas moins vain, s'est, par cette regle, trouvé resserré dans la ligne circulaire d'un fort petit compas. S'il murmure d'être ainsi apprécié; s'il se déchaîne contre ceux qui le mesurent de cette maniere, qu'importe? Le public n'est, du moins, pas la dupe de la vaine fumée de son orgueil.
>
> Suivez donc cette regle, Monsieur. – Ici les limites de la réputation de la sage-femme s'étendoient, comme vous le savez déjà, à une circonférence de six ou sept milles.[18]

Similarly, when Tristram mocks his potential critics through an extended metaphor, Frénais includes a moral dimension by taking the metaphor literally and ignoring Tristram's playfulness with his own critical reception. Tristram creates an analogy between guests at a dinner party and readers. The host (or author) should not order things so badly that 'critics and gentry of refined taste' criticize the entertainment, nor should he leave the critics out of the party, which would ensure vengeful criticism of his book:

> – I guard against both; for, in the first place, I have left half a dozen places purposely open for them; – and, in the next place, I pay them all court, – Gentlemen, I kiss your hands, – I protest no company could give me half the pleasure, – by my soul I am glad to see you, – I beg only you will make no strangers of yourselves, but sit down without any ceremony, and fall on heartily.
>
> I said I had left six places, and I was upon the point of carrying my complaisance so far, as to have left a seventh open for them, – and in this very spot I stand on; – but being told by a critick, (tho' not by occupation, – but by nature) that I had acquitted myself well enough, I shall fill it up directly, hoping, in the mean time, that I shall be able to make a great deal of more room next year.[19]

The dinner party metaphor veers between satire, flattery and self-publicity as Tristram pays court to his 'occupational' critics, giving them space at his table – and in his book – by inviting them to dinner and kissing their hands. He thus takes account of the critical reception he expects and hopes that 'I shall be able to make a great deal of more room next year', in his next instalment.

In Frénais's translation of this passage, Tristram's self-conscious preoccupation with the reception of his work is absent. Frénais interprets the chapter very differently, using the dinner party as an opportunity to eulogize food and wine and bringing into the scene Comus, god of singing, comedy, revelry and sex. The analogies between host and author, and between guests and readers disappear, and the dinner party provides Frénais with an opportunity to discourse on the nature of hospitality and conviviality. He criticizes those who host dinner parties only to mock their guests and ruin the jovial atmosphere:

> J'aime assez le dieu Comus; je loue les bienfaisantes ames qui lui font des sacrifices, & qui invitent leurs amis à y participer. – Vive la bonne chere! – vive le bon vin! & vive le bon feu, quand il fait froid! – Avec tout cela, cependant, il faut de la précaution. Je connois des gens, qui, faute de savoir arranger les choses, ne font la dépense d'un repas, que pour se faire moquer d'eux, & donner prise aux sarcasmes.[20]

This is a straightforward moral point and does not appear to constitute a critique of Sterne's own satiric inclinations. Frénais advises the reader to ignore such critics 'by nature', and Tristram's mock-obsequious welcome of the critics is, finally, turned into a more benign metaphor in which the narrator issues to readers an altogether warmer and more sincere invitation, while providing a clear moral:

> Faites comme moi, mes amis. On n'a pas toujours des cartes toutes prêtes, pour inviter M. un tel, & M. un tel & M. un tel ... Mais en revanche, j'ai toujours eu une demi-douzaine de couverts de plus pour les survenans; & vienne qui pourra, il est bien reçu. Je fais ma cour ensuite à tous ... Soyez les bien arrivés, messieurs. Je vous baise les mains; je suis enchanté de vous voir. Il n'y a point de compagnie qui me fasse plus de plaisir. – Agissez, je vous prie, sans façon; vous êtes ici chez vous: point de gêne. Allons, mettons-nous à table, buvons frais, & vive la joie![21]

Some of Frénais's changes protect national pride and soften any satire directed against France. Dr Slop, for instance, is not simply a 'papist' in Frénais's version, but also a priest. Catholic priests and their corruptions were frequently satirized in French literature, so Sterne's unflattering portrait of Slop would have been more palatable to a French reader if he were a priest rather than simply a Catholic, as his flaws in this case could provide an amusing contrast with his officially holy status. Frénais censors Slop's self-implicating statements, omitting, for instance, his boastful statement to Walter concerning the differences between Protestant and Catholic sermons ('our sermons have greatly the advantage, that we never introduce any character into them below a patriarch or a patriarch's wife, or a martyr or a saint').[22] Even more revealing is Frénais's omission of the two chapters (Sterne's Volume IV, Chapters 21 and 22) which contain Sterne's comic anecdote about the French king Francis I, presumably considering it to be disrespectful, if not subversive.

In addition to the censorship of suggestive language, the introduction of moral observations and the preservation of French nationalist sensibilities, Frénais makes some significant structural adjustments. His overriding response to *Tristram Shandy*'s chaotic structure is to organize it, principally by reorganizing both chapters and volumes. The reconfiguration of divisions between chapters constitutes an important attempt to guide the reader through the book's narrative maze. On the whole, Frénais increases the divisions, raising the number of chapters in Volumes I to IV from 118 to 156. This move serves the purpose of 'tidying' the text and making the narrative structure more closely reflect the events described. While Tristram digresses and frequently changes the subject within a chapter, Frénais's shorter chapters permit fewer, or only single, topics to be discussed at a time. Thus a digression within a chapter will occasion the creation of a new chapter by Frénais. Volume I, Chapter 18, for instance, is divided by Frénais into two (Chapters 19 and 20). The chapter contains Walter's reasons for not permitting his wife to give birth according to her preferences. Frénais's division falls where Tristram suddenly introduces Jenny into the picture. Tristram decides to 'enter a caveat in the breast of my fair reader' shortly before the end of the chapter by warning her not to assume the mysterious Jenny he has mentioned in an earlier chapter to be his wife. Tristram squeezes this in to tease a fictionalized female reader towards the conclusion that Jenny is his mistress, and then to scold her for the assumption. In the French translation, Jenny arouses enough interest to merit a whole chapter to herself.

Frénais also creates new divisions between volumes to clarify the threads of the plot. While Sterne published two-volume instalments, Frénais published the first four volumes at once in the form of two books.[23] The divisions that Sterne establishes between volumes, and particularly between pairs of volumes – Volumes I and II on one hand, and III and IV on the other – do not, therefore, apply in Frénais's text. His first book, furthermore, does not correspond exactly to Sterne's first and second volumes. In fact it ends, not at Chapter 19, where Sterne's second volume terminates, but earlier, at Chapter 17. The consequence of this alteration is that the French Tristram does not play with suspense at the end of each pair of volumes. Sterne ends his second volume by asking the reader to be 'content to wait for a full explanation of these matters till the next year, – when a series of things will be laid open which he little expects'.[24] To accommodate his change in volume distribution and the difference in publication instalments, Frénais omits the reference to 'next year':

– Ce sont-là des énigmes trop difficiles à développer. Il y faut mon secours [...] Mais attendez, s'il vous plaît, que j'en aie le tems; il viendra, & vous verrez alors une suite de choses que vous n'attendez sûrement pas. – .[25]

Frénais's first book ends when Trim has finished reading Yorick's sermon and Tristram relates the history of the sermon's adventures. By redistributing the divisions between volumes, he ensures that his second book begins with a new topic: it does not correspond to Sterne's third and fourth volumes, but begins as soon as Obadiah returns with Dr Slop's bag of instruments after the reading of the sermon is completely finished, an incident which, in Sterne, occurs in Volume II, Chapter 18.

Frénais's second book similarly ends in a 'tidier' fashion – at Sterne's Volume IV, Chapter 30 (Frénais's Chapter 102). Chapters 31 and 32 are simply omitted. Again, this has the effect of ordering the novel's events and narrative structure, since Sterne's Chapter 30 marks the end of the visitation dinner during which Walter discovers that he cannot change Tristram's baptism name. Sterne's thirty-first chapter begins a different subject, Walter's new and endless dilemma as to how to spend Aunt Dinah's legacy: whether to fence in the Ox-moor land or to send his eldest son Bobby on a Grand Tour of Europe. This dilemma ends, as does the chapter, with news of Bobby's death. In the thirty-second chapter, 'the chapter of THINGS', Tristram only tells the reader what he has still to write about. Frénais's omission of these two chapters means that Bobby's death, the greatest in a series of misfortunes for Walter regarding his children, is left for the new volume, in which Shandy Hall's reactions to Bobby's death are also described (these appear in Sterne's fifth volume and are translated by Bonnay and La Beaume). Frénais alters the end of Chapter 30 since it now becomes the final chapter of the book, though his elaboration of the exchange between Walter and Toby is rather gratuitous:

> Et moi, dit mon oncle Tobie, je suis d'avis, quoi qu'en disent ces Messieurs, qu'il y avoit une espece de consanguinité entre la Duchesse de Suffolk & son fils.
> Le Public le croit comme vous; mais le Public est un sot, & les Savant [sic] sont des Savants.
> D'accord: mais les Savants sont une partie du Public, reprit mon oncle Tobie.
> Mon pere crut voir une pointe dans cette réflexion de mon oncle Tobie. Il détestoit les pointes; mais c'étoit la premiere qui fut jamais sortie de la bouche de son frere, il sourit.[26]

By changing the volume divisions between the different instalments, Frénais naturally loses some of Sterne's play with suspense. But it permits him to 'tidy' the structure of the novel and organize the novel thematically so that each of his two books, or volumes, ends with the completion of a particular episode. This formal reorganization and its consequences for the significance of the novel highlight Sterne's own consideration of the reader's expectations and use of suspense at the end of each pair of volumes through the introduction of a new subject or momentous event shortly before it ends.

Emphasizing Originality

While Frénais tidies *Tristram Shandy*, he also demonstrates a contradictory propensity to exaggerate of some of Tristram's original narrative techniques. This usually occurs through the addition of passages and even whole chapters that imitate Tristram's playful eccentricities. Typographically, Frénais's text

The Translations of Tristram Shandy   71

looks more bizarre than Sterne's, and there are some striking additions, such as the insertion of a short chapter in the second book. Entitled 'Rien', it consists of the sentence 'Je laisse en lacune tout ce que je pourrois dire ici' followed by nine and a half lines of suspension points, then a final sentence 'Le chapitre suivant l'éclaircira ...'.[27] Similarly, after the 'Déploration de mon Pere' ('My father's lamentation') in Chapter 86 of Book II, Frénais adds a passage (see Figure 1 and the transcription below).[28]

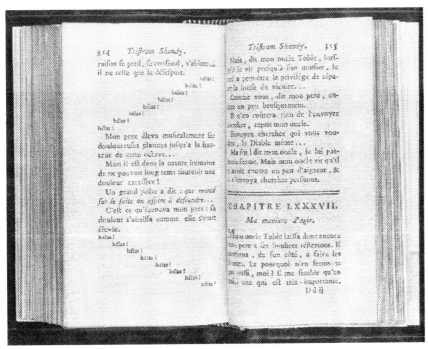

Figure 1

A ce nom, à ce nom vil, à ce nom humiliant, ignomineux, toute raison se perd, se confond, s'abîme ... il ne reste que le désespoir.

                                                                                                    hélas!
                                                                     hélas!
                                                        hélas!
                                    hélas!
                        hélas!
              hélas!
      hélas!
hélas!

Mon pere éleva musicalement ses douloureuses plaintes jusqu'à la hauteur de cette octave ...

Mais il est dans la nature humaine de ne pouvoir long tems soutenir une douleur excessive!

Un grand Poëte a dit: *que monté sur le faite on aspire à descendre* ...

> C'est ce qu'éprouva mon pere: sa douleur s'abaissa comme elle s'étoit élevée.
> hélas!
>   hélas!
>   hélas!
>   hélas!
>   hélas!
>   hélas!
>   hélas!
>   hélas!
>
> Mais, dit mon oncle Tobie lorsqu'il le vit presqu'à son unisson, le curé a peut-être le privilége de réparer la sottise du Vicaire ...
> Comme vous, dit mon pere, encore un peu brusquement.
> Il n'en coûtera rien de l'envoyer chercher, reprit mon oncle.
> Envoyez chercher qui vous voudrez, le Diable même ...
> Ma foi! dit mon oncle, je lui parlerois ferme. Mais mon oncle vit qu'il y avoit encore un peu d'aigreur, & il n'envoya chercher personne.[29]

The section after the display of 'alases' is a free adaptation of the chapter's final two sentences:

> We will send for Mr. *Yorick*, said my uncle *Toby*.
> – You may send for whom you will, replied my father.[30]

Frénais's version reduces the scene's tragic overtones by comically exaggerating Walter's grief. The rising and falling 'alases' emphasize Walter's comedic status, and his reply to Toby is ruder than in Sterne. Frénais's Walter is, in this chapter at least, less sympathetic than Sterne's, but the change seems to serve little purpose other than to increase the text's typographical eccentricities.

Frénais does not stop at typographical imitations, but also occasionally adds his own fragments. One creative instance is the insertion of a poem in the middle of Sterne's Volume III, Chapter 18, in which Walter lectures Toby on Locke's ideas of duration. Frénais creates his own chapter for the poem, aptly named 'Mes offres':

> Le chevalier d'Acilly disoit un jour à sa belle:
>   Philis, rien pour rien.
>   Donnez-moi du vôtre.
>   Qui donne un bijou,
>   Au moins, s'il n'est fou,
>   En demande un autre
> Je ne sais quels étoient ces bijoux. Moi, Monsieur, je vous offre de mon cœur mon bonnet & mes pantoufles.
> A CONDITION
> Que vous serez attentif à tout ce chapitre.[31]

This very free adaptation of the first few lines of the chapter is amusing enough but, again, does not appear to have any further function. Such additions are at odds with Frénais's attempt to tidy the narrative, and instead contribute to the fragmentary nature of the text. He confidently reconfigures chapter and volume divisions, substitutes obscene words and inserts ethical precepts in order to guide the reader through the narrative twists and turns. But he simultaneously multiplies minor typographical originalities and introduces his own fragments, further complicating the narrative in an apparent drive to amuse and entertain the reader. It is unfortunate that his translation omits the marbled page which, on many levels, represents *Tristram Shandy*'s originality. Its very appearance within the book's pages is surprising. Tristram calls it the 'motly emblem of my work' while prodding the reader to interpret its 'moral'. It is motley not only because of its mixed colours, but also because it suggests the jester in his multicoloured clothing. As an artefact, it is also literally original and unique, since each marbled page had to be hand-made separately. Frénais's omission of it should not, however, be interpreted as an indication that he was unwilling to consider the novel's multi-layered meanings or its articulation of profound ideas through jest. It is more likely to have been a printer's decision based on the expense of producing marbled pages and, in fact, the more easily produced black page does appear in the translation. Whatever the precise reason, its omission meant that the French reader was excluded from one of Tristram's most charmingly meaningful eccentricities.[32]

Despite the contradictory nature of his translation, one innovation does come close to providing an overriding methodical principle. The addition of chapter titles is Frénais's most consistent contribution, and arguably the most important. First, it has an organizing effect on the narrative because the titles are generally descriptive of the contents. The opening chapters of the novel, for instance, are named 'C'étoit bien à cela qu'il falloit penser' during Tristram's conception, 'L'embryon' when he describes the effect of interruption on the homunculus and 'En voilà l'effet' when the product of the dispersed homunculus turns out to be the little boy's 'unaccountable obliquity' in the way he sets up his top. The titles clarify the themes of the chapters and highlight the narrative's progression by describing the movement from initial mistake, through its immediate effect, to its evident final consequences in little Tristram. They encourage the reader to expect some narrative development and provide a clue as to what might happen in each chapter. Sterne does not give titles to his chapters, so his reader remains in the dark a little longer before discovering what they contain. Second, the addition of chapter titles creates an association between *Tristram Shandy* and picaresque or comic-satiric works. Used by Rabelais, Cervantes and his seventeenth and eighteenth-century French and English translators, Scarron, Lesage and Fielding, chapter headings amuse or tease the reader, give him a clue about what might happen next only to comically deflate the expectation, or simply provide a description of the chapter's contents. Frénais's decision to treat Sterne's book as a *roman comique* through the use of chapter titles constitutes its incorporation into the familiar traditions of picaresque and comic-satiric fiction.

Bonnay and La Beaume

Although his translation of Volumes I to IV was well received and quickly reprinted three times, Frénais never translated the remaining volumes of *Tristram Shandy*.[33] Critical discussions continued to focus on its originality, and it inspired enough curiosity to warrant the publication of the two different and unrelated translations of Volumes V to IX in 1785. Each of the translators, the Marquis de Bonnay and Griffet de La Beaume, expresses his aims in relation to his predecessor.[34] Bonnay presents himself as a great admirer of Sterne who wishes to complete Frénais's translation simply in order to understand the rest of the novel:

> L'extrême plaisir que m'a causé sa traduction m'en a fait vivement desirer la suite. Amateur passioné de Stern, j'attendois avec impatience que M. Frénais achevât de me le faire connoître.
>
> A la fin, j'ai pris le texte anglois et un dictionnaire. – *Et moi aussi*, j'entends Stern, ai-je dit. – Peu-à-peu, et presque sans y songer, je suis venu à bout de traduire ce qui restoit de *la Vie et des Opinions de Tristram Shandy*.[35]

The 'accidental' nature of this translation is emphasized by the personal reasons for having undertaken it in the first place (his love of Sterne and a desire to read and understand the rest of the book), and he seems not to care too much about an audience: 'Ceux qui ont aimé autant que moi le commencement de l'Ouvrage, me sauront gré de l'avoir continué; les autres ne m'importent guere'. He is equally casual about his methods: 'M. Frénais avoue qu'il a fait beaucoup de retranchemens, auxquels il a suppléé de son propre fonds. – J'ai usé de la même liberté que lui, et je desire que ce soit avec autant de bonheur'.[36] The dilettantish attitude is refreshingly straightforward. Unlike Frénais, who engages in a debate about translation, weighs the advantages and weaknesses of different procedures, justifies his changes, and competes with a rival translator, Bonnay is an aristocratic amateur who participates in the world of *belles-lettres* for the pleasure of it. Yet despite his free approach to translation, which allows him to add a few of his own colourful details to the text, his translation is remarkably faithful and, with one exception that is discussed below, he does not make substantial alterations in the same way as Frénais. He claims to follow his predecessor, but the freedom he calls for as a translator is exercised stylistically rather than through omissions, insertions and structural reorganization. Sterne's individual sentences on the whole remain intact and Bonnay's own elaborations remain true to Sterne's spirit because they complement, rather than falsify, the text.

La Beaume, on the other hand, is not as carefree as Bonnay. He does not write his own preface, and the 'Avertissement des editeurs, pour servir d'introduction' creates a very different tone from Bonnay's 'Avis'. The editors are concerned to present the translation as serious and scholarly. Justifying the need for a continuation of Frénais's translation, they claim that the later volumes will be appreciated by French readers because they are more interesting, varied and philosophical than the early ones. They also praise its originality and compare its sentimental episodes with those of *A Sentimental Journey*:

> Elle contient des épisodes qui ne le cèdent en rien, pour la touche, au Voyage Sentimental, tels que l'Histoire de le Fèvre, celle des fameux Amans de Lyon, celle de la pauvre Marie, et plusieurs traits recueillis par M. Stern, dans un de ses voyages en France. Quant à l'originalité, à la gaieté et à l'excellence de la critique et des bonnes plaisanteries qui caractérisent l'Auteur, elles s'y trouvent abondamment répandues dans les détails de ce même Voyage, dans ceux sur la mort du frère Bobi, dans la *Tristra-pédie*, ou Système d'éducation de M. Shandy, à l'usage de son fils unique, et dans les *Campagnes de l'oncle Tobie*. Ce dernier morceau du Roman est surtout d'une originalité singulièrement plaisante: il étoit au gré de l'Auteur, le meilleur de son Ouvrage; et il trouvera certainement beaucoup de partisans chez les Lecteurs François.[37]

The editors present their edition as being rich in content as well as representative of Sterne's work as a whole, thanks to additional extracts from his other works and to the fidelity of the translation itself. Favouring the original text, they express the hope that La Beaume's version is worthy of it, and to encourage the view that it is, they invoke the authority of the Abbé Raynal, whose response to La Beaume's text is quoted:

> J'ai reçu le présent que vous avez bien voulu me faire. Les Ecrivains les plus prévenus en faveur de notre langue, n'auroient jamais osé espérer, que la gaieté, que l'esprit, que l'originalité de Stern pussent être rendus aussi heureusement que vous l'avez fait.[38]

Concerned with accuracy and the authority of the original, the editors take issue with Frénais's methods and affirm that the best way to convey the author's individuality is through fidelity rather than exaggeration:

> On n'y trouvera rien qui soit étranger à cet Auteur inimitable [...] Et le Traducteur n'a pas cru non plus devoir, à l'exemple de M. Frénais, interpréter et vouloir rendre son Auteur plus original ou plus piquant: Stern l'est, sans doute, assez lui-même; et l'on ne sauroit ajouter à la plaisante singularité, à ses idées et à ses tournures pittoresques.[39]

La Beaume does not, like Frénais, add chapters and short poems of his own composition, nor does he experiment with typography. His translation offers reliability and erudition, and is supported by footnotes scattered throughout the text. These provide biographical details about Sterne and explanations of a particular word, phrase or reference, or express the translator's own views of the work.[40] La Beaume paraphrases far less than Frénais, and his vocabulary and phrasing are closer to the original. This scholarly attitude may be explained in part by his background. From impoverished nobility, his jesuit and humanist education in Classics, German and English led him to pursue a literary career, and he worked as a critic for *Le Censeur universel anglais*, *Le Mercure de France* and *Le Journal encyclopédique*. His approach to *Tristram Shandy* is reverent and respectful, and his most substantial and consistent changes to the text consist of abridgement. Many chapters are shortened, with sentences or paragraphs sometimes entirely omitted. This tendency increases towards the end of the translation, perhaps simply an indication that he was impatient to complete the work.

Minor Modifications: Structure and Typography

As the prefaces to their translations indicate, Bonnay and La Beaume approached the task of translating *Tristram Shandy* very differently. In structural terms neither reorganizes the volumes in the manner of Frénais. Both take up where he ended, beginning their translations with Volume IV, Chapter 31, the penultimate chapter of that volume, and continuing through the division between Volumes IV and V. Bonnay omits the final paragraph of Chapter 32, in which Tristram takes leave of his readers until the following year when, he promises, he will offer them a surprising story. Precise and scholarly, La Beaume leaves this in, which might have confused French readers who were not aware of the original book's publication by instalment. However, he does, like Bonnay, remove the epigraphs and dedication to Lord Viscount Spencer at the head of Volume V, and places them (along with the first volume's dedication to William Pitt) among the 'Mélanges, Pensées, Bons Mots et Mémoires' at the end of the translation. In a similar fashion, Bonnay omits the 'Dedication to a Great Man', which introduces Sterne's ninth volume. This is the second dedication to William Pitt who, since the first, had been elected Prime Minister and appointed Earl of Chatham – hence his 'greatness' and the more ironic tone of the dedication. La Beaume does not get rid of it completely but simply moves it from its prominent position at the head of a volume and places it a little earlier. The chapter divisions also remain intact in both translations and are not redistributed. The only notable change is La Beaume's rearrangement of the eight chapters containing the story of Le Fever, while Bonnay follows Sterne's divisions more closely in this case.[41] The minimal reorganization of volume and chapter divisions in Bonnay and La Beaume does not mean, however, that Sterne's method of leaving the reader in suspense between published instalments is lost. La Beaume in particular is careful to transfer the technique to the division between his two volumes. He terminates the first volume (called Volume III by the publishers since it constitutes the continuation of Frénais) at the end of the first chapter of Volume VIII, which promises to tell the story of Toby's amours, thus recreating the between-volume suspense of which Sterne is so fond.[42]

Bonnay and La Beaume follow Frénais's example with the addition of chapter titles, but since these are more or less identical in both, they are likely to have been publishers' additions. The typography, meanwhile, which inspired Frénais's imitative additions in 1776, is rendered comparatively faithfully in both. Neither introduces further eccentricities and any changes are minor: the points of suspension and asterisks, for instance, do not always match Sterne's and are sometimes used interchangeably, but these may well be printers' variations. Sterne's Rabelaisian lists and catalogues (of things, of auxiliary verbs, etc.) also appear intact in both translations, as does Trim's twirling flourish. The list of love's attributes, however, is translated differently by each translator.[43] The blank page reserved for the male reader's portrait of Mrs Wadman, and the two missing chapters (Chapters 18 and 19) in the ninth volume, are also represented faithfully as blank pages. The only significant typographical infidelity by either translator relates to the squiggly lines traced by Tristram in the final chapter of Volume VI as he reflects on the journey of his narrative (see Figure 2).[44]

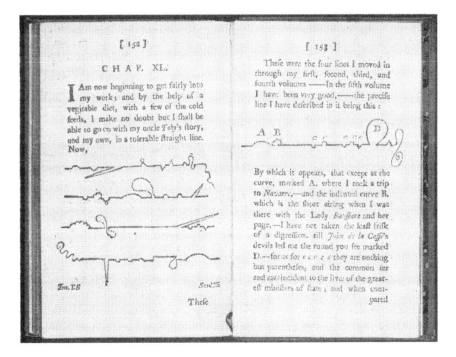

Figure 2

Bonnay simply omits these, while La Beaume, with his scholarly approach, preserves the first two out of the six lines and attempts to adapt them to Frénais's two-volume structure. The squiggle representing Sterne's Volume V is used to represent his own first volume (that is, Volume III of the complete French translation), and he modifies the surrounding text (see Figure 3).[45]

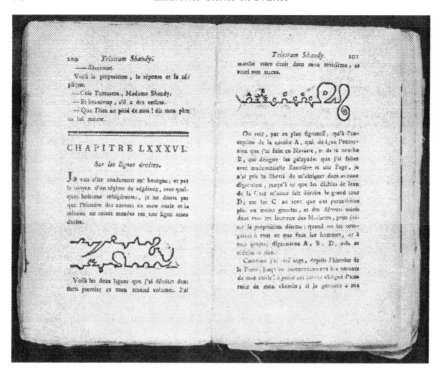

Figure 3

This change would clearly not work if one were to see the lines as pictorial representations of Tristram's narrative. The first line, for instance, may represent the progression (and simultaneous digression) from Tristram's conception to his birth, the first two bumps representing the digressive stories of Yorick and the midwife and of Mrs Shandy's marriage settlement. The sharp downward slope may be regarded as Tristram's musings on the difficulties of writing his life, while the upward loop could be the digression on Toby's character. While it might be a stretch to read the lines according to the narrative twists and turns, La Beaume's reorganization of them to represent different volumes would make it a harder, if not impossible, task. The lines become representative in a more abstract sense and at least retain their entertainment value.

The Fragment on Whiskers

In order to point out some of the key differences in the methods and execution of the translations by Bonnay and La Beaume, it is useful to focus on a specific section of the text. The Fragment on Whiskers, like Yorick's sermon, is one of the many interpolated texts that contribute to *Tristram Shandy*'s disordered nature. Tristram's introduction to this particular fragment plays on the suggestiveness of whiskers and noses:

Upon Whiskers

I'm sorry I made it – 'twas as inconsiderate a promise as ever entered a man's head – A chapter upon whiskers! alas! the world will not bear it – 'tis a delicate world – but I knew not of what mettle it was made – nor had I ever seen the underwritten fragment; otherwise, as surely as noses are noses, and whiskers are whiskers still; (let the world say what it will to the contrary) so surely would I have steered clear of this dangerous chapter.[46]

Sur les Moustaches

De quoi diantre me suis-je avisé? Quelle promesse étourdie! un chapitre sur les moustaches! le public ne le supportera jamais. C'est un public délicat. – Mais je n'avois jamais lu le fragment que voici; je ne le croyois pas aussi scabreux: – autrement aussi sûrement que des nez sont des nez, & que des moustaches sont des moustaches, j'aurois louvoyé de maniere à ne pas rencontrer ce dangereux chapitre.[47]

Sur les Moustaches

Je suis fâché d'avoir fait une promesse aussi inconsidérée: un chapitre sur les *Moustaches!* (1) On ne le supportera pas; car on est délicat aujourd'hui. Je n'en connoissois pas la conséquence, et je n'ai jamais lu le fragment que je vais copier. Bonnes gens, nous le lirons, si vous voulez, ensemble.[48]

The first translation, Bonnay's, is more lively than La Beaume's. It begins by emphasizing Tristram's *in medias res* statement with the slightly more exclamatory 'De quoi diantre me suis-je avisé? Quelle promesse étourdie! un chapitre sur les moustaches!' Bonnay translates loosely without abridging the text. He preserves all the elements, as well as the tone, of the paragraph. La Beaume is more literal in the first sentence but goes on to cut much of the text, replacing the second half of the paragraph ('otherwise, as surely as noses are noses, and whiskers are whiskers still [...]') with a shorter sentence. La Beaume may be precise, but he abridges freely. In a footnote to the first sentence, he makes clear his disapproval of the Fragment on Whiskers, admitting that he would have left it out had it not been for some interesting historical details in the story, which he dutifully but rather unnecessarily researches:

> Je pourrois dire que je suis fâché de l'avoir traduit. Sterne avoit sûrement parié de faire un chapitre bisarre sur un mot donné comme on remplit des bout-rimés. J'ai même failli à le supprimer; mais comme les détails en sont intéressans, quoique le sujet ne le soit pas, le lecteur sera toujours à tems de faire ce que le traducteur nécessairement prévenu, n'a pas la force d'exécuter. Vainement il a voulu éclaircir ce chapitre par des recherches historiques; le seul fruit de ses peines a été de trouver, que Mlles Rebours et la Fosseuse sont citées dans plusieurs livres, et notamment dans les mémoires de Marguerite de Valois, comme maîtresses de Henri IV. Quant aux Guiol, Maronette, Batarelle, etc. etc. le hasard les lui a offertes dans la nombreuse liste des témoins entendus au procès de Girard et la Cadiere.[49]

With his commitment to accuracy, La Beaume reluctantly translates the Fragment although he clearly does not believe it has a purpose. He suggests that writing a chapter on a single word is bizarre, and it seems not to have occurred to him that the story, which is structured around a play on words, comically exposes the philosophical espousal of fixed definitions.[50] John Ferriar also points out that La Beaume was not familiar with Robert Burton, from whom Sterne freely borrowed this episode.[51]

Tristram concludes the Fragment on Whiskers by mocking the poor Lockean curate d'Estella. The curate realizes that the meaning of any word can vary according to its context and the intention of the speaker. However, nobody understands or pays attention to his book, which does not have the desired effect of regulating and fixing the meaning of words:

> The best word, in the best language of the best world, must have suffered under such combinations. – The curate of *d'Estella* wrote a book against them, setting forth the dangers of accessory ideas, and warning the *Navarois* against them.
>
> Does not all the world know, said the curate *d'Estella* at the conclusion of his work, that Noses ran the same fate some centuries ago in most parts of *Europe*, which Whiskers have now done in the kingdom of *Navarre* – The evil indeed spread no further then, – but have not beds and bolsters, and night-caps and chamber-pots stood upon the brink of destruction ever since? Are not trouse, and placket-holes, and pump-handles – and spigots and faucets, in danger still, from the same association? – Chastity, by nature the gentlest of all affections – give it but its head – 'tis like a ramping and roaring lion.
>
> The drift of the curate *d'Estella*'s argument was not understood. – They ran the scent the wrong way. – The world bridled his ass at the tail. – And when the *extreams* of DELICACY, and the *beginnings* of CONCUPISCENCE, hold their next provincial chapter together, they may decree that bawdy also.[52]

Unlike La Beaume, Bonnay understands and enjoys the ambiguities in which Sterne revels, and even inserts his own contributions. In the case of the Fragment on Whiskers, he livens up the text with a subtle addition: '*Moustaches!* s'écria encore la reine, pouvant d'autant moins se persuader d'avoir bien entendu, qu'il s'agissoit d'un de ses pages qu'elle voyoit tous les jours [...]'.[53] In Sterne there is no mention that the queen knows the page to whom La Fosseuse refers: 'Whiskers! cried the queen, laying a greater stress upon the word, and as if she had still distrusted her ears – .'[54] Bonnay adds the detail that the queen sees the page every day – perhaps in order to suggest a more intimate relationship between them. In another instance, Bonnay breaks the flow of the story within the story when the queen touches her eye with the tip of her forefinger as if to say 'I understand you all'. In Bonnay, the old lady (the listener of the tale, like the reader) interrupts the storyteller (the old gentleman) with a question:

> 'Et qu'entendoit- elle? dit la vieille dame, en soulevant sa gaze & regardant le vieux gentilhomme' –

'Ce que vous entendez vous-même, répondit le vieux gentilhomme;' & continua de lire.[55]

By making more explicit the fact that the reader may be asking the same question as the old lady and that the narrator is not replying but forcing her to guess, Bonnay shows that he has fully absorbed Sterne's methods of playing with meaning and with the reader's expectations through the use of a fictionalized reader, a subject which will be considered in Chapter 6.

'Le Pauvre et son chien'

Bonnay's claim to be as free as Frénais in his translation is fulfilled by the addition of a spurious chapter in Volume VII, in which Tristram takes his Grand Tour and which is divided, in Bonnay, between Volumes III and IV. The extra chapter, entitled 'Le Pauvre et son chien', occupies a prominent position at the head of Volume IV, and consists of a sentimental episode in the style of *A Sentimental Journey*. Tristram tells of his encounter with a poor old man whose misfortunes are met with his initial refusal to help, then with his remorse, and finally with belated charity. As the critic Mallet du Pan pointed out, the episode recalls Yorick's encounter with the monk at Calais and, I would add, with the old man mourning his dead ass.[56]

Travelling through France, Tristram's carriage is forced to stop so that the horses may be fed, since the courier of an approaching berlin carriage has already reserved the fresh horses. Impatient at the delay, Tristram dismisses the poor old man when he asks for charity. He describes the appeal as an inconvenience that worsens his mood. Stylistically, the episode recalls Sterne: Tristram's words of refusal, 'Je n'ai rien, mon bon-homme, lui dis-je', throw the reader into the middle of the situation and leave him to wonder momentarily what the question to this answer is, and who is asking the question. As in the exchange between Yorick and Father Lorenzo, the appeal hardens the narrator's mood. The ensuing description of the poor man resembles the portraits of Lorenzo, the mourning man and even Maria. His physical appearance and the meaning of his expression and gestures are sketched with a few details:

> C'étoit [Tristram's reply] à un vieillard couvert de haillons, qui s'étoit avancé jusqu'à deux pas de la portiere, son bonnet de laine rouge à la main. – Son geste & ses yeux demandoit, sa bouche ne parloit pas. – Il avoit un chien qui tenoit, ainsi que son maître, ses yeux fixés sur moi, & qui sembloit aussi solliciter ma charité.[57]

Bonnay's Tristram, like Sterne's Yorick, experiences rapid changes of thought and mood as he regrets his cruelty and blushes with shame, then blames the old man's bad timing to justify his own behaviour to himself. The old man, meanwhile, like Father Lorenzo, exhibits only goodness as he blesses Tristram and humbly retires. When the berlin carriage arrives and its rich passengers also refuse to help the old man, Tristram can further justify his meanness. But again he has second thoughts: 'Bon Dieu! m'écriai-je, leur dureté excuse-t-elle la mienne?' He then observes the old man in sentimental pose, sitting on a stone bench with his dog's head gently resting in his lap. A travelling soldier, with his own dog, joins them on the bench, and Tristram reflects on the friendship between man and dog:

> Ce bon vieillard, méprisé, délaissé, rebuté par le monde entier, trouve en toi [the dog] un ami qui l'accueille, & qui lui sourit: – & sur le lit de paille qu'il partage avec toi, sa misere lui paroît moins affreuse, il n'est pas seul au monde tant que tu lui restes encore.[58]

The people in the berlin throw out some leftover meats from their lunch and both dogs run towards them. In a dramatic turn, one is run over: 'La berline parut: un seul chien fut écrasé. – C'étoit celui du pauvre. Le chien jetta un cri. – Ce fut le dernier. Son maître s'étoit précipité sur lui. – Son maître dans le plus sombre désespoir!' The dog's death motivates Tristram to throw a six-franc coin to the old man, whose misfortunes have at last elicited his benevolence. But in a further twist, the soldier offers the old man his own dog, his only worldly possession, a gesture which puts to shame Tristram's meagre offering. Tristram's final exclamation clarifies the moral lesson in case it were not already evident: 'Brave & galant homme, m'écriai-je! Eh! qui suis-je auprès de toi? Je n'ai donné à ce malheureux que de l'argent: tu viens de lui rendre un ami'.

The dog's road accident might appear somewhat ludicrous to modern readers, and the moral lesson it extracts predictable. Despite his remorse, moreover, the Tristram of this episode, who never leaves his carriage and reports the whole incident from its safety, is an altogether haughtier and less generous character than either of Sterne's narrators. As a purely sentimental story, it cannot compare with Sterne's more self-conscious sentimentalism with its mixture of sincerity and comic self-criticism.[59] Because Bonnay generally communicates with subtlety Sterne's ironies and ambiguities, it is worth questioning whether he really is the author of this straightforward sentimental tale. It may simply be an anonymous imitation added by the publisher, which would indicate that the translation of *Tristram Shandy* was, to some degree, a collaborative entreprise.

Tristam Shandy and Ideas of Translation

The story of 'Le Pauvre et son chien' sparked a minor argument when Mallet du Pan did not recognize it as spurious but rather praised it as particularly representative of Sterne's writing.[60] He clearly had not compared the translation with the original. A few months after his article appeared in the *Mercure de France*, a letter was published in the same journal complaining about the oversight. Its author objects to the fact that Mallet chose only to review Bonnay's translation, and defends La Beaume's against accusations that it is awkwardly literal:

> On a affirmé, par un avis répandu dans plusieurs Journaux, qu'il ne faut pas confondre cette Traduction avec celle de M. le Marquis de **; que celle de M. de L. B. est d'un style lâche & rampant, & que les idées de Stern y sont si gauchement rendues, qu'on croiroit cette Traduction l'ouvrage d'un Ecolier forcé de faire une version.[61]

The concerned author argues that La Beaume's translation is more accurate and offers additional extracts from Sterne's letters and sermons (the 'Mélanges, Lettres, Pensées, Bons-mots, & Mémoires'). The complaint appears to have worked, for it forced Mallet to look at the original and admit his mistake. In a second article on the subject, Mallet justifies his earlier praise of Bonnay, this time comparing the two different translations and referring to the English text. He acknowledges that the story of the poor man and his dog is nowhere to be found in *Tristram Shandy*, but declares that this need not prevent him from admiring it since its style is perfectly coherent with Sterne's – the proof being that he mistook it for Sterne:

> la justice m'oblige à déclarer que le Chapitre du *Chien tué sous la berline*, et que j'ai rapporté, est absolument de l'invention de M. le Marquis de ***. Pour s'en assurer, on peut feuilleter toutes les Editions Angloises de *Tristram Shandy*, dans aucune on ne trouvera ce morceau si pathétique, et dont le mérite, à mon gré, surpasse celui de dix Traductions. L'Auteur s'est tellement confondu avec *Sterne* lui-même, qu'aucun Lecteur ne s'est douté qu'ici, M. le Marquis de **** fut original. En effet, ce Chapitre, et celui de la tabatière du Moine à Calais, dans le *Voyage Sentimental*, paroissent écrites de la même main.[62]

Mallet defends his admiration of the spurious chapter with the argument that the translator's pen is indistinguishable from the original author's, but the exchange of letters demonstrates that some readers disagreed and wanted to be able to rely on the accuracy and authenticity of a translation. It also suggests that between Frénais's translation of 1776 and the two continuations of 1785, ideas of translation, which continued to be aired in the public arena of the periodicals, had definitively changed.

Frénais's text is classical in the sense that it attempts to accomodate the text to the taste and expectations of a French audience. Like Prévost and La Place, he claims the right to translate freely and improve the original. He clarifies ambiguities, censors jokes, attempts to order the narrative chaos and guide the reader through its digressions with varying degrees of success. But *Tristram Shandy* resists corrective translation and Frénais's attempts to subdue it are countered by his own creative additions and typographical exaggerations, which signal an acknowledgement that its originality is both integral and appealing. Less than a decade later, both Bonnay and La Beaume are more accurate than Frénais. La Beaume's scholarly attitude shows a serious concern to produce a faithful representation of the original and a recognition of its unique value. La Beaume nevertheless cannot help expressing his opinion in intrusive footnotes and abridging the text in an overzealous drive for clarity. He ultimately does not produce as entertaining, subtle and thereby, arguably, as faithful a translation as Bonnay, even though the latter claims to follow in Frénais's footsteps. Both cases show that as theories of translation begin to privilege the original author, the translator is increasingly required to facilitate the reader's comprehension of a foreign text rather than to fulfill his expectations by modifying irregularities. *Tristram Shandy* might have hastened this shift because it could not be rendered more elegantly or conventionally, and because its interest and value lay in this peculiarity.

Part III

Fiction

Chapter 5

Sentimental Journeys

While *Tristram Shandy*'s reception is represented by the conflicting attitudes and methods of its three very different French translations, the reception of *A Sentimental Journey* took place within the wider arena of popular narrative fiction. The shorter novel owed much of its success in France to the ease with which it was integrated into the vogue for sentiment between 1760 and 1800. As we saw in Chapter 2 in relation to Madame Suard's letter, *A Sentimental Journey* was a focal point for a new critical idiom that embodied a changing taste and sensibility. This chapter examines how it passed into popular literary culture via a substantial body of imitative fiction that adopted several of its sentimental features. These works constitute a subgenre, which I shall call *voyages sentimentaux*, and may be described as 'imitations' because they are consciously modelled on *A Sentimental Journey* and, sometimes, on Volume VII and various sentimental episodes of *Tristram Shandy*.

The terms 'sentimental', 'sentimentalism' and 'sensibility' will be used in reference to the general tendency to privilege pathos in narrative fiction during the second half of the eighteenth century. There have been many studies and definitions. Ann Jessie Van Sant, for instance, discusses the history and development of the words themselves and attempts to distinguish between them, while David Denby proposes a formal definition of sensibility and studies how sentimental writing is rooted in social attitudes.[1] Anne Vincent-Buffault identifies sympathy in France from the eighteenth to the twentieth centuries as an historical phenomenon, and Anne Coudreuse examines pathos linguistically, at the meeting point of rhetoric, the history of ideas and the history of pictorial representation.[2] In English studies, Michael Bell focuses on the ambivalent legacy left by the eighteenth century in its theorization of sentiment (both as feeling and as principle), and examines the relationship between sentimental fiction and the moral philosophy of the period.[3] John Mullan believes that literary critics have too easily equated sympathy as a term in the period's moral philosophy with the sympathy represented in popular novels. He studies the language and 'sociability' of feeling, and criticizes Brissenden's application of the word 'sentimental' to very different discourses, from the philosophy of Hutcheson to the novels of Mackenzie (though Brissenden distinguishes between early 'sentiment' and a later, degenerated 'sensibility').[4] According to Mullan, 'the congruence of philosophical doctrine and narrative preoccupation is taken for granted. But in novels which rely on the depiction or demonstration of sentiment, sympathy is not that which is always and everywhere given'.[5] To avoid the confusion of which Mullan speaks, my own terminology refers to narrative fiction, though some philosophical ideas necessarily enter the picture and will be mentioned. On a more specific level, a notion of sentimentalism will emerge within the chapter through an examination of how it functions within the texts inspired by Sterne, both individually and as a group in which certain common themes and narrative techniques are employed in order to move the reader emotionally. I will identify the elements these texts borrow from *A Sentimental Journey* and the sentimental episodes of *Tristram Shandy*, analyse their use of pathos and make textual comparisons between them and Sterne in order to demonstrate the ways in which they remain distinct.

French Sterneiana

The presence of *A Sentimental Journey* in late eighteenth-century France is apparent. The sentimental journey became such a common *topos* that the title *Voyage sentimental* was frequently taken up, sometimes without any awareness of its origin. Saint-Amans's *Fragmens d'un voyage sentimental et pittoresque* (1789) and Brune's *Voyage pittoresque et sentimental dans plusieurs provinces occidentales de la France* (1788), for instance, are indebted to Rousseau's wanderings in nature and have little to do with Sterne's sentimental travelling.[6] Some authors exploit Sterne's celebrity by attributing their work to him: Rutledge's *La Quinzaine anglaise à Paris* (1776), a cautionary tale about how British tourists can lose their money in Paris, masqueraded as a posthumous work by Sterne, and the anonymous *Tableau sentimental de la France depuis la Révolution* (1792) claimed to be the translation of a work by Sterne's nephew, Yorick.[7] The English author even inspired a musical comedy, *Sterne à Paris, ou Le Voyageur sentimental*, performed in the vaudeville theatre in 1799.[8] Incorporating episodes from *A Sentimental Journey* and anecdotes about Sterne's visits to France, it cheerfully indulges in French stereotypes about the English and patriotically asserts French identity during the post-revolutionary period.

This chapter focuses on texts which share rather more common ground with their English model and which demonstrably set out to imitate it. The overwhelming tendency to sentimentalize Sterne differs from the response of imitators in Britain. Although several sentimental imitations were published in Britain, as well as an extremely popular selection of sentimental extracts entitled *The Beauties of Sterne* (1782) that went into at least 13 editions and reprints before 1800, there also appeared a substantial quantity of comic and satiric parodies inspired by *Tristram Shandy*.[9] In the early pamphlet *The Clockmaker's Outcry* (May 1760), for example, a group of clockmakers complain about Mrs Shandy's association of the winding of the clock with sex, both of which take place in the Shandy household, like clockwork, on the first Sunday of each month.[10] Respectable ladies, claim the clockmakers, can no longer look at a clock, and winding up a watch in the presence of a lady is tantamount to a proposition. Another early publication, the anonymous *A Genuine Letter from a Methodist Preacher* (1760), directs its satire against both *Tristram Shandy* and its own narrator, a disapproving Methodist critic.[11] Keenly aware that these pamphlets could increase his celebrity, Sterne was delighted by them, as he admitted to Stephen Croft: 'I wish they would write a hundred such'.[12] There were no comparable parodies in France before the end of the eighteenth century, and the vast majority of imitations employed sentiment as their principal mode of expression, usually with ideological purposes.

Sentiment and Ideology: the *Tableau sentimental*, François Vernes and Pierre Blanchard

The imitative *voyages sentimentaux* adopt Sterne's *topos* of sentimental travelling, in which a first person narrator travels around rural France and relates his observations and experiences. These take the form of individual episodes which are linked together by the traveller-narrator's point of view. They typically depict his chance encounters with members of the lower social orders or impoverished nobles and offer a touching story or scene of pathos. The tale of 'Le Pauvre et son chien' in Bonnay's translation, described in the previous chapter, is typical of such episodes. The characters sometimes narrate their own stories but the emphasis is on the traveller-narrator's feelings and reactions to what he sees and hears. Usually male, his identity is merged with that of the imitating author and conflated with Yorick, Tristram and Sterne himself. The descriptions of his emotional responses to the tales of unfortunate victims in turn aim to elicit sympathy from the reader. As Bell points out in his discussion of the tale within the tale, an important self-reflexive device of sentimental fiction, 'the listener within the fiction is aroused to sympathetic compassion as a surrogate for the real reader who is thereby offered an intensifying model of response'.[13] The narrator is constantly shown to be responding to a moving scene or story – a *tableau*, *récit* or *historiette* – that depicts some sort of misfortune.

The representation of misfortune is closely related to eighteenth-century humanitarian and philanthropic concerns. Sentimental fiction focuses on social categories that were traditionally under-represented in literature as well as in society: the poor, the mad, the old, the infirm, women, children.[14] For this reason Denby has asserted that sentimental literature should be read, 'not just as a corpus of themes but as a phenomenon possessing real social referents and historical meanings'.[15] It represents, furthermore, the acceptance of the socially excluded:

> sentimental literature represents the discovery, and above all the popularisation and repeated celebration of the humanity of the excluded, and as such is part of the global project of Enlightenment humanism. What the sentimental text enacts is the recognition of the universal category of humanity in each individual case of suffering

encountered: this child, this mother, this destitute old man are exponents of a universal value system, applying equally to all.[16]

Yet although sentimental fiction encouraged widespread interest in humanitarian issues, the 'universal value system' to which Denby refers frequently revealed itself to be the value system of the privileged. Ideological questions arise when we examine the formulaic nature of sentimental fiction in general and, for the purposes of this chapter, of the *voyages sentimentaux*. What is the social position of the observing traveller-narrator in relation to the objects of his sympathy, and to what ideological ends does he guide or manipulate the reader's emotions? Even if sympathy permits a transcendence of social hierarchy, does its fictional representation actually challenge this hierarchy or simply perpetuate a system in which the aristocracy or educated bourgeoisie are privileged enough to feel pity? The *voyages sentimentaux*, written before and during the revolutionary period, are permeated by political concerns. While they assume many features from *A Sentimental Journey*, their politically motivated and frequently naïve use of pathos differs from Sterne's highly self-conscious sentimentalism, which dramatically explores its own ideology rather than simply reflecting it.

Sentimentalism is used to convey a patently political message in the anonymous *Tableau sentimental de la France depuis la Révolution* (1792). As mentioned above, the author of this imitation makes a strange claim. He presents himself as the mere translator and invents an elaborate story to make his text appear genuine, claiming that this sentimental journey is by Yorick, Sterne's nephew, and that it was read and approved by Sterne. It is narrated by 'Sterne', who is revisiting Paris after the revolution and finds it changed. The travel motif is used, with its meandering narrative structure that moves capriciously between the narrator's encounters, observations and *rêveries* as he wanders around Paris or remains in his lodgings: 'Je me promenois sans savoir où j'allois, c'est ma coutume, on le sait ... quand j'écris, c'est la même chose. Je prends ma plume et je suis le fil de mes pensées, je vais jusques où il me mène'.[17] The text's political message is apparent in the way its sentimentalism functions. One of the central episodes consists of the story of a young woman named Dugg, whose suffering and misfortune render her noble and interesting, and attract the traveller-narrator's attention:

> Une jeune personne d'une figure noble et intéressante, passa avec un paquet sous le bras. La douleur étoit peinte sur sa figure; elle s'arrêtoit de temps en temps; elle prononçoit quelques mots mal articulés et sans suite ... à cette vue qu'on juge de mon émotion: j'approchai en tremblant, car l'infortune inspire une sorte de respect ... j'étois à portée d'entendre.[18]

Dugg's directionless wandering and fragmentary and irrational sentences are signs of her psychological and emotional distress. She may be compared with 'poor Maria', one of Sterne's best-known sentimental figures, who makes her first appearance in Volume IX of *Tristram Shandy*. There is an evocative lead-up to Tristram's encounter with her, in which his emotions are aroused by the sweet sound of her flute and the coach driver's expression of pity for her. Nevertheless, during their meeting, when she looks at Tristram and at her goat, he cannot refrain from asking whether she finds a resemblance between them, a question that disrupts the gravity of the scene:

> I do intreat the candid reader to believe me, that it was from the humblest conviction of what a *Beast* man is, – that I ask'd the question; and that I would not have let fallen an unseasonable pleasantry in the venerable presence of Misery, to be entitled to all the wit that ever Rabelais scatter'd – and yet I own my heart smote me, and that I so smarted at the very idea of it, that I swore I would set up for Wisdom and utter grave sentences the rest of my days – and never – never attempt again to commit mirth with man, woman, or child, the longest day I had to live.
>
> As for writing nonsense to them – I believe, there was a reserve – but I leave that to the world.[19]

Tristram's sentimental *tableau* is not straightforward because it contains the potential to become ridiculous. The portrayal of Maria in *A Sentimental Journey*, though more drawn out and affecting, similarly incorporates a comically self-conscious element in Yorick's description of their shared tears:

> I sat down close by her; and Maria let me wipe them away as they fell with my handkerchief. – I then steep'd it in my own – and then in hers – and then in mine – and then I wip'd hers again – and as I did it, I felt such undescribable emotions within me, as I am sure could not be accounted for from any combinations of matter and motion.[20]

Yorick frequently invokes his sensibility as proof that he does not merely function according to the materialism expounded by the *philosophes*. Such self-consciousness about the underlying processes and motivations of his thoughts, emotions and actions in the description of his tearful exchange with Maria suggests an emotional distance, which is also dramatized by the comically repetitive, and possibly sexually charged, wiping of tears.

For Battestin, Sterne's sensibility nevertheless refutes both materialism and egotistical self-love, and constitutes a genuine manifestation of his religious faith, even if the religion permeating *A Sentimental Journey* is more secularized as a result of his exposure to the materialist ideas of his French friends.[21] We saw in Chapter 2 that many eighteenth-century critics found Sterne's sentimentalism to be his most redeeming feature, even while it made others (like Mademoiselle de Sommery) laugh. Its sincerity has provoked varied opinions ever since.[22] It would be difficult to claim that Sterne was beyond the influence of earlier and contemporary theories of sentiment, particularly those of Shaftesbury and of his followers, in which morality and feeling came closer together, or that he could place himself outside the context of Latitudinarianism. The latter, whose influence, as New has argued, was integral to Sterne's religious views, advocated good works and benevolence partly in reaction to the Calvinist doctrine of predestination, with its attendant conception of the futility of human endeavour.[23] While the sincerity of his sentimentalism should therefore not be doubted, it is also possible to agree with Bell that he was one of the earliest writers of popular sentimental fiction to demonstrate an awareness that sentimentalism had both moral and aesthetic aspects.[24]

In Sterne, faith, benevolence, mirth and sexuality are inextricably bound together. Maria's beauty encourages Yorick's pity and inspires his wish that she 'should lay in my bosom' – as a daughter, he adds somewhat belatedly, a delay that hints at his sexual interest.[25] His vulnerability to temptation by various ladies along his journey is nevertheless not incompatible with virtue, as long as temptation is ultimately overcome. Indeed, it motivates the sentimental Don Quixote to be virtuous because he is constantly 'in quest of melancholy adventures [...] I am never so perfectly conscious of the existence of a soul within me, as when I am entangled in them'.[26] Yorick's self-consciousness about his feelings of sympathy does push them towards the edge of sincerity: reflecting on the existence of his soul while evoking the touching scene with Maria necessitates a certain amount of distance from the perfectly shared feeling of common humanity he is describing, and even suggests the potential solipsism of his sentimentalism. Without going, like Mullan, to the extent of seeing Sterne's sentimentalism as damagingly private and fundamentally pessimistic because it does not offer a wide-ranging and practical response to the existence of misfortune, such as an improved social system, it may be said that Yorick's manner of being virtuous is at least partly self-regarding, and knowingly so. This does not mean that Sterne did not believe in sensibility as an expression and vehicle of morality, even while he questioned its assumptions and processes through comic self-awareness.[27]

In the *Tableau sentimental*, there is no such self-reflexivity, and sentiment is employed in the promotion of a political viewpoint. 'Sterne' talks to Dugg, and learns that she has arrived in Paris to save her innocent father from prison but has run out of money. It is evident to him that she was once more fortunate, so he buys her bundle of clothes in an act of charity. He learns her story from the love letters he finds in the bundle, gaining a sentimental *récit* in return for his benevolence. He discovers that her boyfriend 'Sylv...' (probably named after Maria's dog Sylvio, a replacement for her own lost lover) is a young hothead who has been led astray by the republican cause. One night, he leads a hoard of republicans in an attack on her father's château. Ignoring her pleas, cruel Sylv... throws her father into prison and gloats triumphantly. The sympathy extracted from the reader is used to political effect: the republicans are monsters because they are insensible to Dugg's distress and inner sensibility, and unmoved by her attempts to gain their sympathy through what she calls 'mes efforts, mes pleurs, mes gémissemens'.[28]

The text as a whole expresses disapproval of the revolution and its chaotic results, and is dedicated to Raynal who, in a *Lettre à l'Assemblée nationale*, criticizes the disorder and violence of the revolutionary government.[29] When he observes post-revolutionary Paris, 'Sterne' is nostalgic about the city he visited during the *ancien régime* and sheds a tear for his faithful servant La Fleur, now dead, who represents happier times. As a political mouthpiece, he is even made to qualify the horror of the Bastille that the real Sterne had shown in *A Sentimental Journey* (now that it is actually destroyed), and to express support for a reformed monarchy and rejection of patricide, which implies the killing of kings as well as of Dugg's father: 'L'abus que le pouvoir arbitraire faisoit de la Bastille affligeoit l'humanité en y renfermant des victimes innocentes, j'en conviens ... mais les scélérats, les parricides, les assassins pour qui on l'avoit construite, où les mettra-t-on?'[30]

Less piecemeal and more interesting as a piece of fiction than the *Tableau sentimental*, François Vernes's *Le Voyageur sentimental, ou ma promenade à Yverdun* (1786), expresses a sentimentalist vision that is also politically motivated – this time on the side of republicanism.[31] Vernes was from the rising Protestant bourgeoisie of Geneva and believed in the 'patriotic' reform of the state. He admired Rousseau, both from a literary point of view and as a fellow Genevan: *Le Voyageur sentimental* contains a panegyric to Rousseau, and he even appears in the narrator's dream.[32] The narrator is a young man, very much based on Vernes himself, who undertakes what begins as a quixotic journey with his appropriately named friend La Joye.

On setting out, he establishes the kinship between his text and Sterne's by asserting his own journey's originality. It will be full of sentiments rather than guide-book descriptions:

> Pardon, Lecteur; à l'exemple des voyageurs, j'aurais dû vous donner la description topographique du lieu de notre départ; vous marquer exactement sa latitude, sa longitude, sa distance de la capitale; vous parler de son église, de son château, de sa bibliothèque, ect. [*sic*] J'avoue, à ma honte, que ce superbe genre d'érudition n'est pas le mien; vous ne le verrez que trop dans tout le cours de mon *Voyage*. Hélas! une nuance de sentiment me frappe et m'attache plus que tous les *Panthéons* et les *Colones Trajanes*. *L'homme au mouton*, par exemple, l'*aveugle* et *sa fille*, le *béquillard*: voilà mes folies![33]

We can compare this with Yorick's famous explanation of sentimental travelling to the Count de B:

> I have not seen the Palais royal – nor the Luxembourg – nor the Façade of the Louvre – nor have attempted to swell the catalogues we have of pictures, statues, and churches – I conceive every fair being as a temple, and would rather enter in, and see the original drawings and loose sketches hung up in it, than the transfiguration of Raphael itself [...] 'tis a quiet journey of the heart in pursuit of NATURE, and those affections which rise out of her, which make us love each other – and the world, better than we do.[34]

Vernes's book begins abruptly, like Sterne's, and moves at a fast pace. We meet the narrator in bed one dark, snowy morning. He does not feel like getting up and braving the long, cold journey to see Mademoiselle de Blas at a ball in Yverdun, but he quickly changes his mind. The journey begins with echoes of Cervantes and Sterne: the narrator rides a puny horse called Rosse, whom he compares to Rosinante, and throughout the narrative he likens himself and La Joye to Don Quixote and Sancho Panza.[35] Like Sterne, Vernes takes a lively interest in the opposite sex and has flirtatious encounters along his journey. The narrative also moves quickly from episode to episode, throwing the reader into the middle of different situations. There are several comic moments and a light, humorous tone. But the connections between *A Sentimental Journey* and *Le Voyageur sentimental* soon peter out. Vernes celebrates youth and health: the two energetic young men undertake the dangers of a long journey in the snow and wind for the pleasure of dancing. While Tristram and Yorick also pursue their own types of pleasure, they are older men who travel to warmer climes for their health. More importantly, Vernes's text becomes increasingly preoccupied with political issues and expresses a darker, more melancholy type of sentimentalism.[36] While in the *Tableau sentimental*, republicans are represented as unfeeling thugs who terrorize innocent aristocrats, here the noblest souls belong to the republicans, as well as to the unfortunate victims of poverty, grief and madness.[37]

Pierre Blanchard's *Le Rêveur sentimental* (1795) takes place entirely in the mind.[38] The text consists of a random mixture of the author-narrator's *rêveries*, which include memories, passing thoughts, imagined scenarios and fantasies. Blanchard is an educated and idealistic young republican soldier who appreciates sentimental literature and acknowledges a debt both to Rousseau and to Sterne. In his ideal library, 'J. J. Rousseau occuperoit la première place [...] Sterne sera aussi sur ma table'.[39] From Rousseau, he borrows the idea of mental travelling and *rêverie*, while Sterne provides him with the disordered narrative structure punctuated by a number of sentimental episodes in which the narrator's feelings are centre stage: he is moved by a poor old couple's hospitality; he refrains from seducing an attractive peasant girl because he learns the story of her sister Adélaïde, who died of grief after becoming pregnant and being abandoned; he sighs over blind young Isadore, who leaves his beloved, unwilling to impose his disability on her.

These stories are usually remembered by Blanchard as he sits at home. They lead to various *rêveries*, which are a mixture of memory and imagination, and are recounted without organization or structure:

> Quand j'ai commence à écrire, je ne savois guères ce que j'écrirois; quand j'ai eu fini, je n'ai guères pu songer à mieux faire. Je donne cet Ouvrage comme un de ces songes informes que par leur bizarrerie même peuvent amuser un instant. Heureux si j'ai pu y semer à propos quelques-uns de ces sentimens qui flattent toujours le cœur et qui sont autant de fleurs qui quelquefois font tout le prix d'un ouvrage![40]

The purpose he claims here is neither ambitious nor moral. Blanchard is more concerned to indulge the wanderings of his imagination than to meet and sympathize with others. This is manifest in his imagined portrait of a prisoner, which allows him to praise the faculty of the imagination:

> le malheureux qui y est enséveli [in prison] doit faire des rêves bien fortement exprimés [...] il n'a que son cœur pour consolateur, il n'a que son imagination pour univers; il rêve, la vue pesamment attachée sur la paille où il est couché. Son rêve est achevé, il relève la tête; je le vois se traîner vers le long soupirail que lui donne un rayon de lumière; il considère l'herbe qui lui dérobe une partie de son jour. Oh! que sa figure est sombre et mélancholique! c'est l'expression de ses pensées noires et lugubres [...].[41]

The prisoner, like the author himself, needs to dream and use his imagination in order to overcome the limitations of reality. The portrait is modelled on that of the captive in *A Sentimental Journey*, who is imagined in order that Yorick may contemplate slavery and 'the miseries of confinement'. Yorick's portrait, however, is very different because it is aware of the ways in which sentiment is used to express and inspire sympathy for the victims of slavery. Yorick realizes that he cannot begin to feel anything about slavery as an abstract concept, but needs to focus on one particular victim in order to 'bring it near' him:

> I was going to begin with the millions of my fellow creatures born to no inheritance but slavery; but finding, however affecting the picture was, that I could not bring it near me, and that the multitude of sad groups in it did but distract me –
> – I took a single captive, and having first shut him up in his dungeon, I then look'd through the twilight of his grated door to take his picture.
> I beheld his body half wasted away with long expectation and confinement, and felt what kind of sickness of the heart it was which arises from hope deferr'd. Upon looking nearer I saw him pale and feverish: in thirty years the western breeze had not once fann'd his blood – he had seen no sun, no moon in all that time – nor had the voice of friend or kinsman breathed through his lattice – his children –
> – But here my heart began to bleed – and I was forced to go on with another part of the portrait.
> He was sitting upon the ground upon a little straw, in the furthest corner of his dungeon, which was alternately his chair and bed: a little calendar of small sticks were laid at the head notched all over with the dismal days and nights he had pass'd there – he had one of these little sticks in his hand, and with a rusty nail he was etching another day of misery to add to the heap. As I darkened the little light he had, he lifted up a hopeless eye towards the door, then cast it down – shook his head, and went on with his work of affliction. I heard his chains upon his legs, as he turn'd his body to lay his little stick upon the bundle – He gave a deep sigh – I saw the iron enter into his soul – I burst into tears – I could not sustain the picture of confinement which my fancy had drawn – I startled up from my chair, and calling La Fleur, I bid him bespeak me a *remise*, and have it ready at the door of the hotel by nine in the morning.
> – I'll go directly, said I, myself to Monsieur Le Duke de Choiseul.[42]

Yorick is perfectly conscious of the need to use the imagination and fiction in order to encourage – and even manipulate – the reader's emotional response in relation to slavery. His comic ability to work himself up into tears emphasizes that selfishness and manipulation are inherent within the sympathetic process: he can only feel for someone with whom he can identify, so he must draw the captive realistically and make him familiar to the person who beholds him – the reader, or Yorick himself. The context of the invented portrait is also important, as Yorick is inspired to contemplate confinement because he is threatened with imprisonment in the Bastille for travelling in France without a passport. It is not adequate, though, to dismiss Sterne's sentimentalism, or sentimentalism as a whole, as selfish and self-regarding. Yorick's manipulative sympathy has much in common with the conscious sympathy evoked in Adam Smith's *The Theory of Moral Sentiments* (1759).[43] Smith, as Mullan points out, believed that a certain amount of self-preservation and self-love plays a vital and positive role in the motivation of benevolence:

> [Sympathy] is not necessarily narcissistic and indulgent; it confesses itself to be inventive and purposeful: a necessary fiction. It confesses also that even the fiction requires the idea of a particular sympathy – that an undifferentiated fellow-feeling is scarcely imaginable.[44]

Yorick's sympathy for the imagined captive arises from his own situation, and also inspires him to action: he decides to call on the Duc de Choiseul and save himself – if not his fellow human beings – from imprisonment. The intentional ambiguity of Yorick's motives demonstrates at least that Sterne was aware of the complexities and processes of sympathy as well as the problems intrinsic to the fictional representation of misfortune and suffering.

Blanchard's portrait of the dreaming prisoner reveals little about the workings of sympathy itself. It is drawn with the simple purpose of praising the liberating quality of the imagination. Blanchard's response to Sterne's representation of the Bastille is direct and uncomplicated: it symbolizes the political oppression of the *ancien régime*, while imagination and *rêveries* can overcome this oppression. Sentimental dreaming is presented as a democratic act because it permits everyone to be equal, but there is something escapist rather than liberating about it. While Blanchard can remember, dream about and describe touching scenes and stories, his sensibility is cultivated in an armchair by the fireplace, with his faithful friend Constant dozing next to him:

> On veut penser aux malheureux, parce qu'il y a de la douceur à les plaindre. Comme la vertu est vivace dans nos cœurs, et même en dépit de nous! on veut être bon, ne fut-ce qu'en songe.[45]

Blanchard's fine feelings are cut off from reality. Perhaps he has seen enough of revolution and civil war, and dreams of being virtuous rather than actively behaving virtuously. With little real power to change political events, he fantasizes about a better future, taking hope as his motto.[46] His description of the captive suggests that dreaming is a way to escape reality; it is the 'bonheur des infortunés'.[47] Yorick, by contrast, never escapes the reality of sentimental representation but draws attention to its manipulative methods, even while succumbing to them with tears. In his armchair, Blanchard can have little influence over political and social injustices and he can only imagine or dream about being an absolute ruler – in which case he would, he claims, enlighten his people, liberate women and expose the hypocrisy of the church. Yorick avoids lapsing into escapism precisely because he knows that self-love is part of sympathy. Sympathy is a conscious manipulation, an act of imagination that allows one to feel the suffering of others. Yorick's sentimentalism has the witty self-consciousness of an author seeking to understand human nature and the nature of sympathy, while Blanchard's armchair dreaming is both passive and random. This suggests a resignation to his inability to act usefully in real life, though there is a touch of ambiguity as to whether he believes that dreaming is the best thing to do, or simply the only thing he can do:

> Rêver est volontiers l'ouvrage des paresseux et de ceux qui n'ont pas mieux à faire; quant à moi je rêve, parce que je ne puis faire mieux. J'écris mes rêves, et je les donne pour ce qu'ils sont.[48]

Sentimental dreaming is perhaps the only form of engagement possible at a time when France was undergoing total upheaval: *Le Rêveur sentimental* was published in the middle of the revolutionary decade and conveys the sense of ineffectuality felt by a disillusioned young writer with republican sympathies.

Julie de Lespinasse

One of Sterne's earliest French readers and imitators was Julie de Lespinasse (1732–76), the protégée of Madame du Deffand until she went on to host her own *salon*. Immortalized in Diderot's *Le Rêve de d'Alembert* (1769), she was a close friend of d'Alembert, and engaged in a passionate correspondence with the Comte de Guibert, who credited her with spreading the reputation of *A Sentimental Journey*. He also claimed that she was the first to read all of *Tristram Shandy*:

> C'était elle qui avoit fait à Paris la réputation du Voyage sentimental. Les ouvrages inégaux, imparfaits, bizarres même, obtenoient grâce à ses yeux, pourvu qu'elle y trouvât quelque trait de génie ou de sensibilité. C'est ainsi qu'elle avoit eu la patience de défricher la première, tout Tristram Shandy.[49]

Guibert's statement emphasizes Lespinasse's ability to focus on Sterne's genius and sentimentalism. For her, these qualities redeemed his irregularities and imperfections. Her own imitation of Sterne is inspired by his sentiment, and takes account neither of his 'bizarre' side (such as structural irregularities and bawdy jokes), nor of his self-conscious explorations of the processes of sympathy.

Lespinasse's *Deux chapitres dans le genre du Voyage sentimental de Sterne* was written in the early 1770s and published posthumously in 1809 in the first edition of her letters.[50] In the first chapter, entitled 'Qui ne vous surprendra pas', the narrator 'Monsieur Sterne' – a conflation of Yorick, Tristram and Sterne – relates an experience. A young deliveryman arrives at his Paris lodgings with his order of two marble vases. One of them, however, is broken. The deliveryman explains that it was accidentally broken by his friend, Jacques, who was too fearful of the consequences to bring it himself. He urges Monsieur Sterne to take pity on Jacques, for if their employer were to discover the breakage, Jacques would be fired and his wife and four children would starve. Monsieur Sterne is moved by the sentimental appeal and promises to keep the secret, his soul 'animée par sa propre sensibilité ou par celle des autres'. He recounts the situation to his servant La Fleur, who declares, 'il faut que nous délivrions Jacques de son malheur!', so he charges La Fleur with twelve francs for Jacques and six for the friend who delivered the vase.[51] The act of charity alleviates Sterne's soul:

> Que je me sentis soulagé par le peu de bien que je venois de faire! je me sentois encore doucement ému par la bonté active de Lafleur ... L'honnête créature, disois-je! Pourquoi la Providence ne l'a-t-elle pas placée dans la classe des hommes qui peuvent secourir et soulager leurs semblables, et dont la plupart ont le cœur inaccessible aux malheureux?[52]

Today's reader would undoubtedly note Monsieur Sterne's self-satisfaction and question the social system that depends to such a degree on private benevolence. Lespinasse, however, appears to have unquestioning faith in sensibility and in the charity that it demands. Her main criticism is directed against those who are not charitable when they can afford to be, and she contrasts them with humble but generous souls such as La Fleur's. The sympathy she offers, which at least leads to practical action through charity, does not seek social change. Her sensibility operates within an established social structure in which workers depend on the mercy of their employers and the benevolence of the rich.

She does not, therefore, take from Sterne an awareness of sensibility's manipulative nature and potential self-indulgence. The complex exploration of alms-giving in the Lorenzo scenes in *A Sentimental Journey* demonstrates that Yorick is quite ironic about the role of pure feeling in acts of charity. The reliability of the 'ebbs and flows of our humours' as a basis for moral responsibility is constantly challenged, as is that of pure reason. Yorick's initial fine sentiments on landing in France are at least partly brought on by a drink to the French king's health, but as soon as they are tested by a real situation in the shape of the mendicant Lorenzo, he fails to act charitably. In fact, it is a rational and wilful – albeit arbitrary – determination not to be charitable that wins, and Yorick's subsequent witty arguments against making a donation to the monk further distance him from the possibility of sympathy. The distinction between feeling and reason, manifested alternately in spontaneous generosity and wilful determination, is not very clear at all. Yorick tells of his lack of sympathy towards Lorenzo and draws a tender portrait of him in retrospect, after having had time to reconsider his behaviour rationally. It is also suggested that Yorick's later softening towards Lorenzo comes about thanks to the presence of a beautiful lady before whom he wishes to appear in the best possible light. During their reconciliation, Yorick and Lorenzo exchange compliments, apologies and snuffboxes, but the act of charity never materializes, which also suggests that sympathetic feeling and practical charity remain distinct.[53]

The second of Lespinasse's imitative chapters, 'Que ce fut une bonne journée que celle des pots cassés', recounts a soirée at Madame G's *salon*, where Monsieur Sterne is invited.[54] As narrator, Sterne is a mouthpiece for Lespinasse's own straightforward type of sensibility, and is made to dismiss wit and eulogize his uncle Toby's simple morality:

> O mon cher oncle Tobi! je n'ai pas l'ame aussi bonne, aussi douce que toi; cependant je l'avouerai, je n'écoute avec intérêt que ce qui parle à mon ame. Je ne louai jamais un trait d'esprit; mais j'ai toujours une larme à donner au récit d'une bonne action ou à un mouvement de sensibilité: ce sont là les seules touches qui répondent à mon cœur.[55]

Monsieur Sterne loves only sensibility, and particularly a sentimental *récit*. He was moved by the *récit* of Jacques's friend in the first chapter, and now, after dinner, he listens to another story, in which his hostess explains why she is serving sour milk with the coffee. Madame G's young milkmaid had broken down in tears and revealed that she was unable to bring any milk because her cow had died. The cow had provided a living for the milkmaid, her bedridden husband and old parents. Madame G swiftly calms her: 'votre douleur me fait une plaie. Je vous donnerai une vache, vous l'acheterez aussi belle que vous pourrez, et j'espère qu'elle remplacera celle que vous avez perdue ...'[56] The milkmaid's gratitude is described in painstaking detail as Madame G draws out maximum pathos from her situation. Madame G then asks the young woman about her life, and is moved by another *récit* in which the girl speaks of her love for her family and describes her care for the dying cow. The story allows the lady to suffer imaginatively along with the milkmaid, to whom she offers a second cow in consolation.

The dinner guests praise her generosity and Sterne is now called upon both as a character and as literary model. When Madame G asks whether he is pleased with her narrative, he sheds a tear, extols her benevolence and addresses his compatriots, telling them to visit her in France in order to witness goodness:

Allez en France, allez voir madame G... vous verrez la bienfaisance, la bonté; vous verrez ces vertus dans leur perfection, parce que vous les trouverez accompagnées d'une délicatesse que ne peut venir que d'une ame dont la sensibilité a été perfectionnée par l'habitude de la vertu.[57]

As a character in Lespinasse's tale, Monsieur Sterne is both a literary model for Lespinasse, and a moral model for her heroine Madame G. Lespinasse thus creates a sentimental relationship between the two characters, Madame G and Monsieur Sterne, as well as between her text and *A Sentimental Journey*. Overwhelmed by his authoritative approval, Madame G cries 'Je suis donc bonne! M. Sterne, vous venez de m'en récompenser, je veux vous embrasser pour le bien que vous m'avez fait ...'. Monsieur Sterne's admiration for her story leads to sentimental rapture as the two characters share an embrace:

Elle se baissa, je me levai avec transport, je la serrai dans mes bras ... Oui ma Lisette, je sentis pour la première fois de ma vie, que les mouvemens qu'inspire la vertu, ont leurs délices comme ceux de l'amour; mon ame eut un moment d'ivresse ... Son retour fut pour toi ... j'en serai plus digne de ma Lisette, me dis-je. Elle pleurera avec moi lorsque je lui conterai l'histoire de la laitière de madame G...[58]

The embrace borders on the erotic but remains sentimental. As the climax of the relationship between the two characters, it also represents a sentimental literary relationship between Lespinasse and Sterne. While Monsieur Sterne approves of Madame G's sensibility, *A Sentimental Journey* gives weight to Lespinasse's sentimental text. It is an exploitative relationship, as it takes Sterne's sentimentalism at face value and ignores its more self-conscious complexities.

Lespinasse's sentimentalism is ideological in the sense that it defends the existing social order. The privileged can be generous and encouraging of each other's sensibility within closed social circles, and Sterne functions as a symbol for a benevolent aristocratic system. The story is also implicitly patriotic, since the respect of a well-known English man of feeling demonstrates that virtue can be found in France, and particularly in an enlightened Parisian *salon*. A sentimental narrative, or *récit*, always accompanies charity, for it is the ability to be moved by a story of misfortune that motivates Madame G's belevolence and in turn inspires the sympathy of her friends. The character of Monsieur Sterne is made to praise Madame G, while the author Sterne is equally used by Lespinasse and incorporated into her text through imitation in order to sanction her own ideological sentimentalism. Despite the moving embrace between the two characters, the relationship between the two texts is more one-way, since Sterne's sentimentalism is idealized and ideologized.

Jean-Claude Gorjy

Unlike the *Deux chapitres*, the *Nouveau voyage sentimental en France* (1784) by Jean-Claude Gorjy (1753–95) does not choose between sentiment and comic irony, but incorporates both.[59] Neither does it shy away from eroticism, as the author explains in his preface, which is placed unexpectedly, and in Sternean manner, in Chapter 8:

> ce n'est pas que, dans aucune de mes esquisses, j'aie trop laissé voir le nud: mais à l'exemple de statuaires antiques, j'ai mouillé les draperies, pour concilier la décence avec la vérité des formes.[60]

Gorjy casts Yorick as the traveller-narrator in this new sentimental journey, with La Fleur as his accompanying servant. The narrative begins somewhere in the French countryside, as Yorick's wandering thoughts are interrupted by La Fleur's observation that they are physically, as well as mentally, off track. Like *A Sentimental Journey*, it opens with an interruption, with the reader thrown into the middle of Yorick's thoughts and travels. Yorick encounters locals who offer him hospitality or tell him a story of misfortune, and he responds with sympathy, displaying all the traits of a man of feeling.

In encounters with women, Gorjy's Yorick has a mischievous sense of humour and is less coy than Sterne's sentimental traveller. When his carriage lightly knocks over a woman by the side of the road, he can enjoy watching her skirts fly up without any self-consciousness. After offering her a lift, they sit staring at each other, embarrassed by the rhythmic movement of the carriage. In another episode, Yorick finds himself attracted to young Javotte, the daughter of a fellow guest at his Paris lodgings. When another resident, a mysterious and reclusive woman, becomes ill, he and Javotte sit by her bedside overnight. To pass the time, she talks about her forbidden love for a poor but intelligent clerk, but they end up playing a game that entails touching each others' hands and other, unnamed parts of the body. Gorjy's bawdy encounters are more direct and farcical than the teasing flirtations between Janatone and Tristram or between the *fille de chambre* and Yorick. The French author is more openly knowing and does not always feel the need to overcome temptation. Another important difference is that Sterne's comedy is evident during the most touching moments of pathos, while Gorjy's comic episodes are entirely separate from the sentimental *tableaux* and do not affect them in any way; sentiment and comedy are juxtaposed but there is no link between them.

Gorjy's *Nouveau voyage*, like Lespinasse's *Deux chapitres*, is also ideologically motivated. This is most apparent in the story of the Chevalier d'Orbeville, a melancholy young man with a story of thwarted love.[61] His father tries to force him to marry an heiress, but he is in love with a poor widow who thinks she is a burden to him and disappears. When his father dies, he sets off to find her. Yorick meets the chevalier in a café as he is on his way to purchase his late father's lands after their seizure by revolutionaries. Yorick accompanies him and describes a sentimental reunion between the village people and their 'bon seigneur', who is joyfully reinstated at the château. The reunion is blessed by a local priest, Orbeville's first preceptor. At the same time, the love story is also resolved: by happy coincidence, the mysterious lady at Yorick's Paris lodging turns out to be Madame Dubois, Orbeville's original love, and they are reunited. The Orbeville narrative suggests a belief in political reform rather than revolution. The ideal social structure is that of a peaceful union between peasants and benevolent landed gentry. The revolution, according to Gorjy, began in the corrupt cities by the middle classes, while the real backbone of the nation lay in the countryside and was based on an alliance between aristocracy and peasants.

Orbeville's story foreshadows the more sustained political analogy of Gorjy's later work, the *Tablettes sentimentales du bon Pamphile pendant les mois d'août, septembre, octobre et novembre 1789* (1791), which also affirms an idealized and paternalistic union between nobles and peasants.[62] Although it is a travel narrative with an episodic structure, it has both thematic and structural coherence, and ends with resolution. A noble family is reinstated at the château which had been brutally destroyed by peasants under the influence of the revolutionary bourgeoisie from the city. Pamphile, the traveller-narrator, nurses a hopeless and chaste love for the lady of the château, whom he finds wandering around the countryside in a state of psychological torment after her traumatic experience. She is only brought to mental health when she returns to the château. The narrative thus portrays the psychological and political restoration of the lord of the manor and his union with the peasants who work for him. Gorjy also used Sterne for the title of his *Ann'quin Bredouille, ou le petit cousin de Tristram Shandy* (1792), which is not, however, an imitation, but a long satire and political allegory.[63] The principal character, very loosely modelled on uncle Toby, travels through a fictional land called Néomanie, clearly meant to represent revolutionary France.

Gorjy's sentimentalism is not consistently used for political purposes. It sometimes leans towards the gothic with its occasionally excessive depictions of emotional suffering. One example of this in the *Nouveau voyage sentimental* is the episode of the *limonadier*'s (or café owner's) daughter. After listening to Orbeville, Yorick is inspired to tell his own sad tale, an exaggerated version of Sterne's story of Maria's doomed love and subsequent madness. It is overheard by the *limonadier*'s daughter, who begins to weep. Orbeville explains to Yorick that she had just learned that her own lover, a prisoner of war in Prussia, married the rich German woman who had paid his ransom. This turns out to be a villain's lie, but the truth is discovered too late to save the poor girl from committing suicide immediately after hearing Yorick's tale of Maria's misfortunes.[64] While the milkmaid's tale in Lespinasse at least leads Madame G to act charitably, in Gorjy, Yorick's story has the opposite effect. The *limonadier*'s daughter can neither relieve Maria's suffering nor Yorick's sadness, and the story only exacerbates her own sadness, leading directly to her suicide. Sensibility thus becomes purely aesthetic, offering neither practical relief in the form of charity nor comfort, and is ultimately destructive. Yorick experiences his most exquisite and melancholy sentiments at the fatal expense of the unhappy girl – the ultimate victim of a sentimental tale.

Sentimental Travelling and the Cult of Rousseau: Louis Damin

Most of Sterne's imitators were also influenced by Rousseau. We have seen that Blanchard acknowledges a debt to both writers and bases his text around a series of fragmentary *rêveries*. Vernes expresses admiration for fellow-Genevan Rousseau and, like him, is prone to dream-like mental flights, particularly when travelling in the countryside. Gorjy's experimentation with a more introspective and melancholy type of sensibility is inspired by Rousseau and, in one scene, his Sternean narrator has a Rousseauist *rêverie* in which external nature and his own imagination are intermingled.[65] The association of Sterne with Rousseau is not particularly surprising. Yorick's focus on psychology and sentiments at the expense of facts, sites and buildings is loosely comparable with Rousseau's preoccupation with his own thoughts and feelings when confronted by nature, as in this passage from *Les Rêveries du promeneur solitaire* (1782):

> La campagne encore verte et riante, mais défeuillée en partie et déjà presque déserte, offrait partout l'image de la solitude et des approches de l'hiver. Il résultait de son aspect un mélange d'impression douce et triste trop analogue à mon âge et à mon sort pour que je ne m'en fisse pas l'application. Je me voyais au déclin d'une vie innocente et infortunée, l'âme encore pleine de sentiments vivaces et l'esprit encore orné de quelques fleurs, mais déjà flétries par la tristesse et desséchées par les ennuis. Seul et délaissés, je sentais venir le froid des premières glaces, et mon imagination tarissante ne peuplait plus ma solitude d'êtres formés selon mon cœur. Je me disais en soupirant: qu'ai-je fait ici-bas?[66]

Yorick's positive evocation of the simple, natural country life, which comes after some excessive socializing and flattering in Parisian society, also has elements in common with the depiction of virtuous and generous country dwellers in *La Nouvelle Héloïse*.[67] Rousseau's towering figure is present in most of the sentimental fiction of the period, and the reception of Sterne in France took place within this context. Rousseau had a large following during his lifetime and it only increased after his death in 1778.[68] For republicans, he was the founding father of the revolution and constitution, a martyr against the forces of tyranny and privilege. Ritualistic *fêtes* were held in his honour during the revolutionary period and there was a ceremonial transfer of his body, declared to be national property, from Érmenonville to the Panthéon in 1794 (year III of the revolution).[69] The posthumous publication of the first part of his *Confessions* in 1782 led to innumerable articles, poems, biographies, plays and portraits, mostly in his favour but also against him.

The last *voyage sentimental* to be discussed in this chapter, *Le Voyageur curieux et sentimental* by Louis Damin (1769–?), is a mixture of Sternean and Rousseauist features.[70] These coexist awkwardly, however, and unsurprisingly, Damin does not manage to reconcile the two different types of sentimental travelling. In the *Confessions*, Rousseau's long, solitary walks represent freedom from attachment to the city and its corruption, and from imprisonment by human institutions:

> La marche a quelque chose qui anime et avive mes idées; je ne puis presque penser quand je reste en place; il faut que mon corps soit en branle pour y mettre mon esprit. La vue de la campagne, la succession des aspects agréables, le grand air, le grand appétit, la bonne santé que je gagne en marchant, la liberté du cabaret, l'éloignement de tout ce qui me fait sentir ma dépendance, de tout ce qui me rappelle à ma situation, tout cela dégage mon âme, me donne une plus grande audace de penser, me jette en quelque sorte dans l'immensité des êtres pour les combiner, les choisir, me les approprier à mon gré, sans gêne et sans crainte.[71]

Rousseau enjoys losing himself in nature and is attracted to the more spectacular aspects – mountains, rocks and waterfalls – that engross the observer's attention. Rather than imposing his own ideas on nature, he lets it impress itself on his mind:

> on sait déjà ce que j'entends par un beau pays. Jamais pays de plaine, quelque beau qu'il fût, ne parut tel à mes yeux. Il me faut des torrents, des rochers, des sapins, des bois noirs, des montagnes, des chemins raboteux à monter et à descendre, des précipices à mes côtés qui me fassent bien peur.[72]

Yorick and Tristram, meanwhile, receive pleasure and inspiration precisely in a tamer landscape and even in a 'pays de plaine':

> How far my pen has been fatigued like those of other travellers, in this journey of it, over so barren a track – the world must judge – but the traces of it, which are now all set o'vibrating together this moment, tell me 'tis the most fruitful and busy period of my life; for as I had made no convention with my man with the gun as to time – by stopping and talking to every soul I met who was not in a full trot – joining all parties before me – waiting for every soul behind – hailing all those who were coming through cross-roads – arresting all kinds of beggars, pilgrims, fiddlers, friars – not passing by a woman in a mulberry-tree without commending her legs, and tempting her into conversation with a pinch of snuff – In short, by seizing every handle, of what size or shape soever, which chance held out to me in this journey – I turned my *plain* into a *city* – I was always in company, and with great variety too: and as my mule loved society as much as myself, and had some proposals always on his part to offer to every beast he met – I am confident we could have passed through Pall Mall or St. James's Street for a month together, with fewer adventures – and seen less of human nature.[73]

While Rousseau seeks solitude and isolation within nature, Sterne's sentimental traveller is fundamentally sociable and constantly reaches out to other people, turning the nature through which he journeys into a city. Both Sterne and Rousseau reflect on human nature during their travels, but Yorick does so through communication with others, while Rousseau examines his own nature in a creative communication with external nature. The 'promeneur solitaire' with his earnest thoughts and rigorous self-examination remains very different from Sterne's eccentric sentimental travellers.

In *Le Voyageur curieux et sentimental*, Damin uses a loosely Sternean sentimental journey framework but expresses a Rousseauist interest in nature which allows him to experience several reveries. He is also influenced by the secular literary pilgrimage, a minor form of writing which intersected with descriptions of landscaped gardens and appeared when Rousseau's tomb in Ermenonville became a site for members of the public and distinguished visitors, such as Marie-Antoinette, Robespierre, Mercier and Bernardin de Saint-Pierre. There were so many visitors, in fact, that Rousseau's friend and the owner of Ermenonville, the Marquis de Girardin, turned the estate into a literary tour. Words were engraved on stones and trees for people to read as they walked to the tomb itself on the Ile des Peupliers and explored the estate on which Rousseau spend his last few months, walking and reflecting. Girardin's son wrote a guidebook for the literary pilgrims entitled *Promenade ou Itinéraire des jardins d'Ermenonville* (1788).[74] Some of the visitors followed suit with their own works. Le Tourneur's *Voyage à Ermenonville* (1788), for instance, which prefaced Rousseau's *Œuvres complètes*, consisted of a description of the estate and, more importantly, presented an account of Le Tourneur's own feelings as he meandered towards Rousseau's tomb, inspired by the natural monuments that had constituted Rousseau's everyday surroundings.[75] Le Tourneur journeys part of the way with two Englishmen who represent the newer aesthetic in landscape gardening. They convey their dislike for the straight paths and geometric shapes of classical French gardens, preferring Ermenonville's sinuous curves and varied features, which resemble those of English gardens. In an English garden, they tell Le Tourneur, the eyes are made to wander around the landscape, and one's footsteps follow unfamiliar routes and lead to surprising discoveries: 'La direction n'en sera pas toujours en ligne droite; elle aura je ne sais quoi de vague, comme la démarche d'un homme oisif qui erre en se promenant'.[76] All three men pay homage to Rousseau and share 'le doux et mélancolique plaisir' with which Ermenonville penetrates their souls.[77]

Damin adopts Sterne's sentimental travelling, Rousseau's country meanderings and Le Tourneur's sentimental pilgrimage guidebook, and his text veers unevenly from one to the other. It is divided into two parts, the first of which, *Le Voyage de Chantilly et d'Ermenonville* (1796), concerns us.[78] It begins humorously, with some irony directed against the traveller-narrator. The tone changes gradually as the journey progresses and is increasingly filled with descriptions of natural landscapes and the narrator's emotional states. Before long, the travellers, Damin and his friend Valere, are on their way to Ermenonville to pay their respects to Rousseau. They initially undertake the journey to Chantilly in order to alleviate their boredom. The narrative pace is quick and recalls Yorick's trip across England and the Channel. One moment they decide to go and the next (also the next chapter), they are on their way in a *diligence*. The comic journey continues on horseback. Damin, envying the rapidity of a passing vehicle, pushes his horse to go faster. He overtakes it but loses balance and falls:

> Me voilà donc pied à terre, jurant contre cette maudite selle que je cherche à remettre en place; lorsque cette diligence, que nous avions dévancée avec tant de fierté, arrive à point nommé pour être temoin de ma disgrace et de ma confusion je laisse à penser si je fus brocardé [...] Ma selle rajustée tant bien que mal, je rejoignis Valere, qui me demanda, avec l'air d'intérêt le plus perfide, si je me trouvois pas mal de ma chute. Je répondis en affectant de sourire, et trotai de nouveau, mais plus prudemment.

Valere's relationship with his friend recalls that of Eugenius and Tristram and, to a lesser degree, of Don Quixote and Sancho Panza, since Valere, Eugenius and Sancho provide an ironic viewpoint to counter the occasional idealism, pride, or stupidity of the 'hero'. Here, Valere points out that pride goes before a fall and compounds his friend's embarrassment. The comic irony is incorporated into the next chapter, which begins, 'Tout en réfléchissant sur l'instabilité des grandeurs humaines, nous arrivons au pont de Neuilly'.[79] Valere's maxim is expressed as a joke to mock his narrating friend, but most of the comic episodes give rise to a moral lesson such as this.

The tone begins to change from episodic sentimental journey to tourist guidebook when the travellers arrive at Chantilly. Descriptions of the gardens take over and these eventually intermingle with the narrator's own half-dreamed experiences as the text increasingly fills with reveries. Some of these suggest the existence of some thrilling and mysterious force: one night, for instance, he thinks that a woman has entered his hotel room, but is not entirely sure whether he is dreaming. A flicker of Sternean comic bawdiness remains to neutralize the darker, sexually charged atmosphere, such as when he bumps into a lady on the dark hotel staircase. But the continuation of the journey to Ermenonville drops both Sternean and gothic influences and instead turns into an emotional pilgrimage to Rousseau's tomb which is filled with descriptions of the landscapes and panegyrics to 'Jean-Jacques'. Like Le Tourneur, Damin asks local inhabitants for details about Rousseau's life in Ermenonville and visits the areas he frequented. These landmarks include Rousseau's cottage ('le temple de la philosophie'), a dry and rocky area ('le desert'), and a lush, green section ('le bocage'). Wandering through the different landscapes, Damin experiences a variety of moods, and when he finally arrives at Rousseau's tomb, he feels a 'saisissement religieux, un sentiment mêlé de respect et d'attendrissement, un saint enthousiasme'.[80] He weeps when contemplating Rousseau's death and, in verse, calls on all men of feeling, 'hommes sensibles', to make the pilgrimage to Rousseau's tomb and weep there.[81]

Towards the end of the text, the comic tone reasserts itself. The vague love plot between the author-narrator and the mysterious lady becomes the primary narrative. The woman he believed to have entered his room, the lady he bumped into on the dark staircase and the lovely young girl staying at the inn turn out to be one and the same. The mystery is solved and he begins to court her with her mother's blessing. The thrilling and dream-like aspect of the narrator's sexuality is thus reconciled with socially acceptable courtship. The hint of gothic and the literary presences of Rousseau, Sterne and Le Tourneur are, however, less easily reconciled within the narrative and remain quite separate. Damin's narrative may be compared with the varied features of the grounds at Ermenonville: just as the narrator experiences an array of moods and emotions as he walks through them, the reader also samples several styles as he journeys through the narrative: 'C'est pour notre bonheur que le maître du monde,/ De peines, de plaisirs entremêle nos jours;/ D'épines et de fleurs en parseme le cours'.[82] The odd juxtaposition of picaresque journey, lyricism, travel guide, pilgrimage and gothic thriller symbolizes the coexistence of different aesthetic and cultural developments. *A Sentimental Journey* was received into this varied and tentative landscape, and experimentations such as Damin's clearly demonstrate that it was absorbed and integrated into the popular literary imagination.

A Sentimental Journey was a substantial presence within the sentimental fiction of the late eighteenth century. Certain recognizable features recur: the motif of the sentimental journey, an episodic narrative structure, humble characters, everyday situations, and the first person traveller-narrator who describes his own responses to the people he encounters and the stories he hears. The *voyages sentimentaux* take over these features and use them to express their own sentimental and ideological visions. Like Rousseau, Sterne was adopted by enlightened monarchists, liberals and revolutionaries alike. The anonymous *Tableau sentimental*, Vernes's *Le Voyageur sentimental* and Blanchard's *Rêveur sentimental* express different political perspectives, but in all three, sentimentalism functions ideologically. Lespinasse uses Sterne to authorize her own sensibility, which affirms the existing social order as represented by an enlightened and sentimentalized *salon*. Gorjy's mixture of comedy, bawdiness and sentiment serves a benevolent monarchist agenda, and Damin's eclectic text, less directly political than the others, employs a naïve sentimentalism to pay homage to Rousseau. Unlike Sterne, the imitations do not dramatically explore the sentimentalism they espouse, but are generally reflective of ideology. For this reason, they remain historically remote and cannot really be recovered as aesthetically interesting works of fiction in their own right. But they do clearly show the extent to which sentimental travelling became a naturalized motif in late eighteenth-century France. They provide, finally, a context for the discussion in the following chapter of *Jacques le fataliste*, and a counterpoint from which to view and appreciate Diderot's achievement.

Chapter 6

Tristram Shandy and *Jacques le fataliste*

Closely tied to the social and political contexts in which they were written, the *voyages sentimentaux* are to be read today primarily as a testimony to the aesthetic ideology of their time. Diderot's *Jacques le fataliste et son maître*, by contrast, holds an eminent position not only in French literature, but also in European and world literature. Brashly original yet self-consciously imitative, it outlived the *voyages sentimentaux* and gradually forged for itself a place in a far wider tradition. The modern interest in parodic, fragmentary and self-referential texts is manifest in the numerous readings of the 1960s and 1970s which affirmed *Jacques*'s continued relevance to criticism and its canonical literary status. Maurice Roelens has pointed out that many of these tended to identify unifying structures within the text, and that they were for the most part a reaction to earlier views of it as a disordered and marginal work within Diderot's *œuvre*.[1] Critics also saw it as an *antiroman*: Robert Mauzi described the ways in which it parodies the eighteenth-century novel,[2] and a decade later, Thomas Kavanagh's structuralist and linguistic reading interpreted *Jacques* as a subversion of the mimetic techniques which embody the belief that reality exists outside the realm of language.[3] More recently still, Milan Kundera has emphasized its importance in the history of the world novel, placing it 'à côté de *Don Quichotte* ou de *Tom Jones*, d'*Ulysse* ou de *Ferdydurke*'.[4] In favouring a Bakhtinian notion of the novel, he associates *Jacques* with *Tristram Shandy* through the idea of writing as *divertissement* with ludic origins.

Diderot certainly set out to do more than simply imitate Sterne, though some early critics, such as J. S. Andrieux, thought that this is exactly what he did:

> Je respecte beaucoup les grands noms; mais je tâche de n'en pas être la dupe. Qu'importe que ce soit Diderot ou un écolier qui ait fait ce livre? Il s'agit de savoir si l'ouvrage est digne d'un maître ou d'un écolier [...] Vous connaissez *Rabelais*? vous connaissez *Sterne*? Si vous ne les connaissez pas, je vous conseille de les lire, sur-tout le dernier. Mais si vous voulez connaître une très-faible imitation du *Tristram-Shandy*, vous n'avez qu'à lire *Jacques le Fataliste*.[5]

The relationship between the two texts is no longer a particular focus of critical attention. The principal works on this topic in fact also date from the 1960s: Alice Green Fredman emphasizes the biographical links between Sterne and Diderot and claims that they had common interests but different starting points and aims;[6] Rainer Warning, meanwhile, examines *Tristram Shandy* and *Jacques* as equally independent and unique works, focusing on their narrative methods and discussing their similarities and differences in terms of two related concepts, oddity in *Tristram Shandy*, and the bizarre in *Jacques*.[7] Since then, several scholars have touched upon the relationship more briefly, but Walter E. Rex's point that Sterne provided Diderot with a beginning (the thematic framework of Jacques's battle wound leading him to meet Denise) and an end (the near 'climactic' conclusion of Denise's knee massage), through which Diderot parodies the French unity of place, is succinctly perceptive.[8] Ernest Simon's discussion of fatalism in *Jacques* (a purely intellectual opinion allowing Jacques to behave differently) in relation to Sterne's conception of the hobby-horse (which incorporates a character's ego) also remains persuasive.[9] Sterne is, of course, only one source among several others in *Jacques*, which include Cervantes, Scarron, Le Sage, Rabelais, Voltaire, Montaigne, La Fontaine, Molière, Goldoni, Prévost and Charles Collé.[10] It would be a largely speculative task to identify all the elements in *Jacques* that might have been borrowed from or influenced by *Tristram Shandy*, and to distinguish them from those inspired by other works, since the connections between them encompass broader literary influences that cross cultural borders and historical periods. As McMorran notes:

> literary history is no teleological narrative, in which each work simply continues the work of its most recent precursor. The *Quijote* is as alive to Diderot as *Tristram Shandy*, and the world of travel that the former represents is as significant an influence upon *Jacques* as the mental wanderings of the latter.[11]

It is tempting, and valid, to ask which of the two texts is more original and, from a modern perspective, more radical and groundbreaking. Diderot had Sterne's innovations to work with, so the predecessor has an advantage through mere chronology. As we saw in previous chapters, Sterne's earliest French readers recognized his originality, a quality that continues to surprise modern readers.[12] And yet the relationship between Sterne and Diderot is not a straightforward one of original and imitator. There is a paradox inherent in the enterprise of imitating an original, and this particular case may be described appropriately in Joseph Wharton's words on Pope's imitations: 'The geniuses, apparently most original, borrow from each other'.[13] In this chapter, *Tristram Shandy* and *Jacques* will be read alongside each other rather than as original and imitation, with a focus on significant meeting points between them. These will be identified and discussed in relation to the wider debates that have already emerged in this study concerning originality and imitation in literary creation, the connections between British and French culture, and the genre and history of the novel. The discussion will thus provide us with some important conclusions to much of the foregoing material.

Imitating Originality, Plagiarizing the Plagiarist

While *Jacques* cannot be read as a mere imitation, it establishes a relationship with *Tristram Shandy* through a playful exploration of originality, imitation and plagiarism. Diderot's thematic debt to Sterne consists in his adoption of Trim's amours from Volume VIII of *Tristram Shandy* for the story of Jacques's amours, which initially appears to be the text's principal story, apart from the framing journey of Jacques and his master. Jacques shares with Trim a Christian name (James), an indulgent master, a brother who comes to a bad end in Lisbon, a fatalistic captain, and a love story that is frequently interrupted. While Trim's amours are related within a few pages, Jacques's span the whole text and, in that regard, resemble Tristram's digressive *Life and Opinions* as a whole. The most direct reference to *Tristram Shandy* appears towards the end of *Jacques* and constitutes the second of its three conclusions, delivering what was promised on the first page, the story of Jacques's loves. This describes the knee massage which Jacques receives from Denise and which leads to his falling in love. It closely follows Trim's tale of falling in love with the beguine,[14] and is introduced as a plagiarism:

> Voici le second paragraphe, copié de la Vie de *Tristram Shandy*, à moins que l'entretien de Jacques le Fataliste et de son maître ne soit antérieur à cet ouvrage, et que le Ministre Stern ne soit le plagiaire, ce que je ne crois pas, mais par une estime toute particuliere de M. Sterne, que je distingue de la plupart des Littérateurs de sa nation dont l'usage assez fréquent est de nous voler et de nous dire des injures.[15]

This is a curious paragraph filled with ironies. To begin with, the speaking voice, here the editor, who has just taken over from the narrator, sets up a rivalry between *Jacques* and *Tristram Shandy* in terms of their originality. While he suspects the narrator of having copied Sterne, he also considers the possibility of the reverse situation in which *Jacques* predates *Tristram Shandy* and is therefore an object of Sterne's plagiarism. This scenario is proposed, however, only to be dismissed by the editor, who has an 'estime toute particuliere de M. Sterne'. The doubt has nevertheless been voiced and, in any case, it is unclear on what the editor's esteem is based.

Our suspicions should be aroused. Sterne was certainly more sympathetic towards the French than other British Grand Tour writers, but he was not entirely immune to the anti-French and anti-Catholic sentiments that were common in Britain during the period, nor to the association of France with absolutism, oppression and injustice.[16] Another complaint is one that he voiced in France and that Arthur Cash, based on Joseph Craddock's account, suggests had damaged his popularity there, though any such setback was also likely to have been caused by the early negative reviews of *Tristram Shandy*.[17] This complaint consisted, as we saw in Chapter 2, in his use of a coin metaphor to distinguish the English and the French to the latter's disadvantage. In the fictionalized version of this exchange in *A Sentimental Journey*, which takes place between Yorick and the Comte de B, Yorick declares that the English are original and varied, 'like antient medals', that pass through few people's hands. Keeping apart, they 'preserve the first sharpnesses which the fine hand of nature has given them – they are not so pleasant to feel – but in return, the legend is so visible, that at the first look you see whose image and superscription they bear'.[18] The French, meanwhile, are excessively polite, thanks to their constant, sociable, rubbing together, like smooth King William shillings that have lost their impressions. Such politeness is different from a 'politesse de cœur' which 'inclines men more to human actions, than courteous ones'.

Diderot employs Sterne's famous coin metaphor to describe Jacques's originality:

> tandis que le Marquis des Arcis causait avec le maître de Jacques, Jacques de son côté n'était pas muet avec M. le Secrétaire Richard qui le trouvait un franc original, ce qui arriverait plus souvent parmi les hommes, si l'éducation d'abord, ensuite le grand usage du monde ne les usaient comme ces pieces d'argent qui à force de circuler perdent leur empreinte.[19]

The allusion is subtle and Diderot had already explored originality through the character of Rameau's nephew, but the plagiarized second conclusion to *Jacques* suggests that he was sensitive to the criticism inherent in Sterne's coin metaphor, perhaps even offended, for he playfully casts doubt on Sterne's own originality. After all, Sterne himself borrowed from innumerable sources, as John Ferriar pointed out early on in *Illustrations of Sterne* (1798).[20] Sterne's borrowings continue to be identified and have been noted extensively in the Florida edition. He was imitative in open and indirect ways, both echoing or alluding to other works and directly referring to specific texts and passages. Thus *Don Quixote* inspires Sterne's 'Cervantick' humour, ironic tolerance of eccentric characters and picaresque motifs,[21] while Rabelais influences his ribaldry, wordplay, lists and mockery of philosophical positions, particularly through comic concretization. Swift and the Scriblerians are his more scathing Augustan predecessors with their satire directed against individuals and their ideas, and the theme of the birth and education of an unusual child also echoes *Gargantua, Pantagruel* and the *Memoirs of Martinus Scriblerus*.[22] He is indebted to Shakespeare for Yorick and his tragicomic humanity, and Tristram's procrastination recalls and parodies Hamlet's. The intimacy that grows between Tristram and his readers, particularly in his reflections on the problem of simultaneously writing about a life and living it, is reminiscent of Montaigne, and although the extremes of Locke's philosophy are mocked, Tristram's associative way of writing is nevertheless Lockean. The world of Burton's *Anatomy of Melancholy* (1621), constructed though books, with quotations, references, elaborations on every subject and an extraordinary exuberance for words, is apparent in Walter's love of systems and Tristram's own learned approach to constructing his life. Texts appear in diverse forms and may be acknowledged or diguised: Obadiah Walker's *Of Education* (1673) and

Xenophon's *Cyropædia* provide models for the *Tristrapaedia*, while Hogarth's *Analysis of Beauty* (1753) is invoked in the composition of Dr Slop and the description of Trim's posture during the reading of the sermon. There are echoes of Pope's *Dunciad* (1743) in Slop's burlesque fall, and Chambers's *Cyclopædia* (1728) provides the vocabulary for Toby's fortifications. Fragments of texts appear frequently, the *Mémoire* of the Sorbonne doctors is quoted in its entirety, and contemporary, biblical and classical sources are present on every page in a variety of ways.

Jonathan Lamb has analysed some of the uses of imitation in Sterne and identified 'a system of double imitation', in which both the structure and matter of his situations are borrowed, frequently from different sources.[23] The combinations can be complex: Yorick's death, for example, is a situation that resembles Don Quixote's because it consists of a beating, then a loss of illusions and of life, 'but it is accomplished in Sancho's words and recorded in Shakespeare's'. For Lamb, Sterne's sentimentalism, irregularities and apparently original progressive-digressive method of writing can be traced as far back as Longinus's *On the Sublime*, a text that enjoyed great popularity in the mid-eighteenth century, while his sermons may be seen as imitations of the divine original scriptural texts (as well as of several other Latitudinarian texts), testifying to the sympathetic power required in the reading of the human heart. Imitation constitutes the very fabric of Sterne's method of writing and, importantly, this was not lost on Diderot, from whose point of view, moreover, Sterne's verdict that the English were more original than the French would have been particularly ironic because so many of his models were French. In addition to Rabelais and Montaigne, there are references to Malebranche, Descartes, Roger de Piles, Pierre Charron, René Rapin, Jean Aimar Piganiol de La Force and, possibly, what Ferriar called the 'ludicrous' writers of the sixteenth century, Béroalde, D'Aubigné, Bouchet and Bruscambille.[24] Sterne's view of the French character as unoriginal, therefore, may partly be considered in the same way as his criticism of plagiarism, which is itself plagiarized from Burton (in turn using borrowed phrases): it is deeply and comically ironic, and brings into question the nature of originality, imitation and plagiarism.[25]

Sterne's exploration of plagiarism is arguably at its most self-reflexive in the reading of Yorick's sermon in Volume II of *Tristram Shandy*. To begin with, the sermon is a real one, and had already been preached by Sterne himself at York cathedral on 29 July 1750.[26] Toby's statement that 'it does not appear that the sermon is printed, or ever likely to be' is comic, given its publication in *Tristram Shandy*, and the sermon was published a second time in 1760 in a volume of Sterne's sermons.[27] There had been some outrage that Sterne should publish his sermons under the name of Shakespeare's fool, and this led him to add a preface to the second edition in order to 'ease the minds of those who see a jest, and the danger which lurks under it, where no jest was meant'.[28] There is also a degree of self-promotion in Sterne's decision to publish his sermons under the name of one of his, and Shakespeare's, characters. For an author who wrote 'not to be *fed*, but to be *famous*',[29] it made sense for him to conflate his own identity as author and priest with his fictional characters, Yorick and Tristram, who had made him famous and were fashioned out of his own life and readings.

The decision shows that Sterne's use of imitation was also at play between his life and works, and French critics picked up on this when they commented on the similarity between his original character and original writings.[30] The idea of original authorship was evidently a complicated one for Sterne, as is revealed by the farcical destiny of Yorick's sermon in *Tristram Shandy*:

> Ill-fated sermon! Thou wast lost, after this recovery of thee, a second time, dropp'd thro' an unsuspected fissure in thy master's pocket, down into a treacherous and tatter'd lining, – trod deep into the dirt by the left hind foot of his Rosinante, inhumanly stopping upon thee as thou falledst; – buried ten days in the mire, – raised up out of it by a beggar, sold for a halfpenny to a parish-clerk, – transferred to his parson, – lost for ever to thy own, the remainder of his days, – nor restored to his restless MANES till this very moment, that I tell the world this story.
>
> Can the reader believe, that this sermon of *Yorick*'s was preach'd at an assize, in the cathedral of *York*, before a thousand witnesses, ready to give oath to it, by a certain prebendary of that church, and actually printed by him when he had done, – and within so short a space as two years and three months after *Yorick*'s death. – *Yorick*, indeed, was never better served in his life! – but it was a little hard to male-treat him before, and plunder him after he was laid in his grave.[31]

This accelerated mock picaresque tale of the sermon's adventures challenges the idea that one can easily distinguish original work from imitation, or indeed acceptable imitation from plagiarism.[32] The plagiarizing prebendary of York cathedral was, of course, Sterne himself, who thus completes the circularity of Tristram's assertion that Yorick's sermon is plagiarized (by its real author). Tristram goes on to defend the plagiarizing minister:

> However, as the gentleman who did it, was in perfect charity with *Yorick*, – and, in conscious justice, printed but a few copies to give away; – and that, I am told, he could moreover have made as good a one himself, had he thought fit, – I declare I would not have published this anecdote to the world; – nor do I publish it with an intent to hurt his character and advancement in the church; – I leave that to others; – but I find myself impell'd by two reasons, which I cannot withstand.
>
> The first is, That in doing justice, I may give rest to *Yorick*'s ghost; – which, as the country people, – and some others, believe, – *still walks*.
>
> The second reason is, That, by laying open this story to the world, I gain an opportunity of informing it, – That in case the character of parson *Yorick*, and this sample of his sermon is liked, – that there are now in the possession of the *Shandy* family, as many as will make a handsome volume, at the world's service, – and much good may they do it.[33]

Yorick's ghost could be said to 'still walk' because his creator was alive – and very able to promote his forthcoming volume of sermons, which contained their own borrowings from seventeenth- and eighteenth-century Anglicans such as John Tillotson, Joseph Hall, John Norris and John Sharp.[34]

In the plagiarized conclusion to *Jacques*, the editor's 'estime' for Sterne becomes deeply and comically ambivalent. Sterne clearly made liberal use of other people's work and ideas. The processes of imitation are integral to his work, and he even manages to plagiarize his own work and imitate his own characters. From Diderot's point of view, in addition to 'stealing' from a plethora of sources, several of which were French, Sterne also insulted the French by claiming that they were not as original as the English. The editor's seemingly academic interpolation concerning the plagiarized passage reveals that Diderot not only created a thematic and stylistic link between *Tristram Shandy* and the digressive story of Jacques's amours, but also that he fully engaged with Sterne's uses of imitation, and absorbed *Tristram Shandy* more generally, as we shall see, for his own literary and philosophical purposes. The insertion of the plagiarized conclusion and the editor's comments on it embody the ironies inherent in a theory of literature based upon the imitation of nature and of literary models, by demonstrating that questions of originality and imitation are far from straightforward, since it is impossible to identify the origin of each idea, theme or style. Like Yorick's sermon, whose adventures take it to several 'masters', it is possible to control neither what happens to a text after it is read, nor the ways in which other writers may use it. Rather than being a humble acknowledgement by an imitator of his source, the explicit plagiarism from *Tristram Shandy* shows that Diderot engages with Sterne as a French original. *Jacques*'s kinship with *Tristram Shandy* is established through a playful exploration of literary originality and imitation, which links them both not only to comic and satiric forms of writing, but also to the classicism which consists in the imitation of models and which they simultaneously mock and practise.

Originality in the Novel

Elements of *Jacques* may have been conceived as early as 1762, shortly after Diderot met Sterne in Paris, or in 1765 after the publication of Volume VIII, which contains Trim's amours. Its existence is first recorded in 1771 in a letter from Meister to Bodmer.[35] After his first trip to France, Sterne asked his publisher, Thomas Becket, to send Diderot a number of books, including the works of Pope and Chaucer, the plays and biography of Colley Cibber, Tillotson's sermons, the complete works of Locke and, as a gift, the six volumes of *Tristram Shandy* that had already been published. Whether Diderot was familiar with *Tristram Shandy* before Sterne went to Paris is questionable, but their meeting certainly led to a literary friendship.[36] He recommended *Tristram Shandy* to Sophie Volland in terms which reveal that he associated it with comic and satiric writing:

Ce livre si fou, si sage et si gai est le rabelais des anglois [...] Il est impossible de vous en donner une autre idée que celle d'une satyre universelle. Mr Stern [sic] qui en est l'auteur est aussi un prêtre.[37]

During the 1750s and early 1760s in particular, Diderot embraced sensibility and experimented with the sentimental *drame bourgeois*. He even entrusted Sterne with the publication of his play, *Le Fils naturel*, in England, unaware that the latter thought it contained 'too much sentiment' and 'too much of preaching'.[38] Diderot was nevertheless attracted to the satirical and self-conscious aspects of Sterne's work rather than to its sentimentalism.[39]

This is apparent, as we saw, in his response to Sterne's uses of imitation, and a comparison of his reading of Richardson with his reading of Sterne also makes this evident. The *Éloge de Richardson* describes a direct and emotional reading experience that contrasts with the more complicated approach demanded by *Jacques*.[40] In *La Religieuse* (published, like *Jacques*, in 1796), Diderot creates a Richardsonian illusion of reality: its memoir form encourages the reader to trust and sympathize with Suzanne, the narrator, who naïvely describes her misfortunes in a convent. Sterne, on the other hand, offered a model for the representation of representation itself. Diderot played with narrative voice and the idea of a listening reader in *Ceci n'est pas un conte* (1773), and *Tristram Shandy* provided an early and fully fledged model for this interest. In *Jacques*, Diderot uses similar self-conscious devices to break down the illusion of reality created by novels and expected by novel-readers. Neither Sterne nor Diderot could anachronistically parody techniques of realism that were not established until the nineteenth century. Both writers did, however, revel in the subversion of linear narrative, and both, in different ways, combined the distancing techniques developed from satiric writing with elements of realism and romance that were already at work in the novel, such as psychological characterization and elaborate plots, thereby continuing the path of picaresque and comic fiction.[41]

The most prominent of these techniques is the use of the self-conscious narrator, frequently employed in comic fiction after *Don Quixote*, for example in the *Roman comique* (1651), the *Roman bourgeois* (1666), *Pharsamon* (1737) and *Tom Jones* (1749). *Jacques* and *Tristram Shandy* develop the device to an extreme degree and expand the role of the fictionalized reader, the person to whom the narrator addresses his discourse and who, like the narrator, becomes a character within the text. Several such fictionalized readers or 'narratees' are regularly brought into the text and addressed by Tristram. They include a general male reader ('Sir'), the aristocratic patron ('my Lord', or 'your Lordship'), the falsely prudish or inattentive female reader ('Madam'), the naïve young female reader ('my dear girl'), the critics ('Messrs. The monthly Reviewers'), the clerics ('your reverences and worships') and Jenny. In his preface, Tristram speaks to a variety of 'serious' readers: 'my dear Anti-Shandeans, and thrice able critics, and fellow-labourers, (for to you I write this Preface) – and to you, most subtle statesmen and discreet doctors (do – pull off your beards) renowned for gravity and wisdom'.[42] While the real reader can exclude himself from this less than flattering list, as we shall see later, one of the consequences of the device is that the real reader is forced into a more distanced relationship with the story. It prevents him from becoming immersed in a fictional world, and the focus of attention turns towards the way in which the story is told. Madam reader is sent back several pages to re-read more carefully, and while she does so, Tristram explains his motives to the remaining narratees (and to the real reader, who may or may not actually turn back a few pages):

> I have imposed this penance upon the lady, neither out of wantonness or cruelty, but from the best of motives; and therefore shall make her no apology for it when she returns back: – 'Tis to rebuke a vicious taste which has crept into thousands besides herself, – of reading straight forwards, more in quest of the adventures, than of the deep erudition and knowledge which a book of this cast, if read over as it should be, would infallibly impart with them.[43]

Despite Tristram's mock confidence in the quality of his own work, his book cannot indeed be read merely for the adventures. While it may be classed within a satirically erudite and philosophical category of books, it is also novelistic in a Bakhtinian sense because it is able to critique itself and parody the autobiographical genre to which it purports to conform, albeit eccentrically. Tristram's life is filled with misadventures, rather than adventures, and with the exception of his travels in Volume VII, they mostly take place at home rather than in the outside world: his interrupted conception, the smashing of his nose at birth with Dr Slop's forceps, the disastrous baptism during which he is wrongly named, the accident with the sash window when he is five years old. Even the long-awaited amours of Uncle Toby and the widow Wadman turn out to be comically unsuccessful.

Tristram's digressiveness, which prevents the reader from reading 'straight forwards' and 'in quest of the adventures', is a consequence of his misadventures, as we immediately learn. He begins the autobiography in the middle of his own conception, taking literally the idea of recounting a life from the beginning. Described by A. D. Nuttall as 'the most brilliant opening ever written', it presents the beginning both of a human life and of a literary *Life*.[44] Tristram initially claims to be following Horace's advice in beginning *ab ovo* (from the egg). This is, in fact, a misquotation, an example of Tristram's faulty 'deep erudition and knowledge', since Horace praised Homer for beginning the *Illiad in medias res*, in the middle of the Trojan war, rather than *ab ovo*, with the birth of Helen, who was hatched from Leda's egg following the union of Leda and Zeus. Tristram goes on to admit that his interpretation is not exactly what Horace meant, but brushes off the misreading:

> But that gentleman is speaking only of an epic poem or a tragedy; – (I forget which) – besides, if it was not so, I should beg Mr. *Horace*'s pardon; – for in writing what I

have set about, I shall confine myself neither to his rules, nor to any man's rules that ever lived.[45]

Tristram's scatterbrain forgetfulness may well be affected, but the misquote is witty, for he ends up not only following Horace's ancient recommendation by beginning *in medias res*, during Mr and Mrs Shandy's love-making, but also observing his own rules by beginning literally *ab ovo*, with his own conception.

As the opening shows, the reader has to interpret the work in an unusual manner. Tristram is an unconventional narrator and hero, conceived by interruption. Mrs Shandy's unfortunate association of ideas causes her husband's animal spirits to disperse fatally, marking Tristram for life as incomplete and prone to interruption, digression, eccentricity and originality.[46] From the 'unaccountable obliquity' with which he sets up his top as a toddler and which convinces his father 'That I should neither think nor act like any other man's child',[47] to his adult talents as a narrator, Tristram is original. Unable to tell his own story without digressing, his lack of conventional narrative progress presents difficulties for his readers, but he takes pride in his ability to surprise them: 'if I thought you was able to form the least judgment or probable conjecture to yourself, of what was to come in the next page, – I would tear it out of my book'.[48] Tristram is not born until Volume III, he takes his Grand Tour as a young man in Volume VII, the book ends several years before it begins, and the narrative jumps forwards and backwards in time as Tristram teases his fictionalized readers, gets carried away by an association of ideas, digresses with a new piece of information or a fragment, or decides to elaborate on a character in the doomed quest to provide a complete explanation for everything. Rather than a novel of adventures, then, the reader is confronted with opinions and, like Locke's *Essay*, with 'a history-book [...] of what passes in a man's own mind'.[49] The narrative is an extension of Tristram's original mind, itself a product of Shandy Hall with its creaking doors, falling sash windows and eccentric characters. The Shandean universe is one of interruptions, accidents, obstacles, frustrations and unheroic failings. Tristram is born into a 'scurvy and disasterous world', the 'continual sport of what the world calls Fortune' and 'sport of small accidents'.[50]

Yet Tristram's digressiveness is simultaneously progressive, for he can 'freeze' uncle Toby as he taps his pipe for several chapters in order to draw a portrait of his character through his hobby-horse.[51] Although he does not adhere to the rules of narrative progression, Tristram nevertheless reveals himself through his work. His opinions prevent him from telling the story of his life in a linear way as he constantly seeks causes, origins and explanations, but they do tell us about his personality and how he thinks. The events and adventures of his life are dwarfed by the manner in which he tells them, which becomes the main subject of his book as well as the event filling his life, for Tristram plans to continue publishing volumes of his *Life and Opinions* for as long as he lives. Like his father, who takes longer to write the *Tristrapædia* than Tristram does to grow up, he will fall further and further behind with his own life story as his original narrative method becomes the theme and world of his book. For Shklovsky, it draws attention to itself by transgressing and 'laying bare' conventional literary devices and rules, encouraging the reader to become more conscious of the methods of fictional representation,[52] while John Traugott sees *Tristram Shandy* as a dramatization of the rhetorical processes which reveal the reader's assumptions and expose the contradictions of Locke's hypotheses of comprehension and communication: through his rhetorically talented narrator, Sterne exposes the processes through which the reader habitually reads and thinks:

> It turns our consciousness not to the end of the argument, but to the process, so that we watch the effects of rhetoric, turn, antithesis, parallel, logic, pathos, inflation, diminution, and so on, as they define characters, motives, attitudes, feelings, in relation to one another and to our own private prejudices and assumptions. Rhetoric becomes the subject of rhetoric, and resolution of the rhetorical logic is not necessary, because we learn by consciousness of the process. The significant continuity of this book is the communication between the reader and his author (through the fool's mask of Tristram), as the author invents his vexed arguments. Always we must know how and why we react to a given stimulus [...] *Tristram* is rhetorical persuasion which yet, peculiarly, creates a world of conception.[53]

At the same time, while *Tristram Shandy*'s world of conception is created out of distancing techniques, it also incorporates intimacy. Sterne's use of a vocal and intrusive narrator and of a community of fictionalized readers may distance the reader from the book's story, pushing him towards an awareness of rhetorical structures or conventions of representation, but it has another, and opposing, consequence: it emphasizes the intimacy between speaker and listener. The real reader can separate himself from any subgroup of narratees, such as the critics or prudish female reader, who are biased or ill-qualified to understand the narrator. The initiated reader, however, is permitted into Tristram's world and even into his study, where he writes 'in a purple jerkin and yellow pair of slippers, without either wig or cap on'.[54] Like 'the truest friendship and cordiality' that exists between the Shandy brothers,[55] who are otherwise locked into their respective worlds and unable to communicate, there is a sympathetic relationship between Tristram and his readers which sustains the familiar tone of the text as a whole, and which he reflects upon through a comparison between reading and travelling:

> As you proceed further with me, the slight acquaintance which is now beginning betwixt us, will grow into familiarity; and that, unless one of us is in fault, will terminate in friendship. – *O diem præclarum!* – then nothing which has touched me will be thought trifling in its nature, or tedious in its telling. Therefore, my dear friend and companion, if you should think me somewhat sparing of my narrative on my first setting out, – bear with me, – and let me go on, and tell my story my own way: – or if I should seem now and then to trifle upon the road, – or should sometimes put on a fool's cap with a bell to it, for a moment or two as we pass along, – don't fly

off, – but rather courteously give me credit for a little more wisdom than appears upon my outside; – and as we jogg on, either laugh with me, or at me, or in short, do any thing, – only keep your temper.[56]

Novel and Anti-Novel

Even if Diderot intended to import *Tristram Shandy*'s originality into France, the result differs from it to such a degree and in such significant ways that, while much is derived from Sterne, it must be regarded as new and original in its own right. *Tristram Shandy* challenges the reader with its self-conscious contraventions of narrative drive and mocks a misguided Enlightenment faith in explanatory systems, while nevertheless creating a sympathetic connection among the characters and between narrator and reader. *Jacques le fataliste* sets out more specifically to unsettle both the eighteenth-century novel and its conventions, at the same time as dramatizing the contemporary debates about the philosophy of determinism through narrative self-reflexivity, as Daniel Brewer in particular has recently demonstrated.[57] Like Sterne, Diderot places the relationship between narrator and narratee in a central position, but does something rather different with it. In this section, I would like to consider this relationship in *Jacques* while also examining the ways in which the text as a whole develops the complicating factors of narrative representation already explored in *Tristram Shandy*.

The narrator–narratee relationship is established at the start of the text, so that it features alongside and as prominently as the relationship between Jacques and his Master:

> Comment s'étaient-ils rencontrés? Par hazard, comme tout le monde. Comment s'appelaient-ils? Que vous importe? D'où venaient-ils? Du lieu le plus prochain. Où allaient-ils? Est-ce que l'on sait où l'on va? Que disaient-ils? Le maitre ne disait rien, et Jacques disait que son Capitaine disait que tout ce qui nous arrive de bien et de mal ici bas était écrit là-haut.[58]

It becomes apparent that the narrator is voicing the questions of a fictionalized reader, answering them flippantly and giving very little away. The questions themselves suggest that the narrative is a picaresque journey, but a very unusual one without origin, destination or aim. The eighteenth-century reader of novels was used to being given, and could reasonably expect, information about location, characters and purpose. Clearly, however, this is no ordinary novel or *roman romanesque*. The narrator quite arrogantly points out that he can construct his text as he pleases rather than according to the fictionalized reader's expectations of novelistic adventures:

> Vous voyez, Lecteur, que je suis en beau chemin, et qu'il ne tiendrait qu'à moi de vous faire attendre un an, deux ans, trois ans le récit des amours de Jacques, en le

séparant de son maitre et en leur faisant courir à chacun tous les hazards qu'il me plairait. Qu'est-ce qui m'empêcherait de marier le maitre et de le faire cocu? d'embarquer Jacques pour les Isles? d'y conduire son maitre? de les ramener tous les deux en France sur le même vaisseau? Qu'il est facile de faire des contes! mais ils en seront quittes l'un et l'autre pour une mauvaise nuit, et vous pour ce delai.[59]

He repeatedly states that he can take the story in any direction he wants ('il ne tiendrait qu'à moi'), and dangles alternative situations in front of the narratee. The expression of power exemplified by this refrain is inextricably linked to other power structures in the text: while the text is controlled by the narrator, Jacques's fatalism asserts that human beings are predestined and act according to what is decreed 'above', and the social relationship between the Master and Jacques entails the subjection of the latter to the decisions of the former. These power structures are tested and explored dramatically through the relationships between narrator and fictionalized reader, between master and servant and ultimately between determinism and free will. The text is thus built upon parallel dialogues in the fictional, philosophical and social realms, all of which are finally narrative. They are set up from the first paragraph when the narrator addresses the fictionalized reader and the basic principles of fatalism are passed from Jacques's captain to Jacques, from Jacques to his Master, and from the narrator to narratee. Diderot's novels, as Brewer points out, are philosophical, and his philosophical works, like *Le Rêve de d'Alembert*, enact their significance like novels.[60] Jacques's philosophy of fatalism is thematized and represented as a text, the *grand rouleau*, or great scroll, but it is also dramatized within the little scroll, *Jacques* itself, through the relationships between Jacques and his Master and between the narrator and narratee.

If the dramatic dialogue between Jacques and his Master explores the question of determinism, the dialogue between narrator and fictional reader mainly explores aesthetic issues that reside in the representation of reality. These have real consequences for Jacques and his Master, since the narrator makes his choices with regard to the events that befall the characters, and responds to or ignores the narratee's demands either to persist with Jacques's love story or to continue with another tale that requires momentary attention. The central claim of Jacques's fatalism is that everything has an origin or cause, that 'chaque balle qui partait d'un fusil avait son billet' or, as Trim and King William put it, that 'every ball had its billet'.[61] For Jacques, there is no need to struggle vainly against destiny, since whatever is written on the *grand rouleau* cannot be changed. His Master, on the other hand, is convinced that human beings do have free will and that they may act consciously and through choice. Ironically, their professed philosophical beliefs have little to do with their actions and personalities. The Master's belief in free will contrasts with his passive nature, while Jacques is an enterprising and active person who thinks quickly, philosophizes, makes decisions, responds to situations as they arise, throws himself into dangerous situations and comes out of them. Jacques finds his Master's lost possessions and entertains him with endless conversation and interesting stories. The nameless Master, on the other hand, is a dull *automate*, totally dependent on his pocket watch, snuffbox and charismatic servant.[62]

Despite his avowed fatalism, Jacques gets by quite well in the world since, as he points out, 'Un paradoxe n'est pas toujours une fausseté'.[63] Although all is determined, he can still be active: he buys time, for instance, when leaving an inn filled with robbers by taking their key – and yet in turn, he does not feel the need to hurry but can walk away calmly. This, he admits, is because human beings cannot know what is written up above, so they are bound to act with some self-determination, which may or may not be reasonable:

> C'est que faute de savoir ce qui est écrit la-haut on ne sait ni ce qu'on veut, ni ce qu'on fait, et qu'on suit sa fantaisie qu'on appelle raison, ou sa raison qui n'est souvent qu'une dangereuse fantaisie qui tourne tantôt bien tantôt mal.[64]

Jacques's belief in an ordered universe in which human beings are predestined, and in which there is a clear relationship between cause and effect, is refuted both by his own actions and by the ways in which events unfold. He is robbed and beaten up, for instance, after giving most of his money to a poor woman, but later 'rewarded' for his virtue by Desglands, who invites him to stay at his château. There are many sudden and incomprehensible reversals of fortune in *Jacques*. Madame de la Pommeraye carefully calculates how to dupe the Marquis but ends up contributing to his happiness, and Richard, who is sent to investigate the Père Hudson's immoral activities, is finally framed for immoral behaviour thanks to Hudson's clever plotting.

Fortune, or Fate, seems to treat the characters as the narrator treats his fictionalized reader. Although the latter is frequently critical and can be impatient, irritable or demanding, the narrator remains in command. He refuses to write a linear narrative whose structure reflects a greater moral and metaphysical order, and constantly interrupts the story of Jacques's amours. Interruptions include external events (the passing of a funeral coach, the theft of the Master's watch and horse, encounters with other characters), other stories (the narrator's, Jacques's, the Master's, those of the people they meet), and the narrator's own commentaries to the fictional reader about his methods of writing. In these commentaries, he frequently points out that he is not writing a novel but telling the truth:

> Pourquoi la jeune paysanne ne serait-elle pas ou la Dame Suzon, ou la Dame Marguerite, ou l'hôtesse du grand Cerf ou la mere Jeanne, ou même Denise sa fille? Un faiseur de roman n'y manquerait pas, mais je n'aime pas les romans, à moins que ce soient ceux de Richardson. Je fais l'histoire; cette histoire intéressera ou n'intéressera pas, c'est le moindre de mes soucis. Mon projet est d'être vrai, je l'ai rempli.[65]

Such assertions parody those of eighteenth-century novelists who claimed to be chronicling history or merely editing letters or memoirs in an attempt to avoid accusations that their work lacked either verisimilitude or moral value. But they also imply that the construction of reality in fiction is arbitrary rather than organized according to greater principles. With his persistent reflections on what he is writing and how he constructs the text, and his insistence that it is not a novel, the narrator exposes the conventions of representation as mere conventions, or 'techniques of illusion' in Vivienne Mylne's phrase,[66] and challenges the mimetic assumption that fiction and art represent an external reality.

The conventional nature of narrative is emphasized by the narrator's refusal to prioritize consistently a single narrative. Jacques's story is interrupted so frequently that it becomes unclear whether there is a principal narrative. The stories proliferate, spreading in different directions and providing ever-widening perspectives. The number of tales and narrating characters complicate the text and contribute to what Mauzi calls its procedures of 'désarticulation'.[67] This has led him to categorize the characters by degrees. The narrator and narratee are 'zero degree' characters (he calls them 'author' and 'reader', though he distinguishes them from the real author and reader). At the first degree are Jacques and his Master. Second degree characters are those encountered by Jacques and his Master on their journey, and those of the third degree only feature in the tales of the zero, first and second degree characters. The stories are told in the first or third person by different characters, sometimes about other characters (hence some are positioned in more than one degree), and interspersed with sections of pure dialogue among the characters or between the narrator and narratee. All the stories, from the picaresque journey of Jacques and his Master, the story of Jacques's duelling captain and his friend, and the bawdy, *dépucelage* adventures of the young Jacques, to the *hôtesse*'s formal and psychological tale of Madame de la Pommeraye, are interrupted by external events or new stories. Each of the partial or complete tales holds the reader's attention for a few lines, paragraphs, or pages before passing into the background and making way for another. Each is also distanced and placed in the context of another, creating disorientating shifts in perspective. The Marquis des Arcis is a principal character in the *hôtesse*'s story of Madame de la Pommeraye, but, like Jacques and his Master, he happens to be staying at the Grand Cerf, and when the weather allows all the guests to leave, the Marquis and his secretary, Richard, travel with Jacques and his Master. The Marquis tells the Master the story of Richard and Père Hudson. Richard, in turn, converses with Jacques and tells him a different story, which we hear from Jacques's mouth when he later recounts it to his Master.

Morality is subjected to a process of destabilization similar to that of metaphysical and narrative structure. As an aspect of the narrator's *antiroman* quest, it constitutes a refusal to subscribe to the claims of eighteenth-century novelists that their work is morally instructive as well as entertaining.[68] But it is also another facet of the investigation into the representation of reality. None of the stories in *Jacques* reveal a clear moral lesson or conclusion, and the novel-reader's expectation of encountering characters who easily can be judged as virtuous or evil is entirely frustrated. The Master comments on this very trait in the tale of Madame de La Pommeraye. He complains – and Jacques agrees with him on this occasion – that the *hôtesse* did not draw a convincing portrait of Mademoiselle Duquesnoi. The lack of consistency in her moral characterization, the Master points out, constitutes a transgression against the aesthetic rules of Aristotle, Horace, Vida and Le Bossu.[69] But the *hôtesse* has an unhelpful, punning reply, declaring her ignorance of such rules and her fidelity only to truth:

> Je ne connais ni bossu ni droit, je vous ai dit la chose comme elle s'est passée, sans en rien omettre, sans y rien ajouter. Et qui sait ce qui se passait au fond du cœur de cette jeune fille, et si dans les momens où elle nous paraissait agir le plus lestement elle n'en était pas secrétement dévorée de chagrin.[70]

She relates what she knows, but this does not seem to be adequate enough for her audience to make a reasonable judgement about the characters. Although she is the narrator of the tale, her knowledge is partial and not entirely reliable, for she does not know what had been going on in Mademoiselle Duquesnoi's mind all along, nor whether she sincerely regretted deceiving the Marquis. The narrator intrudes to join the debate regarding Madame de la Pommeraye's actions:

> Et vous croyez, Lecteur, que l'apologie de Mme de la Pommeraye est plus difficile a faire? [...] Vous entrez en fureur au nom de Mme de la Pommeraye et vous vous écriez, ah! la femme horrible! ah! l'hypocrite! ah! la scélérate! Point d'exclamation, point de courroux, point de partialité; raisonnons.[71]

He proceeds to defend Madame de la Pommeraye, blaming the fictionalized reader for judging her too quickly. Her desire for revenge is understandable, he argues, considering how much she sacrificed for the Marquis, who only repaid her with betrayal. The narrator adds another piece of information as evidence in her favour, which he has gained 'par les voies les plus sures', as he tells us tantalizingly, to prove that she was not driven by desire for wealth or titles.[72] Even if her motivations are understandable, the narrator also anticipates the narratee's discomfort with the extent and depth of her vengeance, suggesting that she has exceptional character and depth of feeling. The real reader is left to his own interpretation, the most logical of which would surely be to consider all the evidence and incorporate all elements of the debate while recognizing that some pieces of information are missing. Yet the reading experience itself is one of paradox. Diderot is able to create a situation in which the reader can hold two contradictory positions: he can be both disapproving of Madame de la Pommeraye and sympathetic towards her, both relieved that her harsh revenge fails and angry that she was so capriciously betrayed by the Marquis.[73] Whatever the final judgement, if there can be one at all, the narrator's interventions and discussion of the story with the narratee, together with the aesthetic conversation between Jacques, his Master and the *hôtesse*, force the reader into a distanced and paradoxical consideration of the story that emphasizes the way in which it is told and examines its relation to truth.

In its focus upon the playfulness of narrative, *Jacques* is at once a quintessentially Enlightenment text that intersects with contemporary philosophical debates, and a novel which marks a significant development in the genre, and presses it to its limits. The distancing procedures that operate in and constitute *Jacques* not only demand a constant awareness of its representational methods, but also dramatize questions about the nature of the reality that is being represented. Just to complicate matters, the text refers to several historically identifiable anecdotes, events, characters and locations. For instance, the doctors Dufouart and Louis, Julien le Roy, Le Pelletier, doctor Tronchin, some of Jacques's previous employers, Père Ange, Gousse, Prémontval, Madame Pigeon and Père Hudson, among many other characters are, to varying degrees, based on real people. The narrator's individualistic insistence that he is free to take the narrative wherever he likes contrasts with the very act of writing, in which choices must be made and written down. His story is also limited by the fact that it depends on the reader's desire to listen. In order to hold the reader's attention, he needs to remain, at least some of the time, within the bounds of conventionality. Despite the frustrating interruptions that force the reader to read fiction more philosophically, the numerous tales in *Jacques* are engrossing, entertaining and tightly structured. Given their variety and the skill with which they are told, they both satisfy and fuel the reader's very human appetite for teleologically driven stories, and particularly for love stories.

Thus while the narrator apparently tries to write an *antiroman*, Diderot's work is both *antiroman* and *roman*. The existence of three endings certainly mocks the teleological narrative drive of more conventional novels, but the third ending turns *Jacques* into the familiar *roman romanesque* that it parodies and claims not to be, and reveals, as Simon and McMorran have pointed out, that Jacques's story is embedded within the Master's.[74] This tells of the betrayal by his friend, the Chevalier de St Ouin. Unaware that Agathe is pregnant with St Ouin's child, the lovers hatch a plan to encourage the Master to fall in love with her and make him legally responsible for the child. The real reason for the journey of Jacques and his Master becomes clear shortly before the three conclusions: the Master is going to visit the child in his foster home. Finding St Ouin there, he finally has his revenge, kills St Ouin and escapes, leaving Jacques to be arrested and imprisoned. In the third ending, however, Jacques is freed from prison by Mandrin's gang and, after becoming a gang member, is eventually reunited with his Master at Desglands's castle, where Denise lives. The conclusion to Jacques's love story (his reunion with Denise) turns out to be dependent on the Master's story (his betrayal by and revenge on St Ouin), which is the framing narrative, and the book ends according to *romanesque* principles. The traditional master–servant hierarchy is reasserted, the Master's story privileged, virtue rewarded and vice punished. Finally, Jacques marries

Denise, and this happy outcome marks the end of a belatedly conventional novel. In the meantime, of course, the conventional novel has been seriously challenged and reworked so that the story becomes that of itself, of how a story is told. With irrepressible playfulness, the editor introduces a small question mark regarding the happiness of Jacques's marriage and Denise's fidelity, but he admits that he has no further information, and the text ends.

Jacques le fataliste, a novel that has become so important in French literature, is also the product of a complicated cross-cultural symbiosis, which has, in turn, continued to influence the modern novel throughout Europe and beyond. My focus on its relationship with *Tristram Shandy* is only one aspect of this continual two-way process, and aims to contribute to our understanding of the fact that national cultures can never exist in isolation. If, as Jauss believes, the meaning of a work is created by its readers over time, an exploration of the first French critics, readers, translators and writers who responded to Sterne offers new perspectives on his work. Sterne's own consideration of his French audience is an important and previously neglected area. His visits to France gave him direct contact with his actual and potential readers (*philosophes*, journalists and critics, cosmopolitan elites, translators, minor writers and middle-class readers), which led him to incorporate French readers into his work with a sympathetic, but also playful, view of their national characteristics. He approached the French as a subject, addressed them as readers, and self-consciously rewrote the contemporary Anglo–French relationship. An exploration of Sterne's early French reception must also engage with recent Sterne criticism and help to show that there are surprising similarities, as well as inevitable distances, between current and eighteenth-century French interpretations. What stands out is that *Tristram Shandy* and *A Sentimental Journey* were read immediately in a variety of ways, both in relation to older comic, satiric and philosophical writings, and as novels. *Tristram Shandy* in particular was identified as original and unique, paradoxically contributing to, or even forming, a subgenre or class of books whose common characteristic was their inimitability, and in which *Jacques le fataliste* was subsequently included. The reception of a literary text also reflects the extraordinary diversity of the recipient culture itself and, importantly, helps to form it. This book has emphasized the shifting nature of the 'horizon of expectations' of late eighteenth-century France. Rather than attempting to describe or 'objectify' it exhaustively – an impossible task – the focus has been on the debates of the period, through which are revealed the richness of and contradictions within the recipient culture. Both literary-aesthetic and socio-political (Jauss has been criticized for neglecting the social aspect of the reading process), these debates are expressions of a national culture in flux. The emphasis placed on points of confrontation between the constantly evolving literary landscape and the work of Sterne has, hopefully, illuminated not only the particular case of Sterne's reception in France between 1760 and 1800, but also the complexities of cross-cultural literary reception itself and the processes by which a new and original work becomes part of a tradition.

Appendix

Articles on Sterne in French Periodicals, 1760–1800

This contains announcements, reviews and critical essays discussed in this study which are specifically on Sterne, as well as articles featured in Howes (1971), and a selection of related pieces. It is not an exhaustive list, and gaps should be filled by The Reception of British and Irish Authors in Europe project, which, in addition to its published volumes (Series Editor Elinor Shaffer), including one on Sterne (edited by Peter de Voogd and John Neubauer), comprises a database and bibliography facility, to which additional information will continue to be added.

Année littéraire (1754–91)

AL, 6 (1776), Letter 1, pp. 3–25.
Review and summary of Frénais's translation of *Tristram Shandy*, and summary of Frénais's life of Sterne.

AL, 6 (1784), pp. 120–8.
Review of Gorjy's *Nouveau voyage sentimental*.

AL, 7 (1785), Letter 3, pp. 49–55.
Review and summary of *Nouveau voyage en France*, i.e. Volume VII of *Tristram Shandy*, followed by the *Histoire de Le Febvre* and *Lettres familières*.

AL, 6 (1786), Letter 25, pp. 313–21.
On Vernes's *Voyageur sentimental*.

AL, 7 (1786), Letter 9, pp. 108–12.
Review of the new edition of Frénais's *Voyage sentimental* which contains the partially spurious *Lettres d'Yorick à Eliza et d'Eliza à Yorick*.

AL, 1 (1789), p. 137.
Contains Colin d'Harleville's poem *Imitation libre de Sterne*, first printed in the *Almanach des muses*, 1789.

Gazette littéraire de l'Europe (1764–6)

GLE, 5 (20 March 1765), pp. 39–43.
Review of the English publication of *Tristram Shandy*, Volumes VII–VIII, by Jean-Baptiste Suard, which was translated into English and published in the *London Chronicle*, XVII, No. 1299 (10–18 April 1765), p. 373.

Journal anglais (1775–8)

JA (15 November 1775), pp. 189–90.
Announcement of the English publication of Sterne's *Letters*.

JA (15 December 1775), pp. 263–75.
Frénais's translation of Slawkenbergius's Tale: *La prise de Strasbourg, ou la Curiosité punie*.

JA (15 February 1776), pp. 12–18.
Review of the *Lettres du Lord Chesterfield à son fils*, translated by Peyron, which contains an extract from the *Lettres d'Yorick à Eliza et d'Eliza à Yorick*.

Journal de Paris (1777–1840)

Also called *Journal de Paris national* (1792–5) then *Journal de Paris* (1795–1811).

JP (18–19 June 1786).
Letter by Amélie Suard on *A Sentimental Journey*, reprinted in Suard, *Mélanges de littérature* (Paris: Dentu, An XII/1803), III, pp. 111–22.

JP (20 October 1787), pp. 1263–4.
Announcement of La Beaume's translation of Sterne's selected *Sermons*.

Journal de politique et de littérature (1774–8)

JPL, 1 (25 April 1777), pp. 568–70.
Voltaire on *Tristram Shandy*.

Journal encyclopédique (1756–93)

Also called *Journal encyclopédique ou universal* (from 1775).

JE, 3.2 (15 April 1760), pp. 150–1.
Announcement and summary of *Tristram Shandy*, Volumes I and II.

JE, 6.1 (15 August 1760), pp. 148–9.
Review of the *Sermons*.

JE, 2.1 (15 February 1761), pp. 137–8.
Announcement of *Tristram Shandy*, Volumes III and IV.

JE (1 May 1761), p. 131.
Review of *Tristram Shandy*, Volumes III and IV.

JE, 2.2 (1 March 1762), pp. 143–4.
Review of *Tristram Shandy*, Volumes V and VI.

JE, 7.2 (15 October 1762), pp. 95–104.
Translation of the Story of Le Fever.

JE, 1.1 (1 January 1766), p. 137.
Review of *Tristram Shandy*, Volumes VII and VIII.

JE, 2.3 (15 March 1767), p. 145.
Review of *Tristram Shandy*, Volume IX.

JE, 5.1 (1 July 1769), pp. 137–8.
Review of Frénais's translation of *A Sentimental Journey*.

JE, 1.2 (15 January 1777), pp. 256–65.
Review of Frénais's translation of *Tristram Shandy*.

JE, 4.1 (15 May 1785), pp. 71–9.
Review of La Beaume's *Nouveau voyage sentimental*, i.e. Volume VII of *Tristram Shandy*, together with the Story of Le Fever and selected *Letters*.

JE, 6.1 (15 August 1785), pp. 173–5.
Review of La Beaume's translation of *Tristram Shandy*.

JE, 1.2 (15 January 1786), pp. 268–77.
Review of Bonnay's translation of *Tristram Shandy*.

JE, 2.3 (15 March 1786), pp. 445–53.
Review of La Beaume's translation of *Tristram Shandy*.

JE, 5.3 (1 August 1786), pp. 524–7.
First part of the essay 'Sur l'esprit et les ouvrages de Sterne, ainsi que sur les traductions françoises de son livre intitulé: La vie et les opinions de Tristram Shandy'.

JE, 6.1 (15 August 1786), pp. 134–42.
Continuation of the essay 'Sur l'esprit et les ouvrages de Sterne'.

Magasin encyclopédique, ou Journal des sciences, des lettres et des arts (1792–3, 1795–1816)

ME, 6 (1795), p. 284.
Announcement of various works, including Rousseau's *Du contrat social*, Goethe's *Werther* and the 1786 edition of Frénais's translation of *A Sentimental Journey*.

ME, 2 (1796).
Announcement of Damin's *Voyage à Chantilly*.

ME, 5 (1799), pp. 334–51.
Review of Dusaulx's *De mes rapports avec J.-J. Rousseau*, which contains a passage on Sterne.

ME, 6 (1799), p. 121.
Review of the musical play, *Sterne à Paris*.

Mémoires littéraires de la Grande-Bretagne (1768–9)

Edited by Jacques Georges Deyverdun and Edward Gibbon.

Mémoires littéraires de la Grande Bretagne, pour l'an 1767 (London: Becket & De Hondt, 1768), p. 223.
Announcement of the publication of *Tristram Shandy*, Volume IX.

Mémoires littéraires de la Grande Bretagne, pour l'an 1768 (London: Heydinger & Elmsley, 1769), pp. 105–34.
Two articles paying homage to Sterne on his death. The first contains several translated extracts from *A Sentimental Journey*; the second, discussion of and extracts from *Tristram Shandy* and the *Sermons*.

Mercure de France (1724–91)

MF (August 1769), pp. 71–4.
Review of Frénais's translation of *A Sentimental Journey*.

MF (January 1777), p. 136.
Review of Frénais's translation of *Tristram Shandy*.

MF (12 November 1785), pp. 71–84.
Mallet du Pan's review of Bonnay's translation of *Tristram Shandy*.

MF (4 March 1786), pp. 30–4.
Review of La Beaume's translation of *Tristram Shandy*.

MF (25 March 1786), p. 185.
Mallet du Pan's defence of Bonnay's translation of *Tristram Shandy*.

Notes

Introduction

[1] Jeremy Black, *Natural and Necessary Enemies: Anglo-French Relations in the Eighteenth-Century* (London: Duckworth, 1986).

[2] In *Britons: Forging the Nation 1707–1837* (New Haven: Yale University Press, 1992), Linda Colley speaks of the forging of Great Britain as a nation between 1707 and 1837, a period consisting of a succession of wars with France: the War of Spanish Succession (1702–13), the War of Austrian Succession (1739–48), the Seven Years War (1756–63), the French Revolutionary War (1793–1802) and the Napoleonic Wars (1803–15). Britons overcame internal differences and defined themselves in relation to the external enemy. Britain equated itself with liberty in politics and economics, in contrast to the feudal and absolutist French system, while in religion, the British defined themselves as Protestants in contrast to the Catholic French, who supported the Catholic Stuart pretenders. Murray G. H. Pittock, *Inventing and Resisting Britain: Cultural Identities in Britain and Ireland, 1685–1789* (Basingstoke: Macmillan, 1997) challenges the idea of a unified British identity in the eighteenth century.

[3] See Josephine Grieder, *Anglomania in France 1740-1789: Fact, Fiction, and Political Discourse* (Geneva: Droz, 1985); Michèle Mat-Hasquin, 'Les Influences anglaises en Europe occidentale au siècle des lumières', *Études sur le XVIIIe siècle* (1981), 191–9; C. Nordmann, 'Anglomanie et anglophobie en France au dix-huitième siècle', *Revue du Nord* 66 (1984), 787–803; Joseph Texte, *Jean-Jacques Rousseau et les origines du cosmopolitisme littéraire* (Paris: Hachette, 1895).

[4] The *Lettres philosophiques* appeared first as *Letters concerning the English Nation* (London: Davis & Lyon, 1733), then in France as the *Lettres philosophiques* (Amsterdam: [n. pub.], 1734); *Le Pour et le contre, ouvrage périodique d'un goût nouveau* (Paris: [n. pub.], 1733–40). Early eighteenth-century translations include Defoe, *La Vie et les avantures surprenantes de Robinson Crusoe*, trans. by Sainte-Hyacinthe and Van Effen, 3 vols (Amsterdam: [n. pub.], 1720); Swift, *Le Conte du tonneau*, trans. by Van Effen, 2 vols (The Hague: Scheurleer, 1721) and *Voyages de Gulliver*, trans. by Desfontaines, 2 vols (The Hague: Gosse & Neaulme, 1727); Milton, *Le Paradis perdu*, trans. by Saint-Maur, 3 vols (Paris: Cailleau, 1729). Mid-century translations of novels include Richardson, *Paméla, ou la Vertu récompensée*, trans. by Prévost or Aubert de la Chesnaye, 2 vols (London [i.e. Paris (?)]: J. Osborn, 1742); Richardson, *Lettres angloises, ou Histoire de Miss Clarisse Harlove*, trans. by Prévost, 6 vols (London [i.e. Paris (?)]: Nourse, 1751); Richardson, *Nouvelles lettres angloises, ou Histoire du Chevalier Grandisson*, trans. by Prévost, 4 vols (Amsterdam: [n. pub.], 1755); Fielding, *Les Avantures de Joseph Andrews*, trans. by Desfontaines, 2 vols (London [i.e. Paris (?)]: Millar, 1743); Fielding, *Histoire de Tom Jones, ou l'Enfant trouvé*, trans. by La Place, 4 vols (London [i.e. Paris (?)]: Nourse, 1750).

[5] *Letters*, p. 411. See also Dr Eustace's letter, p. 403.

⁶ James Boswell, *Life of Johnson*, ed. by Bruce Redford (Edinburgh: Edinburgh University Press and New Haven: Yale University Press, 1998), II, p. 197 (March 1776).

⁷ Thomas Middleton Raysor, ed., *Coleridge's Miscellaneous Criticism*, 2 vols (London: Constable, 1936), pp. 121–6.

⁸ Alain Montandon, *La Réception de Laurence Sterne en Allemagne* (Clermont-Ferrand: Association des Publications de la Faculté des Lettres et Sciences Humaines, 1985).

⁹ William Makepeace Thackeray, *The English Humourists of the Eighteenth Century*, in *Works of Thackeray*, Harry Furniss Centenary edn (London: Macmillan, 1911), pp. 160–73.

¹⁰ Friedrich Nietzsche, *Human, All too Human: A Book for Free Spirits*, trans. by R. J. Hollingdale (Cambridge: Cambridge University Press, 1986), cited in *Laurence Sterne's Tristram Shandy: A Casebook*, ed. by Thomas Keymer (Oxford: Oxford University Press, 2006), p. 8.

¹¹ Woolf's Introduction to *A Sentimental Journey*, The World's Classics (London: Oxford University Press, 1928).

¹² Viktor Shklovsky, 'Sterne's *Tristram Shandy*: Stylistic Commentary', in *Russian Formalist Criticism: Four Essays*, trans. and ed. by Lee T. Lemon and Marion J. Reis (Lincoln: University of Nebraska Press, 1965), pp. 25–57.

¹³ Mikhail Bakhtin, *Problems of Dostoevsky's Poetics*, trans. by Caryl Emerson (Minneapolis: University of Minnesota Press, 1984).

¹⁴ Melvyn New, *Laurence Sterne as Satirist: A Reading of Tristram Shandy* (Gainesville: University of Florida Press, 1969).

¹⁵ D. W. Jefferson, '*Tristram Shandy* and the Tradition of Learned Wit', *Essays in Criticism* 1 (1951), 225–48.

¹⁶ Wayne C. Booth, 'The Self-Conscious Narrator in Comic Fiction before *Tristram Shandy*', *PMLA* 67 (1952), 163–85.

¹⁷ Michael Seidel, *Satiric Inheritance: Rabelais to Sterne* (Princeton: Princeton University Press, 1979).

¹⁸ J. T. Parnell, 'Swift, Sterne, and the Skeptical Tradition', *Studies in Eighteenth-Century Culture* 23 (1994), 220–42.

¹⁹ Thomas Keymer, *Sterne, the Moderns, and the Novel* (Oxford: Oxford University Press, 2002).

²⁰ For example, Ian Watt, *The Rise of the Novel: Studies in Defoe, Richardson and Fielding* (London: Chatto & Windus, 1957); J. P. Hunter, *Before Novels: The Cultural Contexts of Eighteenth-Century English Fiction* (New York: Norton, 1990); Michael McKeon, *The Origins of the English Novel 1600–1740* (Baltimore: Johns Hopkins University Press, 1987). McKeon complicates and to some extent reformulates the terms of Watt's argument about the rise of the novel amid the changing circumstances of the emergent bourgeoisie in early eighteenth-century Britain. He objects to Watt's apparently simplistic distinction between novel and romance, suggesting that the critical discussion of genre itself depends for its inception upon a category of the 'literary' which emerges only with the advent of bourgeois modernity. Although McKeon's conclusions are therefore similar in historical terms to Watt's, he arrives at them differently, aiming to show that the concept of literary tradition, against which we might set the terms of the debate about the rise of the novel, is itself a product of the very period in which the novel and middle class first come into history.

²¹ See Georges May, *Le Dilemme du roman au XVIIIe siècle* (Paris: Presses Universitaires de France, 1963) and 'The Influence of English Fiction on the French Mid-Eighteenth-Century Novel', in *Aspects of the Eighteenth Century*, ed. by Earl R. Wasserman (Baltimore:

Johns Hopkins University Press, 1965), pp. 265–81; English Showalter, *The Evolution of the French Novel, 1641-1782* (Princeton: Princeton University Press, 1972); Jean Serroy, *Roman et réalité: Les Histoires comiques au XVIIe siècle* (Paris: Minard, 1981); Marthe Robert, *Roman des origines et origines du roman* (Paris: Gallimard, 1972); Maurice Bardon, *Don Quichotte en France au XVIIè et au XVIIIè siècle* (Paris: Champion, 1931); Henri Coulet, *Le Roman jusqu'à la révolution* (Paris: Armand Colin, 1967; rpt 1991); Jean Fabre, *Idées sur le roman: de Madame de Lafayette au Marquis de Sade* (Paris: Klincksieck, 1979).

[22] Margaret Anne Doody, *The True Story of the Novel* (New Brunswick: Rutgers University Press, 1996); William B. Warner, *Licensing Entertainment: The Elevation of Novel Reading in Britain, 1684–1750* (Berkeley: University of California Press, 1998); Homer Obed Brown, *Institutions of the English Novel: From Defoe to Scott* (Philadelphia: University of Pennsylvania Press, 1997) and 'Why the Story of the Origin of the (English) Novel is an American Romance (If Not the Great American Novel)', in *Cultural Institutions of the Novel*, ed. by Deirdre Lynch and William B. Warner (London: Duke University Press, 1996), pp. 11–43.

[23] Showalter (1972), Ch. 1, traces the break between *roman* and *nouvelle* during the 1660s, and examines these and other terms used for the novel, particularly *histoire*. See also McKeon (1987), pp. 52–64, on the use of *histoire, histoire vraie, mémoires, amours, histoire merveilleuse, vie et aventures*.

[24] *Yorick and the Critics* (New Haven: Yale University Press, 1958); *Sterne: The Critical Heritage* (London: Routledge & Kegan Paul, 1974).

[25] J. C. T. Oates, *Shandyism and Sentiment, 1760–1800* (Cambridge: Cambridge University Press, 1968); *Sterneiana*, 21 vols (New York: Garland, 1974–5).

[26] These include: Serge Soupel, 'Lavieille, Hédouin, Leloir and the *Voyage sentimental*', 2 (1990), 202–13; Agnes Zwanenveld, 'Laurens Sterne in Holland: The Eighteenth Century', and Peter de Voogd, 'Laurence Sterne in Dutch', 5 (1993), 125–49; 150–9; Luis Penegaute, 'The Unfortunate Journey of Laurence Sterne through Spain: The Translations of his Works into Spanish', 6 (1994), 25–53; Shigemitsu Ishii, 'Rorensu Sutahn: Sterne in Japan', and Olivia Santovetti, 'The Adventurous Journey of Lorenzo Sterne in Italy', 8 (1996), 9–40, 79–97; Gabriella Hartvig, 'Lōrincz Sterne in Hungary', 11 (1999–2000), 9–27; Lana Asfour, 'Sterne's First Female Reader in France: Julie de Lespinasse', 12 (2001), 30–6; Urpo Kovala, 'Sterne's Long Journey into Finland', and Grazyna Bystydzienska, 'Wawrzyniec Sterne: A Sentimental Journey in Nineteenth-Century Poland', 13 (2002), 29–45; 47–53.

[27] Montandon (1985); Neil Stewart, *'Glimmerings of Wit': Laurence Sterne und die russische Literatur von 1790 bis 1840* (Heidelberg: Universitätsverlag Winter, 2005).

[28] Paris: Hachette, 1911. See also Charles Sears Baldwin, 'The Literary Influence of Sterne in France', *PMLA* 17 (1902), 221–36.

[29] 1961; rpt Paris: Presses Universitaires de France, 1967.

[30] London: Dent, 1935, pp. 459–63.

[31] New York: Publications of the Institute of French Studies, 1963; rpt New York: Benjamin Blom, 1970.

[32] New York: Columbia University Press, 1960.

[33] Peter de Voogd and John Neubauer, eds, *The Reception of Laurence Sterne in Europe* (London: Continuum, 2004).

[34] Hans Robert Jauss, 'Literary History as a Challenge to Literary Theory', in *Towards an Aesthetic of Reception*, trans. by Timothy Bahti (Minneapolis: University of Minnesota Press, 1982), Ch. 1, pp. 3–45. This was first published in English in 1969 and revised in 1970 in *New Literary History* 1 (1969). Wolfgang Iser, a leading advocate of

Rezeptionsästhetik (the aesthetics of reception), has written a book on *Tristram Shandy* called *Tristram Shandy*, Landmarks in World Literature (Cambridge: Cambridge University Press, 1988). In his theoretical works, Iser concentrates on the individual reader's response to a text, while Jauss focuses on the cumulative experience of historical readers. Iser distinguishes between his own theory of aesthetic response (*Wirkungstheorie*) and theories of the aesthetics of reception (*Rezeptionstheorie*) in the preface to his book, *The Act of Reading: A Theory of Aesthetic Response* (Baltimore: Johns Hopkins University Press, 1978). On Jauss, Iser and reception theory in general, see Robert C. Holub, *Reception Theory* (London: Methuen, 1984).

[35] Jauss (1982), p. 5.

[36] Jauss (1982), pp. 21–2.

[37] A larger study of minor imitations might include later examples, such as Charles Nodier's *L'Histoire du roi de Bohême et de ses sept châteaux* (Paris: Delangle frères, 1830). Xavier de Maistre's *Voyage autour de ma chambre* is also indebted to Sterne and was published in the 1790s, but is most productively considered along with its continuation, the Romantic *Expédition nocturne autour de ma chambre* (Paris: Dondey-Dupré père et fils, 1825). De Maistre and Nodier are discussed in Daniel Sangsue, *Le Récit excentrique: Gautier, de Maistre, Nerval et Nodier. Essai sur la postérité de l'anti-roman à l'époque romantique* (Paris: José Corti, 1987).

Chapter 1: Familiar Categories: Early Reviews of *Tristram Shandy*, 1760–77

[1] 'Swift, Sterne, and the Skeptical Tradition', *Studies in Eighteenth-Century Culture* 23 (1994), 220–42.

[2] Annie Becq, *Genèse de l'esthétique française moderne, 1680–1814* (Pisa: Pacini, 1984; rpt Paris: Albin Michel, 1994), pp. 10–13.

[3] René Wellek, *A History of Modern Criticism, 1750–1950*, 4 vols (New Haven: Yale University Press, 1955), I, p. 6.

[4] Genette's 'open structuralism' studies the ever-changing relationships linking a text with the 'architextual' network through which it produces its meaning. Thus, 'intertexts' (quotations, plagiarisms, allusions), 'paratexts' (chapter titles, prefaces, interviews, announcements, reviews, authors' letters), 'metatexts' (commentary on the text), and 'hypotexts' – what many call 'intertexts', or the major source of a text, which now become the 'hypertexts' (a transformation or imitation) – are all relevant in the creation of meaning in a single literary work. See Genette, *Palimpsestes: La littérature au second degré* (Paris: Seuil, 1982).

[5] Jack R. Censer, *The French Press in the Age of Enlightenment* (London: Routledge, 1994). See also Hugh Gough, *The Newspaper Press in the French Revolution* (Chicago: Dorsey Press, 1988), pp. 1–11, and Jean Sgard, 'La multiplication des périodiques', in *Histoire de l'édition française: Le livre triomphant 1660–1830*, ed. by Roger Chartier and Henri-Jean Martin, 2nd edn (Paris: Fayard/Promodis, 1990), pp. 247–55.

[6] See the Appendix for a list of French articles on Sterne.

[7] Its favourable representation of America and the strict anonymity of its contributors suggest that its editors, a 'Société de gens des Lettres', was close to revolutionary circles. See the *Dictionnaire des journaux 1600–1789*, ed. by Jean Sgard (Paris: Universitas, 1991).

[8] Claude Bellanger et al.; eds, *Histoire générale de la presse française*, 5 vols ed. by Claude Bellanger *et al.*, 5 vols (Paris: Presses Universitaires de France, 1969–76), I, pp. 298–311.

[9] XVII (10–18 April 1765), No. 1299, p. 373.

[10] Censer (1994), pp. 103–7, maintains that despite Fréron's personal hatred of individual *philosophes*, the *Année littéraire* actually agreed with and propounded many of their ideas. See also Jean Balcou, *Fréron contre les philosophes* (Geneva: Droz, 1975).

[11] For a study of this journal's ideas on foreign literature, see Paul Van Tieghem, *L'Année littéraire comme intermédiaire en France des littératures étrangères* (1914; rpt Geneva: Slatkine, 1966).

[12] Raymond Birn, 'The *Journal encyclopédique* and the old régime', *SVEC* 24 (1963), 219–40, argues that this periodical's publishing problems were due mainly to the short-term political policies of the various governments who had control over it rather than to the offensiveness of its material.

[13] Sgard (1991).

[14] J. W. Hemperley, *The* Journal encyclopédique *as an Intermediary of English Literature in France* (Michigan: University Microfilms, 1971).

[15] On the *Journal encyclopédique*'s attempt to present a unified perspective over time in the face of accusations of superficiality and ephemerality, see J. Wagner, 'L'écriture du temps: une difficulté pour la presse périodique ancienne', in *Le Journalisme d'ancien régime* (Lyons: Presses Universitaires de Lyons, 1982), pp. 351–60.

[16] Censer (1994), p. 108.

[17] *La Formation de la doctrine classique en France* (Paris: Nizet, 1927). Bray focuses on French classicism in relation to the *Ars Poetica*, asserting that the *Ars Rhetorica* led to a related but different sphere. I use the general term 'classicism' and avoid 'neoclassicism', which is frequently applied specifically to art and architecture of the late eighteenth and early nineteenth centuries.

[18] Miklós J. Szenczi, 'The Mimetic Principle in Later Eighteenth-Century Criticism', in *Studies in Eighteenth-Century Literature*, ed. by Miklós J. Szenczi and László Ferenczi (Budapest: Akadémiai Kiadó, 1974), pp. 9–54. A. D. Nuttall comments on the strictness of French classicism by describing how Horace's criticism of incongruity is contradicted by his own poetic practice, while Boileau's *Art poétique* remains clearer and more consistent: 'Fishes in the Trees', *Essays in Criticism* 24 (1974), 20–38; rpt in *The Stoic in Love* (New York: Harvester Wheatsheaf, 1989).

[19] John Richardson Miller, *Boileau en France au dix-huitième siècle* (Baltimore: Johns Hopkins Press, London: Oxford University Press and Paris: Société d'édition 'Les Belles Lettres', 1942). See Chapter 2 on the novel's adoption of certain classical rules.

[20] (Paris: Durand, 1746), p. 27.

[21] Jacques Chouillet, *l'Ésthétique des lumières* (Paris: Presses Universitaires de France, 1974) believes that Batteux represents both the culmination of a classical poetics of *mimesis* (in its metaphysical idealization of nature in *la belle nature*) and, simultaneously, the very point of its breakdown, pp. 59–62.

[22] *JE* (15 April 1760), pp. 150–1.

[23] Horace, *The Art of Poetry*, in *Ancient Literary Criticism*, ed. by D. A. Russell and M. Winterbottom (Oxford: Oxford University Press, 1972), p. 279. The comparison between the 'sister arts', painting and poetry, was common during the eighteenth century. See Jean H. Hagstrum, *The Sister Arts: The Tradition of Literary Pictorialism and English Poetry from Dryden to Gray* (Chicago: University of Chicago Press, 1958).

[24] Horace (1972), p. 291.

[25] Boileau, *Art poétique*, in *Œuvres complètes*, ed. by Françoise Escal (Paris: Gallimard, 1966), pp. 155–85, Chant I, ll. 41–4.

[26] Boileau (1966), Chant I, ll. 175–82.

[27] Chouillet (1974), disputes Boileau's status as 'législateur des lettres', on the grounds that he was too late and most of the rules had already been established, p. 25.

[28] Descartes and Malebranche had linked the imagination to the sensual perception of the external world rather than to the tasteful ordering of it, which is the activity of reason. See Becq (1994). Chouillet (1974) traces a line from Descartes, through Malebrache, to eighteenth-century metaphysics and the Père André's idea of the 'Beau essentiel'. This line represents a reaction to pragmatism (in which institutions and conventions create standards for art) and hedonism (in which emotion is a criterion by which to judge art), pp. 47–63.

[29] *JE* (April 1760), p. 150.

[30] See Boileau (1966), Chant I, ll. 49–50 and ll. 59–60, where it is suggested that the writer keep to the point in descriptions and not exhaust a subject before moving on, in order to keep the narrative proportional.

[31] *JE* (August 1760), pp. 148–9.

[32] *MF* (August 1769), p. 71.

[33] *JA* (15 November 1775), p. 189.

[34] *AL*, 7 (1785), Letter 3, p. 49.

[35] *JE* (August 1786), p. 524.

[36] *JP* (20 October 1787), p. 1263.

[37] *Le Grand Robert*, 2nd edn (Paris, 1985); *Dictionnaire du français classique* (Paris: Larousse, 1988); *Dictionnaire historique de la langue française* (Paris: Robert, 1992).

[38] Roland Mortier, *L'originalité: une nouvelle catégorie esthétique au siècle des lumières* (Geneva: Droz, 1982), p. 31. See also the *Dictionnaire historique* (1992).

[39] It was also turned into a substantive in reference to a person, as will be discussed in Chapter 2.

[40] The *Dictionnaire historique* (1992) dates the appearance of this noun to the end of the fourteenth century with the meaning of lineage or extraction, and to 1699 with the meaning of the quality of being original in reference to a literary work, both in a positive and in a negative way.

[41] 'Original', *Encyclopédie*, XI, p. 648.

[42] 'Originalité', *Encyclopédie*, XI, p. 648.

[43] A. G. Baumgarten first employed the term 'aesthetics' in the modern sense in his 1735 dissertation, *Meditationes philosophicæ de nonnullis ad poema pertinentibus* (Magdeburg: Grunerti, 1735) or *Reflections on Poetry*, trans. and ed. by Aschenbrenner and Holther (Berkeley and Los Angeles: University of California Press, 1954), § CXVI. The word was used for the title of his *Æsthetica* (Frankfurt [?]: Kleyb, 1750–8). See Becq (1994); Chouillet (1974); Szenczi (1974); Wladyslaw Folkierski, *Entre le classicisme et le romantisme* (Paris: Champion, 1925; rpt 1969); Walter Jackson Bate, *From Classic to Romantic: Premises of Taste in Eighteenth-Century England* (Boston: Harvard University Press; rpt New York: Harper & Brothers, 1961).

[44] *JE* (May 1761), p. 131.

[45] Bray (1927), p. 354.

[46] Charles Sorel, *De la connoissance des bons livres*, cited in Nicholas Cronk, 'La Défense du dialogisme: vers une poétique du burlesque', in *Burlesque et formes parodiques: Actes du Colloque*, ed. by Isabelle Landy-Houillon and Maurice Menard (Paris: Papers on Seventeenth Century Literature, 1987), p. 326. Seventeenth-century theorists were

equally critical of the heroic novel, and their objections both to it and to the *roman comique* are echoed by eighteenth-century opponents of the novel. See Chapter 2.

⁴⁷ Richmond P. Bond gives a precise definition of burlesque along these lines in *English Burlesque Poetry, 1700–1750* (Cambridge: Harvard University Press, 1932), and his definition is taken up in John Davies Jump's *Burlesque* (London: Methuen, 1972). The more convincing argument that the burlesque was a style rather than a clearly defined genre is presented by: Jean Serroy, 'Introduction', in Paul Scarron, *Virgile travesti*, Classiques Garnier (Paris: Bordas, 1988); Zygmunt Marzys, 'Le Burlesque et les fondateurs de la langue classique', in Landy-Houillon and Menard (1987), pp. 115–23; Cronk in Landy-Houillon and Menard (1987), pp. 321–38.

⁴⁸ See Jean Serroy, *Roman et réalité: les histoires comiques au XVIIIè siècle* (Paris: Minard, 1980) and English Showalter, *The Evolution of the French Novel, 1641–1782* (Princeton: Princeton University Press, 1972). On the critique of novelistic representation in relation to *Tristram Shandy* and *Jacques le fataliste et son maître*, see Chapter 6.

⁴⁹ Boileau (1966), Chant I.

⁵⁰ Guez de Balzac, *Les Entretiens* (1657), cited in Cronk (1987), p. 325. See also Marzys (1987) on Balzac's view of burlesque, pp. 117–18.

⁵¹ *JPL* (25 April 1777), pp. 568–70. Voltaire's article is discussed below.

⁵² *JE* (May 1761), p. 131.

⁵³ *JE* (March 1762), p. 143.

⁵⁴ *JE* (March 1767), p. 145.

⁵⁵ *JE* (January 1766), p. 137.

⁵⁶ *JE* (October 1762), p. 96.

⁵⁷ *JE* (January 1766), p. 137.

⁵⁸ Suard worked on the *Journal Etranger*, the *Journal de Paris*, the *Gazette littéraire de France* and became chief editor of the *Mercure de France*. His success has been attributed to his marriage to Panckoucke's sister. He outlived the Revolution and the Empire, and was head of the Académie Française by the beginning of the Restoration. See Alfred C. Hunter, *J.-B.-A. Suard, Un introducteur de la littérature anglaise en France* (Paris: Champion, 1925).

⁵⁹ *GLE* (20 March 1765), pp. 40–1. This review was translated and published in the *London Chronicle* XVII, No. 1299, 10–18 April 1765, p. 373. Despite this unflattering view of *Tristram Shandy*, Suard nevertheless met, conversed with and seemed to appreciate Sterne, as Dominique-Joseph Garat relates in his *Mémoires historiques sur M. Suard, sur ses écrits et sur le XVIIIè siècle*, 2 vols (Paris: Belin, 1820), II, pp. 146–9.

⁶⁰ *Gargantua*, in *Œuvres complètes*, ed. by Pierre Jourda, 2 vols (Paris: Garnier, 1962), pp. 5–9.

⁶¹ Pierre Le Roy *et al.*, *Satyre ménippée de la vertu du catholicon d'Espagne et de la tenue des estats de Paris* (Paris: Charpentier, 1841; facsimile rpt Cœuvres and Valsery: Ressouvenances, 1997).

⁶² Menippean forms were not specifically Greek and Roman, and there are equivalents in Middle Eastern literatures. Menippus himself was from Gadara, east of the Jordan River. See Otto Immisch, 'Uber eine volkstümliche Darstellungsform in der antiken Literatur', *NeueJahrbücher für das klassische Altertum, Geschichte und deutsch Literatur* 47 (1921), 409–21, cited in H. K. Riikonen, *Menippean Satire as a Literary Genre*, Commentationes Humanarum Litterarum 83 (Helsinki: Societas Scientiarum Fennica, 1987), p. 11.

⁶³ '*Tristram Shandy* and the Tradition of Learned Wit', *Essays in Criticism* 1 (1951), 225–48.

⁶⁴ Wayne C. Booth, 'The Self-Conscious Narrator in Comic Fiction before *Tristram Shandy*', *PMLA* 67 (1952), 163–85, 165.

⁶⁵ Eugene P. Kirk (also known as Korkowski), *Menippean Satire: An Annotated Catalogue of Texts and Criticism* (New York: Garland, 1980). See also Korkowski, '*Tristram Shandy*, Digression, and the Menippean Tradition', *Scholia Satyrica* I:4 (1975), 3–16. Joel C. Relihan, *Ancient Menippean Satire* (Baltimore: Johns Hopkins University Press, 1993), attempts a generic definition of Menippean satire in antiquity by separating it from Cynicism and verse satire, and Riikonen (1987) also outlines a definition in terms of genre, with particular reference to Frye and Bakhtin.

⁶⁶ In *Menippean Elements in Paul Scarron's Roman comique* (New York: Peter Lang, 1991), Barbara Merry returns to the original definition of Menippean satire as a mixture of prose and verse in order to assert a new definition of it that is based on 'rupture'.

⁶⁷ *Anatomy of Criticism: Four Essays* (Princeton: Princeton University Press, 1957; rpt London: Penguin, 1990), pp. 309. Frye's archetypalizing distinctions have been challenged. Margaret Anne Doody, *The True Story of the Novel* (New Brunswick: Rutgers University Press, 1996), for instance, has brought different forms closer together, placing both ancient and modern prose types within a wide and malleable novel genre. The 'novel' encompasses satire, Menippean satire, romance, fantasy, historical novel and memoir, and elements from any combination of these recognizable types are present in texts from different cultures and periods.

⁶⁸ Frye (1957), p. 312.

⁶⁹ In *Menippean Satire Reconsidered: From Antiquity to the Eighteenth Century* (Baltimore: Johns Hopkins University Press, 2005), Howard D. Weinbrot claims that Frye and Bakhtin define Menippean satire too widely. He derives his own list of Menippean texts from a limited corpus of classical models, narrowing the definition to 'satire that uses at least two different languages, genres, tones, or cultural or historical periods to combat a false and threatening orthodoxy', p. xi. Emphasizing its serious intentions to challenge orthodoxy, Weinbrot argues that cheerful writers, such as Apuleius, Sterne and Rabelais should be excluded.

⁷⁰ Mikhail Bakhtin, *Problems of Dostoevsky's Poetics*, trans. by Caryl Emerson (Minneapolis: University of Minnesota Press, 1984).

⁷¹ *GLE* (20 March 1765), p. 40.

⁷² *JE* (January 1766), p. 137.

⁷³ *JE* (March 1762), pp. 143–4.

⁷⁴ The articles in *Questions sur l'Encyclopédie*, including this one, are published as part of the *Dictionnaire philosophique* in the Garnier edition of Voltaire's *Œuvres complètes*, XVIII (Paris: Garnier, 1877–85), pp. 234–40. The Besterman *Œuvres complètes* (Geneva: Les Delices, 1970–) does not incorporate the *Questions sur l'Encyclopédie* into its edition of the *Dictionnaire philosophique*, XXXV–XXXVI (1994), ed. by Christiane Mervaud *et al.*, as it is based on the 1769 edition.

⁷⁵ Voltaire (1877–85), p. 237.

⁷⁶ *JPL* (25 April 1777), pp. 568–70.

⁷⁷ According to Horace Walpole, Bishop Warburton called Sterne 'the English Rabelais' in 1760, before Voltaire. See *Sterne: The Critical Heritage*, ed. by Alan B. Howes (London: Routledge & Kegan Paul, 1971; rpt 1995), p. 56. However, Warburton might have had in mind Voltaire's view of Swift as the English Rabelais, expressed much earlier in the *Lettres philosophiques* (Amsterdam: Lucas, 1734), Letter 22, p. 111. Voltaire even qualifies his epithet: Swift should not be called 'le Rabelais d'Angleterre' because

'il n'a pas à la vérité la gaieté du premier, mais il a toute la finesse, la raison, le choix, le bon goût qui manque à notre Curé de Meudon'.

[78] Johann Jaeger, Ulrich Von Hutton et al., *Epistolae Obscurorum Virorum*, ed. and trans. by Francis Griffin Stokes (London: Chatto & Windus, 1925). See Kirk (1980), pp. 76–7.

[79] These culminated in the Romantic arguments about the relative merits of Shakespeare and classical French drama, as in Stendhal's essays, *Racine et Shakespeare* (Paris: Bossange, 1823).

[80] Voltaire (1734).

[81] *Discours sur la tragédie*, in *Brutus* (1730; Amsterdam: Ledet & Co & Desbordes, 1731).

[82] *Shakespeare*, trans. by Pierre Le Tourneur, 20 vols (Paris: Duchesne et al., 1776–83).

Chapter 2: New Critical Expressions: The Later Reviews, 1776–86

[1] Dominique-Joseph Garat, *Mémoires historiques sur M. Suard, sur ses écrits et sur le XVIIIè siècle*, 2 vols (Paris: Belin, 1820), II, p. 142.

[2] Germaine de Staël-Holstein, *De la littérature considérée dans ses rapports avec les institutions sociales*, 2 vols (2nd edn; Paris: Maradan, An IX/1800), I, Ch. 14: 'De la Plaisanterie anglaise', pp. 344–56; Charles Nodier, *Miscellanées, variétés de philosophie, d'histoire et de littérature*, in *Œuvres complètes* (1832), V, pp. 16–21.

[3] Sterne, *Voyage sentimental*, trans. by Joseph-Pierre Frénais, 2 vols in 1 (Amsterdam: Rey and Paris: Gauguéry, 1769).

[4] *SJ*, p. 116.

[5] *SJ*, p. 219. Since the mid-twentieth century, critics have debated the sincerity of Sterne's sentimentalism: Ernest Dilworth, *The Unsentimental Journey of Laurence Sterne* (New York: King's Crown, 1948) believed that he was satirizing sentiment, while Arthur Cash, *Sterne's Comedy of Moral Sentiments: The Ethical Dimension of the Journey* (Pittsburgh: Duquesne University Press, 1966) saw Sterne neither as entirely sentimental nor as entirely satiriacs, and Melvyn New, *Laurence Sterne as Satirist: A Reading of Tristram Shandy* (Gainesville: University of Florida Press, 1969) proposed that Sterne was a satirist in his view of human nature, in the sense that he measures it according to an external and rational standard, that of Anglican orthodoxy. More recently, Michael Bell has discussed Sterne's critique of sentimentalism through fictional self-consciousness in *Sentimentalism, Ethics and the Culture of Feeling* (Basingstoke: Palgrave, 2000), pp. 67–73, and John Mullan has examined the potential self-indulgence and solipsism of sentimentalist ideas of virtue in *Sentiment and Sociability: The Language of Feeling in the Eighteenth Century* (Oxford: Clarendon Press, 1988).

[6] *Letters*, p. 399, Note 3.

[7] *JE* (September 1766), pp. 86–95. On the differences between *A Sentimental Journey* and Smollet's *Travels*, see Frédéric Ogée, 'Channelling Emotions: Travel and Literary Creation in Smollett and Sterne', *SVEC* 292 (1991), 27–42, and Frank Felsenstein, 'After the Peace of Paris: Yorick, Smelfungus and the Seven Years' War', in *Guerres et paix: la Grande-Bretagne au XVIIIè siècle*, ed. by Paul-Gabriel Boucé, 2 vols (Paris: Presses de la Sorbonne Nouvelle, 1998), II, pp. 311–23. Felsenstein takes issue with Ogée's

consideration of Smollett's *Travels* as a work of fiction and discusses Sterne and Smollett specifically in relation to their views of the Seven Years' War.

[8] *JE* (July 1769), p. 138.

[9] *MF* (August 1769), p. 71.

[10] Arthur Cash, *The Later Years* (London: Methuen, 1986), and Ian Campbell Ross, *Laurence Sterne: A Life* (Oxford: Oxford University Press, 2001).

[11] *Letters*, p. 151. See Alan Charles Kors, *D'Holbach's Coterie: An Enlightenment in Paris* (Princeton: Princeton University Press, 1976).

[12] See Chapter 1 for a discussion of Suard's article on *Tristram Shandy*.

[13] *Letters*, p. 162.

[14] Guillaume Thomas Raynal, *Histoire philosophique et politique des établissemens & du commerce des Européens dans les deux Indes*, 6 vols (Amsterdam: [n. pub.], 1770). A later edition, 4 vols (Geneva: Pellet, 1780), contains Raynal's *Éloge d'Eliza Draper*, I, pp. 318–20. The *Éloge* was frequently published in editions of Sterne's *Lettres* and *Voyage sentimental*, and undoubtedly encouraged interest in his life and enhanced his reputation as a man of feeling.

[15] *Letters*, p. 157.

[16] Garat (1820), II, p. 136.

[17] On Sterne's celebrity in London, see Peter M. Briggs, 'Laurence Sterne and Literary Celebrity in 1760', *The Age of Johnson: A Scholarly Annual* 4 (1991), 251–80. K. E. Smith points out that Yorick's journey diverged from Sterne's actual travels, particularly in the routes he took and in the domesticity of his life among British ex-patriots in the south of France: 'Ordering things in France: the Travels of Sterne, Tristram and Yorick', *SVEC* 292 (1991), 15–25.

[18] *Dictionnaire de l'Académie françoise*, new edn, 2 vols (Avignon: Garrigan, 1777).

[19] *Dictionnaire comique, satyrique, critique, burlesque, libre et proverbial* (Amsterdam: [n. pub.], 1718), p. 374.

[20] *Dictionnaire critique de la langue française*, 3 vols (Paris, 1787).

[21] *Dictionnaire de l'Académie française* (1777).

[22] *AL* (1776), Letter 6.

[23] *JE* (January 1777), p. 256.

[24] Frénais (1769), p. iii.

[25] *SJ*, pp. 232–3.

[26] *GLE*, 5 (20 March 1765), pp. 39–42.

[27] *AL*, 7 (1786), Letter 9, pp. 108–12; Garat (1820).

[28] Montesquieu, *Ésprit des Lois*, in *Œuvres complètes*, ed. by Daniel Oster (Paris: Seuil, 1964), Part III, Book XIV, Ch. 13, 'Effets qui résultent du climat d'Angleterre', p. 617, and Part III, Book XI, Ch. 6, 'De la Constitution d'Angleterre', pp. 586–90.

[29] Josephine Grieder, *Anglomania in France 1740-1789: Fact, Fiction, and Political Discourse* (Geneva: Droz, 1985). See also Paul Langford, *Englishness Identified: Manners and Characters, 1650–1850* (Oxford: Oxford University Press, 2000).

[30] *JE* (January 1777), p. 257. Joshua Reynolds's 1760 portrait (in the National Portrait Gallery) offers a brilliant representation of Sterne's many sides. The sober colours of the clergyman's habit are lifted by the intensity of Sterne's gaze, which is directed straight back at the viewer and suggests his sharp wit. The wig tipped slightly to one side also makes reference to his mischievous humour.

[31] *JE* (January 1777), p. 257. See also *AL*, 6 (1776), Letter 1, p. 8, and Garat (1820), II, p. 148.

[32] With *Le Neveu de Rameau* and the *Paradoxe sur le comédien* (1769–?), Diderot

renounced his earlier advocation of the sentimental *drame bourgeois* and the view that a good actor had to feel the emotions which he depicted. On the meaning of gesture and the idea that it can reveal the inner self, see Angelica Goodden, *'Actio' and Persuasion: Dramatic Performance in Eighteenth-Century France* (Oxford: Clarendon, 1986) and *Diderot and the Body* (Oxford: Legenda, 2001).

[33] Garat (1820), II, p. 148.

[34] A small number of the 1785 to 1786 group are concerned with the problem of translating Sterne and analyse the quality of translation. These are discussed in Chapter 4.

[35] *JE* (January 1777), p. 256; *AL*, 6 (1776), Letter 1, pp. 3–4.

[36] *MF* (12 November 1785), p. 71. René Bray, *La Formation de la doctrine classique en France* (Paris: Hachette, 1927), notes that Ariosto was criticized by seventeenth-century critics for mixing the heroic and the comic: his 'héroi-comique' style was different from the burlesque, which was entirely comic, because it had separate heroic sections and comic sections, pp. 303–6.

[37] *AL*, 6 (1776), Letter 1, p. 9.

[38] *MF* (January 1777), p. 130.

[39] *MF* (January 1777), p. 131.

[40] *AL*, 6 (1776), Letter 1, p. 22.

[41] *AL*, 6 (1776), Letter 1, p. 3.

[42] *JE* (August 1785), p. 174.

[43] *AL*, 8 (1785), Letter 2, p. 35.

[44] *MF* (January 1777), p. 131, p. 136.

[45] Georges May, *Le Dilemme du roman au dix-huitième siècle: étude sur les rapports du roman et de la critique, 1715–1761* (Paris: Presses Universitaires de France and New Haven: Yale University Press, 1963).

[46] Prefatory discourse (1710) to *Les Heros de roman (1665)*, in *Œuvres*, 2 vols (Geneva: Fabri & Barrillot, 1715–16), p. 196.

[47] Pierre-François Guyot Desfontaines *et al.*, *Observations sur les écrits modernes*, 33 vols (Paris: Chaubert, 1735–43), VIII, p. 28.

[48] May (1963). See the next chapter on the dangers of English novels in particular.

[49] English Showalter, *The Evolution of the French Novel, 1641–1782* (Princeton: Princeton University Press, 1972) and Vivienne Mylne, *The Eighteenth-Century French Novel: Techniques of Illusion* (Manchester: Manchester University Press, 1965) examine such techniques of representation, as well as the novel debates. See also Françoise Barguillet, *Le Roman au dix-hiutième siècle* (Paris: Presses Universitaires de France, 1981); Henri Coulet, *Le Roman jusqu'à la Révolution* (Paris: Armand Colin, 1967; rpt 1991); Henri Coulet, ed., *Idées sur le roman: Textes critiques sur le roman français XIIe-XXe siècle* (Paris: Larousse, 1992).

[50] Nicolas Lenglet-Dufresnoy, *De l'usage des romans*, 2 vols (Amsterdam: De Poilras, 1734); Pierre-Daniel Huet, *Traitté de l'origine des romans* (Paris: [n. pub.], 1670). Showalter (1972) argues that the novel was increasingly defended through comparisons with history rather than with epic.

[51] Horace, *The Art of Poetry*, in *Ancient Literary Criticism*, ed. by D. A. Russell and M. Winterbottom (Oxford: Oxford University Press, 1972), p. 288.

[52] Pierre Carlet de Chamblain de Marivaux, *La Vie de Marianne, ou les Avantures de Mme la comtesse de ****, 11 vols (Paris: Prault, 1731–41), Part II, 'Avertissement'.

[53] Claude-Prosper Jolyot Crébillon, *Les Égarements du cœur et de l'esprit, ou Mémoires de M. de Meilcour*, 3 vols (Paris: Prault fils, 1736–8), Preface.

[54] *MF* (12 November 1785), p. 77, 74–5. On the critic himself, see Frances Dorothy Acomb, *Hallet du Pan (1749–1800): A Career in Political Journalism* (Durham, NC: Duke University Press, 1973) and see Chapter 4, pp. 82–4 of this study on Hallet's articles on Sterne in translation.

[55] *AL*, 7 (1786), Letter 9, p. 109.

[56] *AL*, 7 (1786), Letter 9, pp. 109–10.

[57] Edward Young, *Conjectures on Original Composition in a Letter to the Author of Sir Charles Grandison* (London: Millar and Dodsley, 1759); *Œuvres diverses du Docteur Young*, trans. by Pierre Le Tourneur, 6 vols (Paris: Le Jay, 1770), III. Examples of French aesthetic works include the Abbé Dubos's *Réflexions critiques sur la poésie et la peinture*, 2 vols (Paris: Mariette, 1719), which placed greater emphasis on the emotive value of art and poetry, and the Père André's *Essai sur le beau* (Paris: Guérien, 1741), which was aligned with a more rationalist conception of art through its concept of essential beauty. Translated works include: Joseph Addison's *Spectateur, ou le Socrate moderne* (Amsterdam: Mortier, 1714–36); Shaftesbury's *Principes de la philosophie morale, ou Essai sur le mérite de la vertu*, trans. by Diderot (Amsterdam: Chatelain, 1745), and his *Oeuvres*, trans. by Jean Baptiste René Robinet, 3 vols (Geneva: [n. pub.], 1769); Edmund Burke's *Recherches philosophiques sur l'origine des idées que nous avons du beau et du sublime, précédés d'une dissertation sur le goût*, trans. by Abbé Des François, 2 vols (London: Hochereau, 1765); Alexander Gerard's *Essai sur le goût, augmenté de trois dissertations sur le même suject, par Messrs de Voltaire, d'Alembert et de Montesquieu*, trans. by Marc-Antoine Eidous (Paris: Delalain, 1766); Francis Hutcheson's *Recherches sur l'origine des idées que nous avons de la beauté et de la vertu*, trans. by Eidous, 2 vols (Amsterdam: [n. pub.], 1749). However, Adam Smith's *The Theory of Moral Sentiments* (London: Millar and Edinburgh: Kincaid & Bell, 1759) and Joseph Warton's *Essay on the Writings and Genius of Pope* (London: Cooper, 1756) were not translated into French during the eighteenth century.

[58] Young (1759), pp. 9–10.

[59] Young (1759), p. 12. This passage foreshadows later Romantic ideas of organic form, in which literary originality grows from the creator's mind in a continuous act of creation.

[60] Young (1759), p. 18.

[61] Young (1759), p. 31.

[62] Roland Mortier, *L'Originalité: une nouvelle catégorie esthétique au siècle des Lumières* (Geneva: Droz, 1982), p. 87.

[63] Le Tourneur (1770), III, pp. xxxi–xxxii.

[64] Le Tourneur (1770), III, pp. xxxii–xxxiii.

[65] Mortier (1982), pp. 90–1.

[66] See Chapter 3 on theories of translation in eighteenth-century France.

[67] Le Tourneur (1770), III, pp. xxxii–xxxiii.

[68] *AL*, 7 (1785), Letter 3, p. 51.

[69] *JE* (May 1785), p. 71.

[70] *JE* (1 August 1786), pp. 524–7 and (15 August 1786), pp. 134–42. The full title of this pair of articles is 'Notice adressée aux auteurs de ce Journal, Sur l'esprit & les ouvrages de *Sterne*, ainsi que sur les traductions françoises de son livre intitulé: *La vie et les opinions de Tristram Shandy*'.

[71] *JP* (18–19 June 1786). I am using the reprint in Suard, *Mélanges* (Paris: Dentu, 1803), III, pp. 111–22.

[72] *Julie, ou La Nouvelle Héloïse* (Paris: Garnier-Flammarion, 1967), *Entretien*.

[73] Rousseau (1967), p. 574.

[74] For example, in *Lettre à d'Alembert sur les spectacles* (Amsterdam: Rey, 1758).
[75] Suard (1803), p. 111.
[76] See Note 5 above, and Chapter 5.
[77] Suard (1803), p. 114.
[78] Suard (1803), p. 112.
[79] Suard (1803), p. 113.
[80] *Éloge de Richardson*, in *Œuvres esthétiques* (Paris: Garnier, 1959; rpt 1994), pp. 29–48. First published in the *Journal étranger* (January 1762), the *Éloge* was reprinted as an introduction to Prévost's *Supplément aux lettres anglaises de Miss Clarisse Harlowe* in 1762.
[81] Diderot (1994), p. 31.
[82] Diderot (1994), p. 30.
[83] Suard (1803), p. 115. On the physiological roots of sensibility, see Anne C. Vila, *Enlightenment and Pathology: Sensibility in the Literature and Medicine of Eighteenth-Century France* (Baltimore: Johns Hopkins University Press, 1998). Studies that discuss the physical signs of internal sensibility and virtue (such tears, blushes, sighs, fainting) include: Ann Jessie Van Sant, *Eighteenth-Century Sensibility and the Novel: The Senses in Social Context* (Cambridge: Cambridge University Press, 1993); R. F. Brissenden, *Virtue in Distress: Studies in the Novel of Sentiment from Richardson to Sade* (London: Macmillan, 1974); Janet Todd, *Sensibility: An Introduction* (London: Methuen, 1986); Anne Coudreuse, *Le Goût des larmes au XVIIIe siècle* (Paris: Presses Universitaires de France, 1999). See also Note 32 above.
[84] Suard (1803), p. 116.
[85] Diderot (1994), p. 33.
[86] Diderot (1994), p. 31.
[87] Suard (1803), p. 122.

Chapter 3: Theories of Translation and the English Novel, 1740–1800

[1] André Lefevere, *Translation, Rewriting, and the Manipulation of Literary Fame* (London: Routledge, 1992), p. vii.
[2] Translation Studies has flourished since the 1970s to the extent that Susan Bassnett has suggested that it is the new Comparative Literature: *Comparative Literature* (Oxford: Blackwell, 1993), p. 138. A good deal of interesting work has been done on literary translations, and two full-length studies in particular are noteworthy for successfully combining translation theory with criticism of specific texts. In *Pour une critique des traductions: John Donne* (Paris: Gallimard, 1995), Antoine Berman uses translation theory not as a means of judging and evaluating translations, but rather in order to find a new way of discussing both original text and translation. He discusses Donne's English poems and their translations separately, treating the latter as important poems in their own right. Thomas O. Beebee's approach in *Clarissa on the Continent: Translation and Seduction* (Pennsylvania: Pennsylvania State University Press, 1990), meanwhile, provides a sophisticated critical analysis of Richardson's *Clarissa* through readings of its first German translation by Johann David Michaelis and its first French translation by the Abbé Prévost.
[3] See Hubert Gillot, *La Querelle des anciens et des modernes en France* (Paris: Champion, 1914), and A. H. T. Levi, 'The Reception of Greek Sources in Late Seventeenth-Century

France,' *French Studies* 42 (1988), 408–23. On the debate in Britain, see Joseph M. Levine, *The Battle of the Books: History and Literature in the Augustan Age* (Ithaca: Cornell University Press, 1991). More generally, see Richard Foster Jones, *Ancients and Moderns: A Study of the Background of the Battle of the Books*, Washington University Studies: Language and Literature, 6 (1936); Ernst Robert Curtius, *European Literature and the Latin Middle Ages*, trans. by Willard R. Trask (London: Routledge and Kegan Paul, 1979), especially Ch. 14.2; and Gilbert Highet, *The Classical Tradition: Greek and Roman Influences on Western Literature* (1949; New York: Oxford University Press, 1985).

[4] An earlier version of this chapter was published in *La Traduction au XVIIIe siècle*, SVEC 4 (Oxford: Voltaire Foundation 2001), 269–78.

[5] Frequently discussed problems of language included the relationship between thought and language, the possibility of a universal language, the origin of language and the natural order of words. See Pierre Juliard, *Philosophies of Language in Eighteenth-Century France* (The Hague: Mouton, 1970), and Ulrich Ricken, *Linguistics, Anthropology and Philosophy in the French Enlightenment* (London: Routledge, 1994). Both emphasize the importance of debates about language to Enlightenment thought. For a detailed examination of the three articles in the *Encyclopédie* on translation discussed here, see Michel Bellot-Antony, 'Grammaire et art de traduire dans l'Encyclopédie', in *L'Encyclopédie et Diderot*, ed. by E. Mass and P.-E. Knabe (Cologne: Verlag, 1985).

[6] 'Langue', *Encyclopédie*, IX, p. 256.

[7] 'Grammaire', *Encyclopédie*, VII, p. 842.

[8] 'Grammaire', *Encyclopédie*, VII, p. 844.

[9] 'Langue', *Encyclopédie*, IX, p. 257.

[10] 'Traduction', *Supplément*, IV pp. 952–4. This article is by Marmontel. We should not make too clear a distinction between rationalist and sensualist conceptions of translation. In the preface to his translation of Pope's *Essay on Man* (Amsterdam: Changuion, 1787), which is called 'Essai de traduction littérale et énergique', Saint-Simon outlines a theory that consists of a mixture of both. Literal translation is possible and desirable because an image reflects a universal sensation which is shared by all human beings even though it is expressed differently. Rather than reproducing the equivalent thought, a translator must find the equivalent sensation. Saint-Simon believes that while doing this the translator should enrich his language with adopted words so that he contributes towards the creation of a universal language in which the exchange of words is completely free. See Ricken (1994) for a full study of eighteenth-century linguistic topics in relation to the debate between the sensualist and rationalist schools of thought.

[11] Sylvain Auroux, *La sémiotique des encyclopédistes* (Paris: Payot, 1979).

[12] The argument of the 'ordre naturel des mots' is discussed in Ulrich Ricken, *Grammaire et philosophie au siècle des lumières* (Villeneuve d'Ascq: Publications de l'Université de Lille III, 1978).

[13] Auroux (1979), pp. 288–9.

[14] 'Traduction, Version', *Encyclopédie*, XII, pp. 510–12. This article is signed B. E. R. M., generally agreed to be Beauzée, as Auroux (1979) discusses.

[15] The corrective and faithful methods were not, therefore, as clearly opposed as C. B. West claims they were in her article, 'La théorie de la traduction au XVIIIe siècle par rapport surtout aux traductions françaises d'ouvrages anglais', *Revue de littérature comparée* XII (1932), 330–55.

[16] 'Observations sur l'art de traduire en général, et sur cet essai de traduction en

particulier', in *Mélanges de littérature, d'histoire, et de philosophie* (Amsterdam: Zacharie Chatelain & Fils, 1763), III, p. 5.

[17] 'Energie', *Encyclopédie*, V, p. 651. In *L'idée d'énergie au tournant des lumières (1770–1820)* (Paris: Presses Universitaires de France, 1988), Michel Delon discusses the concept of *énergie* in all disciplines of the period; scientific, philosophical, linguistic and literary. In literary terms it refers to the life and 'dynamism' of a piece of work, and Delon concludes that during the years 1770 to 1820, the idea of *énergie* participated in the constitution of an aesthetic of creation and the movement towards Romanticism. See also Jacques Chouillet, *Diderot: poète de l'énergie* (Paris: Presses Universitaires de France, 1984).

[18] D'Alembert (1763), III, pp. 11–12.

[19] 'Traduction', *Supplément*, IV, p. 952.

[20] 'Traduction', *Supplément*, IV, p. 954.

[21] D'Alembert (1763), III, p. 6.

[22] D'Alembert (1763), III, p. 11.

[23] This phenomenon was also due to censorship laws. See Georges May, *Le Dilemme du roman au XVIIIe siècle: Etude sur les rapports du roman et de la critique, 1715–1761* (New Haven, CT: Yale University Press and Paris: Presses Universitaires de France, 1963), Ch. 3.

[24] *Correspondance littéraire* (Paris: Longchamps and Buisson, 1813), I, p. 208. See Chapter 2 of this study on attitudes towards the novel.

[25] *AL*, 6 (1785), Letter 12, pp. 230–1.

[26] *AL*, 6 (1785), Letter 12, pp. 231–2. On the idea of the decadence of literature, see Roland Mortier, 'L'idée de décadence littéraire au XVIIIe siècle', *SVEC* 57 (1967), 1013–29.

[27] *AL*, 7 (1762), Letter 3, pp. 61–2.

[28] *AL*, 6 (1756), p. 243, cited in Van Tieghem's *L'Année littéraire comme intermédiaire en France des littératures étrangères* (1914; Geneva: Slatkine Reprints, 1966), pp. 13–20, in the context of a discussion of the journal's view of translation. With Fréron as editor, this view was prevalent, but after his death the periodical shifted towards the more modern demand that a translation be an accurate reproduction of the original, as is apparent in articles by Geoffroy, discussed later in this chapter.

[29] Roger Zuber, *Les belles infidèles et la formation du goût classique: Perrot d'Ablancourt et Guez de Balzac* (Paris: Armand Colin, 1968).

[30] Samuel Richardson, *Lettres angloises, ou Histoire de Miss Clarisse Harlove*, trans. by Prévost, 6 vols (London [i.e. Paris (?)]: Nourse, 1751), Introduction.

[31] These are discussed in C. B. West (1932).

[32] *Nouvelles lettres angloises, ou Histoire du Chevalier Grandisson*, trans. by Prévost, 4 vols (Amsterdam: [n. pub.], 1755), Preface; Prévost (1751), Introduction.

[33] Henry Fielding, *Histoire de Tom Jones, ou l'Enfant trouvé*, trans. by La Place, 4 vols (London [i.e. Paris]: Nourse, 1750), prefatory *Lettre à M. Fielding*.

[34] Cited in Beebee (1990), p. 10.

[35] Prévost (1751), Introduction.

[36] La Place (1750), prefatory *Lettre à M. Fielding*.

[37] Prévost's changes are discussed in Beebee (1990) and F. H. Wilcox, *Prévost's Translations of Richardson's Novels* (Berkeley: University of California Press and London: Cambridge University Press, 1927).

[38] *AL*, 8 (1783), Letter 6, pp. 87–8.

[39] *AL*, 5 (1776), Letter 1, pp. 7–8.

[40] *Éloge de Richardson*, in *Œuvres esthétiques* (Paris: Garnier, 1959), p. 36. See Chapter 2

for Diderot's view of Richardson's novels in relation to Madame Suard's reading of Sterne.

⁴¹ Armand-Pierre Jacquin, *Entretiens sur les romans: ouvrage moral et critique, dans lequel on traite de l'origine des romans & de leurs différentes espéces, tant par rapport à l'esprit, que par rapport au cœur* (Paris: Duchesne, 1755); Lenglet-Dufresnoy, *Histoire justifiée contre les romans* (Amsterdam: Bernard, 1735). The latter might have been written in order to protect Lenglet-Dufresnoy's reputation after the publication of his pro-novel *De l'usage des romans* (1734) under the pseudonym Gordon de Percel.

⁴² *Julie, ou La Nouvelle Héloïse*, 3 vols (Amsterdam: Rey, 1761), first Preface.

⁴³ May (1963).

⁴⁴ *Amélie, histoire angloise*, trans. by Philippe-Florent de Puisieux, 2 vols (Paris: Charpentier, 1762); *Amélie, roman imité de l'anglais*, trans. by Madame Riccoboni (Paris: Libraires Associés, 1743).

⁴⁵ Puisieux (1762), 'Avertissement du Traducteur'.

⁴⁶ *Clarisse Harlowe*, trans. by Pierre Le Tourneur, 10 vols (Geneva: Barde and Paris: Moutard and Merigot, 1785–6).

Chapter 4: The Translations of *Tristram Shandy*

¹ Laurence Sterne, *Voyage sentimental*, trans. by Joseph-Pierre Frénais, 2 vols (Amsterdam: Rey and Paris: Gaugéry, 1769).

² In 'Laurence Sterne, ses traducteurs et ses interprètes', *SVEC* 4 (2000), 291–8, Soupel claims that both novels were translated equally unfaithfully by Frénais.

³ *La vie et les opinions de Tristram Shandy*, trans. by Frénais, 2 vols (York: Ruault, 1776); I am using (York: Ruault, 1777). *Suite de la Vie et des opinions de Tristram Shandy*, trans. by Bonnay, 2 vols (York: Volland, 1785); I am using 2 vols (London [i.e. Paris: Cazin], 1785). *Suite et Fin de la Vie et des opinions de Tristram Shandy, suivies de mélanges, lettres, pensées, bons-mots, & mémoires*, trans. by Griffet de La Beaume, 2 vols (London [i.e. Paris (?)]: [n. pub.], 1785); I am using La Beaume's translation in *Œuvres de Stern*, trans. by Frénais and La Beaume, 6 vols (Paris: Libraires Associés, 1797).

⁴ *Biographie universelle ancienne et moderne*, XV (Paris: Desplaces and Michaud, 1811; rpt 1856); *Dictionnaire historique du Vendômois de Saint-Venant* (Blois: Nigault and Vendôme: Souilly and Chartier, 1912–17; rpt 1969). The *Dictionnaire de biographie française* (Paris: Letouzy, 1979) claims that he was born in the mid-eighteenth century and died sometime after 1825. The parish registers of Fréteval, however, mention his baptism in 1728 and tell us that his parents were from the wealthy middle classes: his father was the fiscal authority for the noble domain of Rocheux. I am grateful to the departmental archives of Loir-et-Cher for this information.

⁵ *Bulletin de la Société archéologique du Vendômois* (1882), pp. 266–7.

⁶ Frances Moore Brooke, *Histoire d'Emilie Montagne par M. Brooke, imitée de l'anglois par monsieur Frenais* (Paris: Gauguery, 1770). Frénais is sometimes named as the translator of: Susannah Gunning, *L'abbaye ou le château de Barford, imité de l'angois par M...* (London, Paris: Gauguery, 1769); Charles Johnston, *Chrisal ou les aventures d'une guinée, histoire anglaise* (London [?] and Paris: Grangé, 1767); *Supplément à Chrysal ou les nouvelles aventures d'une guinée, traduites de l'anglais par mylord Aleph* (Amsterdam: Rey, Lyon: Cellier and Paris: Dufour, 1769) – though the unflattering reference in the latter to *Chrisal* undermines the idea that both are by the same author; Christophe Martin

Weiland, *Histoire d'Agathon ou tableau philosophique des mœurs de la Grèce* (Lausanne: Grasset and Paris: De Hansy, 1768); Weiland, *La sympathie des âmes* (Amsterdam, Paris, 1768). See Martin, Mylne and Frautschi, eds, *Bibliographie du genre romanesque français* (London: Mansell and Paris: France Expansion, 1977), and the biographies listed above, Note 4.

[7] *Dictionnaire historique du Vendômois de Saint-Venant* (1969). Martin, Mylne and Frautschi (1977) also cite Frénais as the author of *Edelzinde, fille d'Amalazonthe, reine des Goths* (Strasbourg: Gay and Paris: Durant neveu, Bastien, 1780) and *Histoire d'Agathe de St. Bohaire* (Amsterdam: J. B. Henri, 1769). The Bibliothèque Nationale catalogue names him as translator of Joshua Gee, *Coup d'œil rapide sur les progrès et la décadence du commerce & des forces d'Angleterre* (Amsterdam: [n. pub.], 1768), and of Arthur Young, *Le guide du fermier* (Paris: [n. pub.], 1770), while J.-M. Quérard, *La France littéraire, ou Dictionnaire bibliographique*, 12 vols (Paris: Didot, 1827–35) attributes to him Wieland's *Le Tonneau de Diogène* (1802).

[8] Frénais (1770), p. i.

[9] See Chapter 3.

[10] Frénais (1770), pp. ii–iv. According to Martin, Mylne and Frautschi (1977), this rival is Jean Baptiste René Robinet and his translation is *Histoire d'Emilie Montague* (Amsterdam: Changuion and Paris: Le Jay, 1770).

[11] Frénais (1770), pp. vi–vii.

[12] See Chapter 1 on Voltaire and *Tristram Shandy*.

[13] Frénais (1777), p. xiii.

[14] Frénais (1777), pp. xiv–xv.

[15] *Works*, I, p. 4; *TS*, I, 3; Frénais (1777), I, Ch. 3, p. 6.

[16] *OED* and *Works*, III, p. 57, Note 12.2.

[17] Frénais (1777), I, Ch. 7, pp. 17–18; *Works*, I, p. 12; *TS*, I, Ch. 7.

[18] Frénais (1777), I, Ch. 14, p. 51; *TS*, I, Ch. 13.

[19] *Works*, I, p. 97; *TS*, II, Ch. 2.

[20] Frénais (1777), I, Ch. 29, p. 115.

[21] Frénais (1777), I, p. 116.

[22] *Works*, I, p. 165; *TS*, II, Ch. 17.

[23] In order to reduce confusion, Frénais's volumes will be called 'books' and Sterne's 'volumes'.

[24] *Works*, I, p. 181; *TS*, II, Ch. 19.

[25] Frénais (1777), II, Ch. 10, p. 24.

[26] Frénais (1777), II, Ch. 102, pp. 257–8.

[27] Frénais (1777), II, Ch. 31, p. 74. This is inserted in Sterne's Volume III, between Chapters 15 and 16.

[28] Frénais (1777), II, Ch. 86, p. 217–18; the image is from the (London [i.e. Paris: Cazin], 1784) edition, II, Ch. 86, pp. 314–15.

[29] Frénais (1777), II, Ch. 86, pp. 217–18.

[30] *Works*, I, p. 356; *TS*, IV, Ch. 19.

[31] Frénais (1777), II, Ch. 35, pp. 78–9.

[32] On Sterne's marbled page and the process of marbling see Diana Patterson, 'Tristram's Marblings and Marblers', *The Shandean* 3 (1991), 70–97, and Peter de Voogd, 'Laurence Sterne, the Marbled Page, and the "Use of Accidents"', *Word and Image* I.3 (1985), 279–87.

[33] 2 vols in 1 (York: 1777); 2 vols (Neuchâtel: Société Typographique, 1777); 2 vols (York: Van Harrevelt, 1777).

³⁴ Before La Beaume's translation was published, part of it appeared in a single volume entitled *Nouveau Voyage de Sterne en France. Suivi de l'Histoire de le Fevre, & d'un choix de Lettres familieres du même Auteur. Traduit de l'Anglois par M.D.L.****, *Avocat-Général au Parlement de **** (Geneva: Belin, 1784). Later editions include: Paris: J. P. Heubach, 1785; Geneva, 1785; Venice, 1788. This consisted of the translation of Volume VII of *Tristram Shandy*, presented as a new *Sentimental Journey*, along with other extracts. Close comparison reveals that the text is identical to the corresponding sections of La Beaume's *Tristram Shandy*. The identities of the two later translators are sometimes confused because of the similarity of their initials: Bonnay's *Tristram Shandy* was published anonymously, while La Beaume's title-page identifies him only as 'D. L. B'. The BNF catalogue and Martin, Mylne and Frautschi (1977), confuse La Beaume with Joseph-Louis de La Boissière, who they mistakenly name as the translator of the *Nouveau voyage*. La Boissière was indeed Avocat-Général at the parliament of Grenoble (and La Beaume was not), but there is no evidence to show that he was interested in translation, so it appears that the original publishers of the *Nouveau voyage* were incorrect (or, far less likely, that La Boissière was the translator of Volumes V to IX of *Tristram Shandy* rather than La Beaume).

³⁵ Bonnay (1785), III, p. ii.
³⁶ Bonnay (1785), III, p. iii.
³⁷ La Beaume (1797), III, pp. ii–iii.
³⁸ La Beaume (1797), III, p. vi. See Chapter 2, Note 14 on Raynal.
³⁹ La Beaume (1797), III, p. v.
⁴⁰ Examples of La Beaume's footnotes may be found at III, Ch. 10, p. 40; III, Ch.17, p. 53; III, Ch. 44, p. 102; III, Ch. 46, p. 107; III, Ch. 47, pp. 110–11; III, Ch. 58, p. 136; III, Ch. 80, p. 188; IV, Ch. 62, p. 143.
⁴¹ *TS*, VI, Ch. 6–13; La Beaume (1797), III, Ch. 51–9, pp. 117–44; Bonnay (1785), III, Ch. 51–9, pp. 194–235.
⁴² La Beaume (1797), III, Ch. 121, p. 299.
⁴³ Bonnay (1785), IV, Ch. 42, pp. 148–9; La Beaume (1797), IV, Ch. 10, pp. 14–15.
⁴⁴ Taken from the first edition of Volumes V and VI (London: Becket & Dehondt, 1762), VI, Ch. 40.
⁴⁵ La Beaume (1797), III, Ch. 86, pp. 200–1.
⁴⁶ *Works*, I, p. 409; *TS*, V, Ch. 1.
⁴⁷ Bonnay (1785), III, p. 21.
⁴⁸ La Beaume (1797), III, pp. 12–13.
⁴⁹ La Beaume (1797), III, p. 12, Note 1.
⁵⁰ See John Traugott's view that Sterne rhetorically enacts and exposes Locke's philosophy, in *Tristram Shandy's World: Sterne's Philosophical Rhetoric* (Berkeley: University of California Press, 1954).
⁵¹ John Ferriar, *Illustrations of Sterne* (London: Cadell and Davies, 1798), p. 70, pp. 187–8. On Sterne's uses of imitation, see Chapter 6.
⁵² *Works*, I, pp. 414–15; *TS*, V, Ch. 1.
⁵³ Bonnay (1785), III, p. 23.
⁵⁴ *Works*, I, p. 410; *TS*, V, Ch. 1.
⁵⁵ Bonnay (1785), III, p. 30.
⁵⁶ *SJ*, p. 33. Mallet du Pan's article is discussed later in this chapter.
⁵⁷ Bonnay (1785), IV, p. 3.
⁵⁸ Bonnay (1785), IV, p. 6.
⁵⁹ See Chapter 5 on Sterne's sentimentalism.
⁶⁰ *MF* (12 November 1785), pp. 71–84, p. 80.

[61] *MF* (4 March 1786), p. 30.
[62] *MF* (25 March 1786), p. 185.

Chapter 5: Sentimental Journeys

[1] Ann Jessie Van Sant, *Eighteenth-Century Sensibility and the Novel: The Senses in Social Context* (Cambridge: Cambridge University Press, 1993); David J. Denby, *Sentimental Narrative and the Social Order in France, 1760–1820* (Cambridge: Cambridge University Press, 1994).

[2] Anne Vincent-Buffault, *L'Histoire des larmes* (Paris: Rivages, 1986); Anne Coudreuse, *Le Goût des larmes au XVIIe siècle* (Paris: Presses Universitaires de France, 1999).

[3] Michael Bell, *Sentimentalism, Ethics and the Culture of Feeling* (Basingstoke: Palgrave, 2000).

[4] John Mullan, *Sentiment and Sociability: The Language of Feeling in the Eighteenth Century* (Oxford: Clarendon Press, 1988; rpt 1990), p. 14; R. F. Brissenden, *Virtue in Distress: Studies in the Novel of Sentiment from Richardson to Sade* (London: Macmillan, 1974).

[5] Mullan (1990), p. 193.

[6] Guillaume Brune, *Voyage pittoresque et sentimental dans plusieurs provinces occidentales de la France* (London: Letellier, 1788); Jean Florimond Boudon de Saint-Amans, *Fragmens d'un voyage sentimental et pittoresque dans les Pyrénées, ou Lettres écrites de ces montagnes* (Metz: Devilly, 1789).

[7] Rutledge, James, *La Quinzaine anglaise à Paris, ou l'Art de s'y ruiner en peu de temps* (London [i.e. Paris (?)]: [n. pub.], 1776); *Tableau sentimental de la France depuis la Revolution. Par Yoryck sous le nom de Sterne; pour servir de suite au Voyage Sentimental, du même auteur* (London [i.e. Paris (?)]: [n. pub.], 1792).

[8] Auguste Forbin and Pierre-Henri Revoile, *Sterne à Paris, ou le Voyageur sentimental, comédie en un acte et en prose mêlée de vaudeville* (Paris: [n. pub.], 1799).

[9] *The Beauties of Sterne, including all his Pathetic Tales and Most Distinguished Observations on Life, selected for the Heart of Sensibility* (London: Davies, 1782). This was translated into several European languages, and the French translation in 1800 was reprinted numerous times. Sentimental titles inspired by Sterne in Britain include *Sentimental Lubrications, by Peter Pennyless* (1770); *Sentimental Tales* (1771); *Unfortunate Sensibility, in a Series of Letters; dedicated to Mr Yorick in the Elysian Fields* (1784); *Reveries of the Heart during a Tour through Part of England and France* (1781); Leonard MacNally's *Sentimental Excursions to Windsor* (1781). See J. C. T. Oates, *Shandyism and Sentiment, 1760–1800* (Cambridge: Cambridge Bibliographical Society, 1968). English imitations, spin-offs, and parodies are reprinted in *Sterneiana*, 21 vols (New York: Garland, 1974–5). See also Anne Bandry, 'Imitations of *Tristram Shandy*', in *Critical Essays on Laurence Sterne*, ed. by Melvyn New (New York: G. K. Hall & Co., 1998).

[10] *The Clockmakers Outcry Against the Author of the Life and Opinions of Tristram Shandy* (London: Burd, 1760); rpt in *Sterneiana* (1974–5), III.

[11] Anonymous, *A Genuine Letter from a Methodist Preacher in the Country, to Laurence Sterne* (London: Vandenbergh, 1760); rpt in *Sterneiana* (1974–5), V.

[12] *Letters*, p. 107. Early parodies include *Explanatory Remarks upon the Life and Opinions of Tristram Shandy* (1760), *Ways to Kill Care* (1761), and some articles in the *Gentleman's Magazine* and the *Grand Magazine*. After the publication of a forged Volume III, Sterne personally signed further instalments of *Tristram Shandy*.

[13] Bell (2000), p. 67.

[14] Several studies have discussed the link between sentimentalism and philanthropy in Enlightenment France and England, including Van Sant (1993), especially Chapter 2, and Bell (2000). See also Daniel Mornet's *Les Origines intellectuelles de la Révolution française* (Paris: Hachette, 1907), and Paul Van Tieghem's 'Quelques aspects de la sensibilité préromantique dans le roman européen au XVIIIe siècle, in *Edda* 27 (1929), 146–75.

[15] Denby (1994), p. 5.

[16] Denby (1994), p. 96.

[17] *Tableau sentimental* (1792), p. 38.

[18] *Tableau sentimental* (1792), pp. 38–9.

[19] *Works* II, p. 784; *TS*, IX, Ch. 24.

[20] *SJ*, p. 271.

[21] Martin C. Battestin, 'Sterne Among the *Philosophes*: Body and Soul in *A Sentimental Journey*', *Eighteenth-Century Fiction* 7.1 (1994), 17–36.

[22] For example, Thackeray thought Sterne's sentimentalism was affected, *The English Humourists of the Eighteenth Century*, in *Works of Thackeray*, Harry Furniss Centenary edn (London: Macmillan, 1911), pp. 160–73; and Ernest Nevill Dilworth contended that Sterne was satirizing sentiment, *The Unsentimental Journey of Laurence Sterne* (New York: King's Crown Press, 1948).

[23] Melvyn New, *Laurence Sterne as Satirist: A Reading of Tristram Shandy* (Gainesville: University of Florida Press, 1969). See also New's introduction to the notes of the *Sermons*, *Works*, V, in which he discusses the 'theology' of Sterne's sentimentalism.

[24] See, for instance, Bell's discussion of the story of Le Fever, in which he takes issue with A. D. Nuttall's 'anti-sentimentalist' critique of the same tale, Bell (2000) pp. 67–73.

[25] *SJ*, p. 275.

[26] *SJ*, p. 270.

[27] For Mullan (1988), Sterne's sentimentalism 'does not strive, like Richardson's fiction, to outline a capacity for sentiment which is to be a model of moral responsibility. It does not even really celebrate a type of social being, but falls back on the invented voice of one dedicated to a specialized and eccentric experience of society', p. 200. Donald Wehrs, by contrast, advocates the ethical relation in Sterne, which takes the subject outside himself in response to that which is outside and beyond him: 'Levinas and Sterne: From the Ethics of the Face to the Aesthetics of Unrepresentability', in New (1998), pp. 311–29.

[28] *Tableau sentimental* (1792), p. 59.

[29] 31 May 1790 (Paris: Cussac, 1791).

[30] *Tableau sentimental* (1792), p. 5. The text contains several politically symbolic episodes, including a dream in which Sterne visits the moon in an allegory of the 'lunatic' revolution in France. The dream is inspired by a trip to see the play *Nicodème dans la lune* by Cousin Jacques, the *nom de plume* of L. J. Beffroy de Reigny, who was considered a patriot and was known as the comic writer of the Revolution.

[31] *Le Voyageur sentimental, ou ma promenade à Yverdun* (London [?]: Cazin and Neufchâtel: Mourer, 1786). I refer to the (Paris: [n. pub.], 1792) edition.

[32] Vernes (1792), pp. 64–5; pp. 115–16. Vernes is also the author of *Le Voyageur sentimental en France sous Robespierre* (Geneva: Paschoud & Paris: Maradan, An VII/1798–9). Like the first *Voyageur sentimental* discussed here, it is structured around a variety of sentimental vignettes, but it is a longer, more directly political work and does not engage with Sterne's *Sentimental Journey*.

33 Vernes (1792), pp. 6–7.

34 *SJ*, pp. 218–19.

35 'A notre entrée dans *Yverdun*, nous étions, *le pere la Joye* et moi, dans un très-piteux état. Aussi, en approchant de l'auberge, fûmes-nous salués par les huées de quelques personnes, qui crurent que *Dom Quichotte*, *Sancho* et leurs haridelles arrivaient d'Espagne', Vernes (1792), p. 67.

36 See Denby (1994) on the gothic and psychological aspects of this text, and on Vernes's politics, particularly in relation to his early nineteenth-century writings.

37 In *Radical Sensibility: Literature and Ideas in the 1790s* (London: Routledge, 1993), Chris Jones shows that in England, particularly in responses to the French Revolution, sensibility was not directly related to specific political alignments, but it did have certain associations. For William Godwin and Thomas Paine, reason was identified with radicalism, while for Edmund Burke, sensibility was linked with conservatism.

38 Pierre Blanchard, *Le Rêveur sentimental*, 2 vols in 1 (Paris: Le Prieur, An IV/1795).

39 Blanchard (1795), II, pp. 26–8.

40 Blanchard (1795), I, pp. v–vi.

41 Blanchard (1795), I, pp. iii–iv.

42 *SJ*, pp. 202–4.

43 London: Millar and Edinburgh: Kincaid & Bell, 1759.

44 Mullan (1988), p. 194. See also Bell (2000), p. 44:

> Smith, who formed his view before the excesses of sensibility in the latter decades of the century, absorbed the strongest currents of sentimental ethics and was able, from his new vantage-point, to dismiss rather more cogently the earlier views that everything comes down either to Hutchesonian compassion or Hobbesian self-love. On the latter he was particularly scathing. Since he freely admitted self-love as a legitimate motive, his conception of sympathy was more readily defensible from the charge of being merely a secret form of it.

45 Blanchard (1795), I, pp. 26–7.

46 Blanchard (1795), I, p. 52.

47 Blanchard (1795), I, p. 15.

48 Blanchard (1795), pp. i–ii.

49 Jacques-Antoine-Hippolyte de Guibert, *Éloge de Mademoiselle de Lespinasse, sous le nom d'Éliza*, in *Lettres de Mademoiselle de Lespinasse*, 2 vols (2nd edn; Paris: Longchamps, 1811), p. 19.

50 *Deux chapitres dans le genre du Voyage sentimental de Sterne*, in *Lettres de Mademoiselle de Lespinasse, écrites depuis l'année 1773, jusqu'à l'année 1776*, 2 vols (Paris: Collin, 1809), II, pp. 305–22.

51 Lespinasse (1809), p. 309.

52 Lespinasse (1809), p. 310.

53 *SJ*, pp. 99–103.

54 Francis Brown Barton, *Étude sur l'influence de Sterne en France au dix-huitième siècle* (Paris: Hachette, 1911), suggests that Madame G represents Madame Geoffrin, which is possible, as she held Wednesday evening dinners and Sterne might have been among the guests.

55 Lespinasse (1809), p. 312.

56 Lespinasse (1809), p. 315.

57 Lespinasse (1809), p. 320.

58 Lespinasse (1809), pp. 321–2.

⁵⁹ (London: Bastien, 1784). I am using the fifth edition which has an additional first chapter, 2 vols (Paris: Guillot, 1791).

⁶⁰ Gorjy (1791), I, p. 44.

⁶¹ A common theme in sentimental fiction, it was further popularized by Baculard d'Arnaud's *Les Époux malheureux* (Avignon, 1746). This work was inspired by the real-life marriage of the chevalier de La Bédoyère to the actress Agathe Sticotti, which was challenged by his father in *parlement*.

⁶² Paris: Guillot, 1791. Denby (1994) discusses works by Gorjy, Vernes and Baculard d'Arnaud in an attempt to piece together an interpretative model or 'metastructure' of the sentimental text. However, he does not seem to realize the extent to which Gorjy's *Nouveau voyage* (1784) and Vernes's *Voyageur sentimental* (1792) are indebted to Sterne's sentimental journey motif.

⁶³ 6 vols (Paris: Guillot, Cuchet & Louis, 1791–2).

⁶⁴ Gorjy (1784), I, p. 13.

⁶⁵ Gorjy (1784), II, p. 4. Gorjy also mentions a debt to Young.

⁶⁶ *Les Rêveries du promeneur solitaire*, in *Œuvres complètes*, ed. by Michel Launay, 3 vols (Paris: Seuil, 1967), 'Seconde promenade', p. 507.

⁶⁷ On this topic in sentimental fiction, see D. G. Charlton's *New Images of the Natural in France* (Cambridge: Cambridge University Press, 1984).

⁶⁸ The variety of critical, literary and political texts relating to Rousseau are discussed in Raymond Trousson, *Rousseau et sa fortune littéraire* (Paris: Nizet, 1977). See also Jean Roussel, *Jean-Jacques Rousseau en France après la Révolution, 1795–1830. Lectures et Légende* (Paris: Armand Colin, 1972). For a broader exploration of Rousseau's influence, see Thomas McFarland, *Romanticism and the Heritage of Rousseau* (Oxford: Clarendon Press, 1995).

⁶⁹ Trousson (1977), p. 68, points out that he was a model for both republican and anti-revolutionary groups: 'Il y eut un Rousseau girondin à la mode de Mme Roland, un Rousseau jacobin à la Robespierre, un Rousseau communiste à la Babeuf; mais il y eut aussi, et la chose est plus curieuse, un Rousseau conservateur et antirévolutionnaire'.

⁷⁰ *Le Voyageur curieux et sentimental; Ouvrage en deux parties, contenant 1. le voyage de Chantilly et d'Ermenonville; 2. le voyage aux Isles Borromée. Par le citoyen Damin* (Toulouse: Manavit fils, An VIII/1799–1800).

⁷¹ Rousseau (1967), I, pp. 182–3.

⁷² Rousseau (1967), I, p. 186. Charlton (1984) argues that Rousseau preferred mountain slopes to high peaks, and that landscape descriptions are favoured for their impact upon the observer-narrator's inner life rather than for their own external and sublime beauty, pp. 47–8.

⁷³ *Works*, II, p. 648; *TS*, VII, Ch. 43.

⁷⁴ Paris: Mérigot père, 1788.

⁷⁵ Pierre Le Tourneur, *Voyage à Ermenonville*, in Rousseau, *Œuvres complètes*, 36 vols (Paris: Valade, 1788–93; rpt Reims: À l'Écart, 1990). See also Arsenne Thiébaut de Berneaud, *Voyage à l'isle des peupliers* (Paris: Lepetit, An VII/1798–9), a young man's literary pilgrimage and Rousseauist manifesto, and Joseph Michaud's *Ermenonville, ou Le Tombeau de Jean-Jacques* (1794), a short account of his visit addressed to his brother.

⁷⁶ Le Tourneur (1990), p. 117.

⁷⁷ Le Tourneur (1990), p. 175.

⁷⁸ This was first published individually (Paris: Hacquart, An IV/1796). The second narrative, *Le Voyage aux Isles Borromée*, was published along with it in the year VIII edition, and consists of a descriptive, picturesque narrative.

[79] Damin (1799–1800), p. 16.
[80] Damin (1799–1800), pp. 63.
[81] Damin (1799–1800), pp. 65–6.
[82] Damin (1799–1800), p. 79.

Chapter 6: *Tristram Shandy* and *Jacques le fataliste et son maître*

[1] Maurice Roelens, '*Jacques le fataliste* et la critique contemporaine', *Dix-huitième siècle* 5 (1973), 119–37. Roelens refers, among others, to J. Robert Loy, *Diderot's Determined Fatalist* (New York: King's Crown Press, 1950); Lester G. Crocker, '*Jacques le fataliste*, an expérience morale', *Diderot Studies* 3 (1961), 73–99; Francis Pruner, *L'Unité secrète de Jacques le fataliste* (Paris: Minard, 1970); Jean Fabre, 'Sagesse et morale dans *Jacques le fataliste*', in *The Age of Enlightenment: Studies Presented to Theodore Besterman* (Edinburgh: Oliver & Boyd, 1967); Jean Ehrard, 'Lumières et roman, ou les paradoxes de Denis le fataliste', in *Au Siècle des lumières* (Paris: SEVPEN and Moscow: Académie des Sciences de l'URSS, 1970), pp. 137–55.

[2] Robert Mauzi, 'La Parodie romanesque dans *Jacques le fataliste*', *Diderot Studies* 6 (1964), 89–132. See also Roger Kempf, *Diderot et le roman, ou Le Démon de la présence* (Paris: Seuil, 1964).

[3] Thomas Kavanagh, *The Vacant Mirror: A Study of Mimesis through Diderot's Jacques le fataliste*, SVEC 104 (Oxford: Voltaire Foundation, 1973).

[4] Milan Kundera, *Jacques et son maître: hommage à Denis Diderot en trois actes* (Paris: Gallimard, 1981), Introduction, pp. 10–12. This play is Kundera's own 'variation' on *Jacques*. On Kundera's relationship with the eighteenth century, see Jocelyn Maixent, *Le XVIIIe siècle de Milan Kundera, ou Diderot investi par le roman contemporain* (Paris: Presses Universitaires de France, 1998).

[5] *DPLP* (An V/1796), p. 224. On the early reception of *Jacques*, see J. Th. de Booy and Alan J. Freer, eds, *Jacques le fataliste et La Religieuse devant la critique révolutionnaire, 1796–1800*, SVEC 33 (Geneva: Institut et Musée Voltaire, 1965), which shows that early responses to *Jacques* were as political as they were aesthetic.

[6] Alice Green Fredman, *Sterne and Diderot* (New York: Columbia University Press, 1960).

[7] Rainer Warning, *Illusion und Wirklichkeit in Tristram Shandy und Jacques le fataliste* (Munich: Fink Verlag, 1965).

[8] Walter E. Rex, *Diderot's Counterpoints: The Dynamics of Contrariety in his Major Works*, SVEC 363 (Oxford: Voltaire Foundation, 1998), pp. 219–20.

[9] Ernest Simon, 'Fatalism, the Hobby-Horse and the Esthetics of the Novel', *Diderot Studies* 16 (1973), 253–74. Stephen Werner, in a looser discussion, believes that *Tristram Shandy* 'shows all the virtues of scepticism and arabesque', and *Jacques* 'adopts the more problematical stance of fatalism and paradox': *Diderot's Great Scroll: Narrative Art in Jacques le fataliste*, SVEC 128 (Oxford: Voltaire Foundation, 1975), p. 94. Both novels have been discussed in relation to a particular topic: Lilian Furst, *Fictions of Romantic Irony in European Narrative, 1760–1857* (London: Macmillan, 1984), sees them as key texts in the shift towards Romanticism, their self-consciousness marking the emergence of the modern phenomenon of 'literature as product yield[ing] to literature as process', while Will McMorran, *The Inn and the Traveller: Digressive Topographies in the Early*

Modern European Novel (Oxford: Legenda, 2002), considers them in the context of an older tradition of digressive novels.

[10] On the literary sources of *Jacques*, see Paul Vernière, 'Diderot et l'invention littéraire: à propos de *Jacques le fataliste*' (1959), in *Lumières ou clair-obscur?* (Paris: Presses Universitaires de France, 1987), pp. 50–65, and Edouard Guitton, 'La mention du livre dans *Jacques le fataliste*', *Interférences* 11 (1980), 57–71.

[11] McMorran (2002), p. 258. On the influence of *Don Quixote*, see Ronald Paulson, *Don Quixote in England: The Aesthetics of Laughter* (Baltimore: Johns Hopkins University Press, 1998), and Maurice Bardon, *Don Quichotte en France au XVIIe et au XVIIIe siècle* (Paris: Champion, 1931).

[12] Martin Rowson, who has drawn the comic book version of *Tristram Shandy* (London: Picador, 1996), frankly calls it 'unquestionably weird', *The Shandean* 7 (1995), 64.

[13] Joseph Wharton, *An Essay on the Genius and Writings of Pope*, 2 vols (London: Dodsley, 1782), II, p. 54.

[14] *Works*, II, pp. 701–4; *TS*, VIII, Ch. 22.

[15] *JF*, p. 375.

[16] On British perceptions of France, see Linda Colley, *Britons: Forging the Nation 1707–1837* (New Haven: Yale University Press, 1992). Sterne's views of the French could be contradictory. He praises French manners, for instance, in *Letters*, p. 186 and p. 284, but criticizes them in *Letters*, p. 405, and claims the French are too serious and not ironic enough in *Works*, II, p. 634; *TS*, VII, Ch. 34. See Chapter 2 on Sterne's approach to overcoming national prejudice through sentimentalism.

[17] Arthur Cash, *Laurence Sterne: The Later Years* (London: Methuen, 1986), pp. 176–7.

[18] *SJ*, pp. 230–3.

[19] *JF*, p. 254.

[20] John Ferriar, *Illustrations of Sterne, with other Essays and Verses* (London: Cadell & Davies, 1798).

[21] See Paulson (1998) on *Tristam Shandy* and *Don Quixote*, especially pp. 150–8.

[22] On Sterne's debt to Rabelais, as well as to Burton, Swift, Cervantes and Montaigne, see D. W. Jefferson, '*Tristram Shandy* and the Tradition of Learned Wit', *Essays in Criticism* 1 (1951), 225–48.

[23] Jonathan Lamb, 'Sterne's System of Imitation', *Modern Language Review* 76 (1981), 794–810. See also Lamb's *Sterne's Fiction and the Double Principle* (Cambridge: Cambridge University Press, 1989).

[24] Ferriar (1798). Sterne's debt to these authors has been disputed, as noted in *Works*, III, p. 21. See also Van R. Baker, 'Sterne and Piganiol de la Force: the Making of Volume VII of *Tristram Shandy*', *Comparative Literature Studies* 13 (1976), 5–14, and Françoise Pellan, 'Laurence Sterne's Indebtedness to Charron', *MLR* 67 (1972), 752–5.

[25] *Works*, I, p. 408; *TS*, V, Ch. 1; Robert Burton, *The Anatomy of Melancholy* (Oxford: Cripps, 1628), 'Democritus Junior to the Reader', p. 7. See H. J. Jackson, 'Sterne, Burton, and Ferriar: Allusions to *The Anatomy of Melancholy* in Volumes Five to Nine of *Tristram Shandy*', *PQ* 54 (1975), 457–70, for a discussion of Sterne's borrowings from Burton and a critique of Ferriar.

[26] Arthur Cash, *Laurence Sterne: The Early and Middle Years* (London: Methuen, 1975), p. 234.

[27] *Works*, I, p. 146; *TS*, II, Ch. 17; *The Sermons of Mr. Yorick* (London: Dodsley, 1760).

[28] *Works*, IV, p. 1.

[29] *Letters*, p. 90.

[30] See Chapter 2.

[31] *Works*, I, pp. 166–7; *TS*, II, Ch. 17.

[32] The accelerated tale of the sermon's fate may be echoed purposely in Jacques's speedy employment history (*JF*, pp. 220–1), though the acceleration device is used elsewhere, and to devastating effect in Voltaire's *Candide, ou l'Optimisme* (London [?]: [n. pub.], 1759).

[33] *Works*, I, p. 167; *TS*, II, Ch. 17. Frénais's translation does little justice to the joke. While Sterne excuses the plagiarist and plays with the loose distinctions between plagiarism and more acceptable forms of literary borrowing, Frénais makes a straightforward moral judgement against plagiarism: he translates up to the point at which Yorick is said to have been transformed into a ghost or spirit, and adds that plagiarists would not experience the same holy metamorphosis, Frénais (1776), I, pp. 206–7.

[34] Melvyn New discusses these borrowings in his notes to the *Sermons*, *Works*, V.

[35] *Lettres inédites de Madame de Staël à Meister* (Paris: Hachette, 1903), p. 24 (12 September 1771). See Jean Garagnon, 'Diderot et la genèse de *Jacques le fataliste*: sur une lettre de Meister père', *Studi Francesi* 27 (1983), 81–2. *Jacques* enjoyed a limited circulation through Grimm's *Correspondance littéraire* between 1778 and 1780, but was not published until 1796 as its apparent espousal of fatalism was too revolutionary for the *ancien régime*. Its publication history is discussed in *JF*, Lecointre and Le Galliot's introduction.

[36] Fredman (1960) speculates that they enjoyed each other's company because they were both sociable, witty and good raconteurs, pp. 52–4.

[37] Diderot, *Correspondance*, ed. by Georges Roth, 16 vols (Paris: Editions de Minuit, 1955–70), IV (1958), p. 189 (7 October 1762).

[38] *Letters*, p. 166, p. 162. *Le Fils naturel, ou Les Épreuves de la vertu* (Amsterdam: [n. pub.], 1757) was eventually translated into English as *Dorval, or The Test of Virtue* (London: Dodsley, 1767). It was rejected by the Comédie Française in 1757 and was not produced until 1771.

[39] Diderot maintained interest in all of Sterne's work and, despite his materialism, was on the long list of subscribers to Volumes III and IV of the *Sermons*, published in 1766, the same year as Sterne's final journey to Paris.

[40] Diderot, *Éloge de Richardson*, in *Œuvres esthétiques* (Paris: Garnier, 1959; rpt 1994), pp. 29–48.

[41] In *Satire and the Novel in Eighteenth-Century England* (New Haven: Yale University Press, 1967), Ronald Paulson argues that satire and romance came together during the eighteenth century, a process that had begun in sixteenth- and seventeenth-century picaresque. He finds (like Bakhtin) that the novel incorporated poetic or romance elements of the high genres as well as low and forbidden discourses such as satire, and could therefore be parodic in the same way as satire.

[42] *Works*, I, p. 228; *TS*, III, Ch. 20.

[43] *Works*, I, p. 65; *TS*, I, Ch. 20.

[44] A. D. Nuttall, *Openings: Narrative Beginnings from the Epic to the Novel* (Oxford: Clarendon, 1992), p. 152.

[45] *Works*, I, p. 5; *TS*, I, Ch. IV. See Chapter 1 on the *Journal encyclopédique*'s view of *Tristram Shandy* as Horace's monster.

[46] Mrs Shandy's association of ideas is a comic representation of Locke's views in *An Essay concerning Human Understanding*, ed. by Peter H. Nidditch (Oxford: Clarendon, 1975), especially in Book II, Chapter XI, § 12–13, and Book II, Chapter XXXIII, § 4.

[47] *Works*, I, p. 4; *TS*, I, Ch. 3.

[48] *Works*, I, p. 89; *TS*, I, Ch. 25.

⁴⁹ *Works*, I, p. 98; *TS*, II, Ch. 2.
⁵⁰ *Works*, I, p. 8; *TS*, I, Ch. 5; *Works*, I, p. 196; *TS*, III, Ch. 8.
⁵¹ *Works*, I, pp. 70–114 (especially pp. 80–1); *TS*, I, Ch. 21 – II, Ch. 6.
⁵² Viktor Shklovsky, 'Sterne's *Tristram Shandy*: Stylistic Commentary', in *Russian Formalist Criticism: Four Essays*, trans. and ed. by Lee T. Lemon and Marion J. Reis (Lincoln: University of Nebraska Press, 1965), pp. 25–57.
⁵³ John Traugott, *Tristram Shandy's World: Sterne's Philosophical Rhetoric* (Berkeley and Los Angeles: University of California Press, 1954), p. 81.
⁵⁴ *Works*, II, p. 737; *TS*, IX, Ch. 1.
⁵⁵ *Works*, I, p. 88; *TS*, I, Ch. 25.
⁵⁶ *Works*, I, pp. 9–10; *TS*, I, Ch. 6. Nuttall (1992) disagrees with Shklovsky's formalist view that *Tristram Shandy* is a typical novel because it exposes the conventionality of other novels and dispenses with mimetic referentiality. He suggests instead that it expresses a common-sense attitude to the physical world and that its comedy relies on this. Sterne's 'characters of love' reach the reader in spite of Tristram's narrative self-consciousness, and this is what makes Sterne so central to the development of novelistic discourse. I would agree and add that Tristram is also a 'character of love' for the same reason.
⁵⁷ Daniel Brewer, *The Discourse of the Enlightenment in Eighteenth-Century France: Diderot and the Art of Philosophizing* (Cambridge: Cambridge University Press, 1993).
⁵⁸ *JF*, p. 3.
⁵⁹ *JF*, p. 5.
⁶⁰ Brewer (1993), pp. 10–11.
⁶¹ *JF*, p. 3; *Works*, II, p. 693; *TS*, VIII, Ch. 19.
⁶² The political consequences of the subversion of the master–servant relationship blow up when Jacques refuses to obey his Master's order to go downstairs during their stay at the Grand Cerf inn. The situation alludes to the contemporary power struggles between king and parliament, during which parliament was exiled and then reinstated: Jacques and his Master agree to the *hôtesse*'s contract, which stipulates that he will go downstairs, but may return immediately, and the relationship is reinstated as if nothing happened. The 'état de fait' naturally takes over the 'état de droit', and they agree that the master continues to have power in name, while Jacques continues to have the thing itself, *JF*, pp. 223–30. See Brewer (1993), pp. 230–5, who suggests that Jacques is reworking the master–servant relationship in terms of a discursive performativity, thereby resituating the social hierarchy and subjecting it to different regulative principles, rather than simply inversing it. The Master's power is limited by its total dependence on servitude, so the Master has power in name because Jacques can decide how and when this power is played out.
⁶³ *JF*, p. 71.
⁶⁴ *JF*, p. 15.
⁶⁵ *JF*, p. 315.
⁶⁶ Vivienne Mylne, *The Eighteenth-Century French Novel: Techniques of Illusion* (Manchester: Manchester University Press, 1965).
⁶⁷ Mauzi (1964), p. 92.
⁶⁸ See Chapter 2 on the defence of the novel.
⁶⁹ Where one might have expected Boileau's name, Diderot places Le Bossu in the list, perhaps simply to allow for the *hôtesse*'s pun.
⁷⁰ *JF*, p. 209.
⁷¹ *JF*, pp. 211.

[72] JF, p. 211.

[73] On Diderot's contradictory aesthetics and the paradox of art, see Lenore Kreitman, 'Diderot's Aesthetic Paradox and Created Reality', *SVEC* 102 (1973), 157-72.

[74] Simon (1973), p. 266, and McMorran (2002), pp. 223–39, suggest that *Jacques* has a classical ending, in contrast to readings that see it solely as a deconstructive *antiroman*.

Bibliography

This contains most cited texts and other relevant works. When unsigned or unattributed, eighteenth-century articles are listed either by entry or by title of journal or dictionary. Anonymous works appear by title. French translations of English works are listed under English author, while editions may be listed under editor, author or title. Eighteenth-century periodical articles specifically on Sterne are listed only in the Appendix.

Acomb, Frances Dorothy, *Mallet du Pan (1749–1800): A Career in Political Journalism* (Durham, NC: Duke University Press, 1973).
Adams, D. J., *Diderot: Dialogue and Debate* (Liverpool: F. Cairns, 1986).
Adams, Percy G., *Travel Literature and the Evolution of the Novel* (Lexington: University of Kentucky Press, 1983).
Addison, Joseph, *Remarks on Several Parts of Italy in the Years 1701, 1702, 1703*, 2nd edn (London: [n. pub.], 1718).
—— *Spectateur, ou le Socrate moderne* (Amsterdam: Mortier, 1714–36).
Alembert, Jean le Rond, D', 'Energie', *Encyclopédie, ou Dictionnaire raisonné des sciences, des arts et des métiers*, 17 vols (Paris: Biasson, David, Le Breton, Durand, and Neufchastel: Samuel Faulche, 1751–65).
—— 'Observations sur l'art de traduire en général, et sur cet essai de traduction en particulier', in *Mélanges de littérature, d'histoire, et de philosophie*, new edn (Amsterdam: Zacharie Chatelain & Fils, 1763), III.
Allen, Graham, *Intertextuality* (London: Routledge, 2000).
André, Yves Marie de l'Isle, Père, *Essai sur le beau* (Paris: Guérien, 1741).
Andrieux, G. J. S., *La Décade philosophique, littéraire et politique* (An V/1796), pp. 224–30.
Année littéraire, 5 (1776), Letter 1, p. 7.
—— 6 (1785), Letter 12, pp. 230–43.
—— 7 (1762), Letter 3, p. 61.
Ascoli, Georges, *La Grande Bretagne devant l'opinion française au XVIIe siècle*, 3 vols (Paris: [n. pub.], 1927, 1930).
Asfour, Lana, 'Sterne's First Female Reader in France', *The Shandean* 12 (2001), 30–6.
—— 'Theories of Translation and the English Novel in France, 1740–1790', in *La Traduction au XVIIIè siècle*, SVEC 4 (2001), 269–78.
Auroux, Sylvain, *La Sémiotique des encyclopédistes* (Paris: Payot, 1979).
Baker, Van R., 'Sterne and Piganiol de la Force: the Making of Volume VII of *Tristram Shandy*', *Comparative Literature Studies* 13 (1976), 5–14.
Bakhtin, Mikhail, *The Dialogic Imagination*, trans. by Caryl Emerson and Michael Holquist (Austin: University of Texas Press, 1981).
—— *Problems of Dostoevksy's Poetics*, trans. by Caryl Emerson (Minneapolis: University of Minnesota Press, 1984).

—— *Rabelais and his World*, trans. by Hélène Iswolsky (Bloomington: Indiana University Press, 1984).

Balcou, Jean, *Fréron contre les philosophes* (Geneva: Droz, 1975).

Baldwin, Charles Sears, 'The Literary Influence of Sterne in France', *PMLA* 17 (1902), 221–36.

Ballanche, Pierre-Simon, *Du Sentiment considéré dans ses rapports avec la littérature et les arts* (Lyon: Ballanche & Barret, 1801), pp. 218–19.

Bandry, Anne, 'A Bibliography of Sterne in French', *The Shandean* 12 (2001), 91–113.

—— 'The First French Translation of *Tristram Shandy*', *The Shandean* 6 (1994), 66–85.

Bardon, Maurice, *Don Quichotte en France au XVIIè et au XVIIIè siècle* (Paris: Champion, 1931).

Barguillet, Françoise, *Le roman au XVIIIe siècle* (Paris: Presses Universitaires de France, 1981).

Barker-Benfield, G. J., *The Culture of Sensibility: Sex and Society in Eighteenth-Century Britain* (London: University of Chicago Press, 1992).

Barthes, Roland, *S/Z* (Paris: Seuil, 1970).

Barton, Francis Brown, *Étude sur l'influence de Sterne en France au dix-huitième siècle* (Paris: Hachette, 1911).

Bassnett, Susan, *Comparative Literature: An Introduction* (Oxford: Blackwell, 1993).

Bate, Walter Jackson, *From Classic to Romantic: Premises of Taste in Eighteenth-Century England* (Boston: Harvard University Press, 1946; rpt New York: Harper & Brothers, 1961).

Batten, Charles L., *Pleasurable Instruction, Form and Convention in Eighteenth-Century Travel Literature* (Berkeley: University of California Press, 1978).

Battestin, Martin C., 'Sterne among the Philosophes: Body and Soul in A Sentimental Journey', *Eighteenth-Century Fiction* 7.1 (1994), 17–36.

Batteux, Charles, Abbé, *Les Beaux-Arts réduits à un même principe* (Paris: Durand, 1746).

Baumgarten, Alexander Gottlieb, *Æsthetica* (Frankfurt [?]: Kleyb, 1750–8).

—— *Reflections on poetry*, trans. and ed. by Aschenbrenner and Holther (1735; Berkeley and Los Angeles: University of California Press, 1954).

Beauzée, Nicolas, 'Traduction, Version', *Encyclopédie*, XII, pp. 510–12.

Becq, Annie, *Genèse de l'esthétique française moderne 1660–1814: De la raison classique à l'imagination créatrice* (Pisa: Pacini, 1984; Paris: Albin Michel, 1994).

Beebee, Thomas O., *Clarissa on the Continent: Translation and Seduction* (University Park: Pennsylvania State University Press, 1990).

Bell, Michael, *Sentimentalism, Ethics and the Culture of Feeling* (Basingstoke: Palgrave, 2000).

Bellanger, Claude, Jacques Godechot, Pierre Guiral and Fernand Terrou, eds, *Histoire générale de la presse française*, 5 vols (Paris: Presses Universitaires de France, 1969–76), Vol. I.

Bellot-Antony, Michel, 'Grammaire et art de traduire dans l'Encyclopédie', in E. Mass and P.-E. Knabe, eds, *L'Encyclopédie et Diderot* (Cologne: Verlag, 1985).

Benrekassa, Georges, *Le Concentrique et l'excentrique: marge des lumières* (Paris: Payot, 1980).

Berger, Günter, ed., *Pour et Contre le roman: Anthologie du discours théorique sur la fiction narrative en prose du XVIIè siècle*, Biblio 17 (Paris: Papers on French Seventeenth Century Literature, 1996).

Berman, Antoine, *Pour une critique des traductions: John Donne* (Paris: Gallimard, 1995).

Biard-Millérioux, Jacqueline, *L'Esthétique d'Elie Catherine Fréron, 1739–76* (Paris: Presses Universitaires de France, 1985).

Biographie universelle ancienne et moderne, 15 (Paris: Desplaces and Michaud, 1811; 1856).
Birn, Raymond, 'The *Journal encyclopédique* and the Old Régime', *SVEC* 24 (1963), 219–40.
Black, Jeremy, *The British and the Grand Tour* (Beckenham, Kent: Croom Helm, 1985).
—— 'Ideology, History, Xenophobia and the World of Print in Eighteenth-Century England', in *Culture, Politics and Society in Britain, 1660–1800*, ed. by Jeremy Black and Jeremy Gregory (Manchester: Manchester University Press, 1991), pp. 184–216.
—— *Natural and Necessary Enemies: Anglo-French Relations in the Eighteenth Century* (London: Duckworth, 1986).
Blanchard, Pierre, *Le Rêveur sentimental* (Paris: Le Prieur, An IV/1795).
Boileau Despréaux, Nicolas, *Œuvres, avec des éclaircissemens historiques*, 2 vols (Geneva: Fabri & Barrillot, 1715–16).
—— *Œuvres complètes*, ed. by Françoise Escal (Paris: Gallimard, 1966).
Bolingbroke, Henry St. John, Viscount, *Lettres sur l'esprit de patriotisme*, trans. by Claude de Thiard, Comte de Bissy (Edinburgh [i.e. Leipzig (?)]: aux depens de la Compagnie, 1750 and London: [n. pub.], 1750).
Bond, Richmond, P., *English Burlesque Poetry, 1700–1750* (Cambridge: Harvard University Press, 1932).
Bonno, Gabriel, *La Culture et la civilisation britanniques devant l'opinion française de la Paix d'Utrecht aux Lettres philosophiques, 1713–1734* (Philadelphia: American Philosophical Society, 1948).
Booth, Wayne C., *The Rhetoric of Fiction* (Chicago: University of Chicago Press, 1961; rpt 1983).
—— 'The Self-Conscious Narrator in Comic Fiction before *Tristram Shandy*', *PMLA* 67 (1952), 163–85; rpt *Tristram Shandy*, ed. by Melvyn New, New Casebooks (London: Macmillan, 1992), pp. 36–59.
Booy, J. Th. de and Alan J. Freer, eds, *Jacques le fataliste et La Religieuse devant la critique révolutionnaire, 1796–1800*, *SVEC* 33 (Geneva: Institut et Musée Voltaire, 1965).
Boswell, James, *Life of Johnson: An Edition of the Original Manuscript*, ed. by Marshall Waingrow, Bruce Redford *et al.*, 4 vols (Edinburgh: Edinburgh University Press and New Haven, CT: Yale University Press, 1994–).
Bougeant, Guillaume-Hyacinth, *Voyage merveilleux du prince Fan-Férédin dans la Romancie* (Paris: Lemercier, 1735).
Brandon, Isaac [or William Combe], *Fragmens à la manière de Sterne*, trans. by Mellinet aîné (Paris: Du Pont, An VIII/1799).
—— *Fragments in the Manner of Sterne* (London: Debrett and Murray & Highley, 1797).
Bray, René, *La Formation de la doctrine classique en France* (Paris: Hachette, 1927).
Bremner, Geoffrey, *Order and Chance: The Pattern of Diderot's Thought* (Cambridge: Cambridge University Press, 1983).
Brewer, Daniel, *The Discourse of Enlightenment in Eighteenth-Century France: Diderot and the Art of Philosophizing* (Cambridge: Cambridge University Press, 1993).
Briggs, Peter M., 'Laurence Sterne and Literary Celebrity in 1760', *The Age of Johnson: A Scholarly Annual*, 4 (1991), pp. 251–80.
Brink, André, *The Novel: Language and Narrative from Cervantes to Calvino* (Basingstoke: Macmillan, 1998).
Brissenden, R. F., *Virtue in Distress. Studies in the Novel of Sentiment from Richardson to Sade* (London: Macmillan, 1974).
Brooke, Frances Moore, *The History of Emily Montague*, 4 vols (London: Dodsley, 1769).
—— *Histoire d'Emilie Montague*, trans. by Joseph-Pierre Frénais (Paris: Gaugery, 1770).

—— *Histoire d'Emilie Montague*, trans. by Jean-Baptiste-René Robinet (Amsterdam: Changuion, 1770).
Brooks, Peter, *Reading for the Plot: Design and Intention in Narrative* (New York: Knopf, 1984).
Brown, Homer Obed, *Institutions of the English Novel: from Defoe to Scott* (Philadelphia: University of Pennsylvania Press, 1997).
—— 'Prologue: Why the Story of the Origin of the (English) Novel is an American Romance (If Not the Great American Novel)', in *Cultural Institutions of the Novel*, ed. by Deirdre Lynch and William B. Warner (Durham, NC: Duke University Press, 1996), pp. 11–43.
Brune, Guillaume-Marie-Anne, *Voyage pittoresque et sentimental dans plusieurs provinces occidentales de la France* (London: Letellier, 1788).
Bulletin de la Société archéologique du Vendômois (1882), pp. 266–7.
Bunyan, John, *The Pilgrim's Progress*, ed. by James Blanton Wharey, 2nd edn (Oxford: Clarendon Press, 1960).
Burke, Edmund, *Recherches philosophiques sur l'origine des idées que nous avons du beau et du sublime, précédés d'une dissertation sur le goût*, trans. by Abbé Des François, 2 vols (London: Hochereau, 1765).
Byrd, Max, *Tristram Shandy* (London: Allen and Unwin, 1985).
Bystydzienska, 'Wawrzyniec Sterne: *A Sentimental Journey* in Nineteenth-Century Poland', *The Shandean* 13 (2002), 47–53.
Cash, Arthur, '*Laurence Sterne. The Early and Middle Years* (London: Methuen, 1975).
—— *Laurence Sterne. The Later Years* (London: Methuen, 1986).
—— The Sermon in *Tristram Shandy*', *ELH* 31 (1964), 395–417.
—— *Sterne's Comedy of Moral Sentiments: The Ethical Dimension of the Journey* (Pittsburgh: Duquesne University Press, 1966).
Censer, Jack R., *The French Press in the Age of Enlightenment* (London: Routledge, 1994).
Cervantes, Miguel de, *Don Quijote*, trans. by Burton Raffel (New York: Norton, 1999).
Charles, Shelley, 'Le *Tom Jones* de La Place ou la fabrique d'un roman français', *Revue d'histoire littéraire de la France* 6 (November–December 1994), 931–58.
Charlton, D. G., *New Images of the Natural in France: A Study in European Cultural History, 1750–1800* (Cambridge: Cambridge University Press, 1984).
Chartier, Roger and Henri-Jean Martin, eds, *Histoire de l'édition française: Le livre triomphant, 1660–1830* (Paris: Promodis, 1984; rpt Paris: Fayard-Promodis, 1990).
Chouillet, Jacques, *L'Ésthétique des Lumières* (Paris: Presses Universitaires de France, 1974).
—— *Diderot* (Paris: Société d'Édition d'Enseignement Supérieur, 1977).
Cohen, Huguette, *La Figure dialogique dans Jacques le fataliste*, SVEC 162 (Oxford: Voltaire Foundation, 1976).
Cointre, Annie, Alain Lautel and Annie Rivara, eds, *La Traduction romanesque au XVIIIè siècle* (Arras: Presses Universitaires Artois, 2003).
Colley, Linda, *Britons: Forging the Nation 1707–1837* (New Haven: Yale University Press, 1992).
Conrad, Peter, *Shandyism: The Character of Romantic Irony* (Oxford: Blackwell, 1978).
Cook, Malcolm, *Fictional France: Social Reality in the French Novel, 1775–1800* (Oxford: Berg, 1993).
Coudreuse, Anne, *Le Goût des larmes au XVIIIe siècle* (Paris: Presses Universitaires de France, 1999).

Coulet, Henri, ed., *Idées sur le roman: Textes critiques sur le roman français XIIe–XXe siècle* (Paris: Larousse, 1992).
—— *Le Roman jusqu'à la révolution* (Paris: Armand Colin, 1967; 1991).
Crébillon, Claude-Prosper Jolyot de, *Les Egarements du cœur et de l'esprit, ou Mémoires de M. de Meilcour*, 3 vols (Paris: Prault fils, 1736–8).
Crocker, Lester G., *Diderot's Chaotic Order: Approach to Synthesis* (Princeton: Princeton University Press, 1974).
—— 'Jacques le fataliste, an expérience morale', *Diderot Studies* 3 (1961), pp. 73–99.
Cronk, Nicholas, 'La Défense du dialogisme: vers une poétique du burlesque', in *Burlesque et formes parodiques*, Actes du Colloque, ed. by Isabelle Landy-Houillon and Maurice Menard (Paris: Papers on Seventeenth Century Literature, 1987), pp. 321–38.
Curtis, Lewis Perry, ed., *Letters of Laurence Sterne* (Oxford: Clarendon Press, 1935).
Curtius, Ernst Robert, *European Literature and the Latin Middle Ages*, trans. by Willard R. Trask (London: Routledge and Kegan Paul, 1979).
Damin, Louis, *Le Voyage de Chantilly et d'Ermenonville*, in *Le Voyageur curieux et sentimental* (Toulouse: Manavit fils, An VIII/1799–1800).
Damrosch, Leopold, *Modern Essays on Eighteenth-Century Literature* (Oxford: Oxford University Press, 1988).
Davis, Lennard, *Factual Fictions: The Origins of the English Novel* (New York: Columbia University Press, 1983).
Delon, Michel, *L'Idée d'énergie au tournant des lumières, 1770–1820* (Paris: Presses Universitaires de France, 1988).
Denby, David J., *Sentimental Narrative and the Social Order in France, 1760–1820* (Cambridge: Cambridge University Press, 1994).
Derrida, Jacques, 'Des tours de Babel' in *Difference in Translation*, ed. by Joseph Graham (Ithaca: Cornell University Press, 1985).
Desfontaines, Pierre-François Guyot; Jacques Destrées; Pierre-Elie Fréron; Granet; Adrien-Maurice de Mairault; *Observations sur les écrits modernes*, 33 vols (Paris: Chaubert, 1735–43), VIII.
Deyverdun, Jacques Georges and Edward Gibbon, eds, *Mémoires littéraires de la Grande Bretagne, pour l'an 1768* (London: Heydinger & Elmsley, 1769).
—— *Mémoires littéraires de la Grande Bretagne, pour l'an 1767* (London: Becket & De Hondt, 1768).
Dictionnaire de biographie française, ed. by Prévost, Roman d'Annat and Tribout de Morembert (Paris: Letouzy, 1979).
Dictionnaire historique du Vendômois de Saint-Venant (Blois: Nigault and Vendôme: Souilly and Chartier, 1912–17; rpt 1969).
Diderot, Denis, *Correspondance*, ed. by Georges Roth, 16 vols (Paris: Éditions de Minuit, 1955–70).
—— *Œuvres esthétiques*, ed. by Paul Vernière (Paris: Garnier, 1959; rpt 1994).
—— *Jacques le fataliste et son maitre*, ed. by Simone Lecointre and Jean Le Galliot (Geneva: Droz, 1976).
—— *La Littérature de la Révolution française* (Paris: Presses Universitaires de France, 1988).
—— *Œuvres complètes*, ed. by H. Diekemann and J. Varloot, 25 vols (Paris: Hermann, 1975–86).
—— *Quatre Contes*, ed. by Jacques Proust (Geneva: Droz, 1964).

Didier, Béatrice, 'Je et subversion du texte: le narrateur dans *Jacques le fataliste*', *Littérature* 48 (1982), 92–105.

Dieckmann, Herbert, *Cinq leçons sur Diderot* (Geneva: Droz and Paris: Minard, 1959).

Dilworth, Ernest Nevill, *The Unsentimental Journey of Laurence Sterne* (New York: King's Crown, 1948).

Diogenes Laertius, *Lives of Eminent Philosophers*, trans. by R. D. Hicks (London: Heinemann and Cambridge: Harvard University Press, 1970).

Doody, Margaret Anne, *The True Story of the Novel* (London: Harper Collins, 1996).

Dryden, John, 'On Translation', in *Theories of Translation*, ed. by Rainer Schulte and John Biguenet (Chicago: University of Chicago Press, 1992), pp. 17–31.

Dubos, Jean Baptiste, Abbé, *Réflexions critiques sur la poésie et la peinture*, 2 vols (Paris: Mariette, 1719).

Dupas, Jean-Claude, *Sterne, ou Le Vis-à-vis* (Villeneuve d'Ascq: Presses Universitaires de Lille, 1984).

Eagleton, Terry, *The Rape of Clarissa. Writing, Sexuality and Class Struggle in Samuel Richardson* (Oxford: Blackwell, 1982).

Edmiston, William, 'The Role of the Listener: Narrative Technique in Diderot's *Ceci n'est pas un conte*', *Diderot Studies* 20 (1981), 61–75.

Ehrard, Jean, 'Lumières et roman, ou les paradoxes de Denis le fataliste', in *Au Siècle des lumières* (Paris: SEVPEN and Moscow: Académie des Sciences de l'URSS, 1970), pp. 137–55.

Encyclopédie, ou dictionnaire raisonné des sciences, des arts et des métiers, ed. by Diderot and D'Alembert, 17 vols (Paris: Briasson, David, Le Breton, Durand and Neufchâtel: Samuel Faulche, 1751–65).

Encyclopédie, Supplément, ed. by Jean Baptiste René Robinet, 4 vols (Paris: Panckoucke, Stoupe, Brunet and Amsterdam: Rey, 1776–7).

Erickson, Robert A., *Mother Midnight: Birth, Sex and Fate in Eighteenth-Century Fiction: Defoe, Richardson and Sterne* (New York: A. M. S., 1986).

Fabre, Jean, *Idées sur le roman: de Madame de Lafayette au Marquis de Sade* (Paris: Klincksieck, 1979).

—— 'Sagesse et morale dans *Jacques le fataliste*', in *The Age of Enlightenment: Studies Presented to Theodore Besterman* (Edinburgh: Oliver & Boyd, 1967).

Felsenstein, Frank, 'After the Peace of Paris: Yorick, Smelfungus and the Seven Years' War', in *Guerres et paix: la Grande-Bretagne au XVIIIè siècle*, ed. by Paul-Gabriel Boucé, 2 vols (Paris: Presses de la Sorbonne Nouvelle, 1998), II, pp. 311–23.

Ferriar, John, *Illustrations of Sterne, with other Essays and Verses* (London: Cadell & Davies, 1798).

Fielding, Henry, *Amélie*, trans. by Marie-Jeanne Laboras de Mézières Riccoboni (Paris: Libraires Associés, 1743).

—— *Amélie, Histoire angloise*, trans. by Florent de Puisieux (Paris: Charpentier, 1762).

—— *Les Avantures de Joseph Andrews*, trans. by Pierre-François Guyot Desfontaines (London [i.e. Paris (?)]: Millar, 1743).

—— *Histoire de Tom Jones, ou l'Enfant trouvé*, trans. by Pierre-Antoine de La Place, 4 vols (London [i.e. Paris (?)]: Nourse, 1750).

—— *The History of Tom Jones, a Foundling*, ed. by Battestin and Bowers (Oxford: Clarendon Press, 1967).

—— *Joseph Andrews*, ed. by Battestin and Bowers, 2 vols (Oxford: Clarendon Press, 1967).

Fluchère, Henri, *Laurence Sterne: de l'homme à l'œuvre* (Paris: Gallimard, 1961).

Folkierski, Wladyslaw, *Entre le classicisme et le romantisme* (Paris: Champion, 1925; rpt 1969).
Fredman, Alice Green, *Diderot and Sterne* (New York: Columbia University Press, 1960).
Frye, Northrop, *Anatomy of Criticism: Four Essays* (Princeton: Princeton University Press, 1957; rpt London: Penguin, 1990).
Furetière, Antoine, *Le Roman bourgeois*, ed. by Jacques Prévot (Paris: Gallimard, 1981).
—— *Le Roman bourgeois, ouvrage comique* (Paris: Jolly, 1666).
Furst, Lilian R., *Fictions of Romantic Irony in European Narrative, 1760–1857* (London: Macmillan, 1984).
Garagnon, Jean, 'Diderot et la genèse de *Jacques le fataliste*: sur une lettre de Meister père', *Studi Francesi* 27 (1983), 81–2.
Garat, Dominique-Joseph, *Mémoires historiques sur M. Suerd, sur ses écrits et sur le XVIIIè siècle*, 2 vols (Paris: Belin, 1820).
Gearhart, Suzanne, *The Open Boundary of History and Fiction: A Critical Approach to the French Enlightenment* (Princeton: Princeton University Press, 1984).
Genette, Gérard, *Palimpsestes: La littérature au second degré* (Paris: Seuil, 1982).
Gentzler, Edwin, *Contemporary Translation Theories* (London: Routledge, 1993).
Geoffroy, Julien-Louis, *AL*, 8 (1783), Letter 6, p. 87.
Gerard, Alexander, *Essai sur le goût, augmenté de trois dissertations sur le même suject, par Messrs de Voltaire, d'Alembert et de Montesquieu*, trans. by Marc-Antoine Eidous (Paris: Delalain, 1766).
Gillot, Hubert, *La Querelle des anciens et des modernes en France* (Paris: Champion, 1914).
Girardin, Stanislas-Cécile-Xavier-Louis, Comte de, *Promenade ou Itinéraire des jardins d'Ermenonville* (Paris: Mérigot, 1788).
Goodden, Angelica, *'Actio' and Persuasion: Dramatic Performance in Eighteenth-Century France* (Oxford: Clarendon Press, 1986).
—— *Diderot and the Body* (Oxford: Legenda, 2001).
Gorat, Dominique-Joseph, *Mémoires historiques sur M. Suard, sur ses écrits et sur le XVIII è siècle*, 2 vols (Paris: Belin, 1820).
Gorjy, Jean-Claude, *Ann'quin Bredouille, ou le petit cousin de Tristram Shandy*, 6 vols (Paris: Louis, 1792).
—— *Nouveau voyage sentimental en France de Sterne*, 3 vols (London: Bastien, 1784; Paris: Guillot, 1791).
—— *Tablettes sentimentales du bon Pamphile pendant les mois d'août, septembre, octobre et novembre 1789* (Paris: Louis, 1792).
Gough, Hugh, *The Newspaper Press in the French Revolution* (Chicago: Dorsey Press, 1988).
'Grammaire', *Encyclopédie*, VII, p. 842.
Green, F. C., *Minuet: A Critical Survey of French and English Literary Ideas in the Eighteenth Century* (London: Dent, 1935).
Grieder, Josephine, *Anglomania in France 1740–1789: Fact, Fiction, and Political Discourse* (Geneva: Droz, 1985).
Grimm, Frédéric-Melchior, *Correspondance littéraire, philosophique et critique, 1753–1769*, 6 vols (Paris: Longchamps & Buisson, 1813), I, p. 208 (15 August 1754).
Guibert, Jacques-Antoine-Hippolyte, Comte de, *Éloge de Mademoiselle de Lespinasse, sous le nom d'Éliza*, in Lespinasse, *Lettres*, 2 vols (2nd edn; Paris: Longchamps, 1811).
Guitton, Edouard, 'La mention du livre dans *Jacques le fataliste*', *Interférences* 11 (1980), 57–71.
Gunning, Susannah, *L'abbaye ou le château de Barford, imité de l'angois par M...* (London: Gauguery, 1769).
Gunny, Ahmad, 'Voltaire and the Novel: Sterne', *SVEC* 124 (1974), 149–61.

Hartvig, Gabriella, 'Lőrincz Sterne in Hungary', *The Shandean* 11 (1999–2000), 9–27.
Hazard, Paul, *La Crise de la conscience européenne, 1680–1715* (Paris: Fayard, 1961).
Hemperley, J. W., *The Journal encyclopédique as an Intermediary of English Literature in France* (Michigan: University Microfilms, 1971; rpt 1981).
Highet, Gilbert, *The Classical Tradition: Greek and Roman Influences on Western Literature* (1949; New York: Oxford University Press, 1985).
Horace, *The Art of Poetry*, in *Ancient Literary Criticism*, ed. by Russell and Winterbottom (Oxford: Oxford University Press, 1972).
Howes, Alan B., *Yorick and the Critics: Sterne's Reputation in England, 1760–1868* (New Haven: Yale University Press, 1958).
—— ed., *Sterne: The Critical Heritage* (London: Routledge & Kegan Paul, 1971; rpt 1995).
Huet, Pierre-Daniel, *Traitté de l'origine des romans* (Paris: [n. pub.], 1670).
Hulst, Lieven D', *Cent ans de théorie française de la traduction: de Batteux à Littré, 1748–1847* (Lille: Presses Universitaires de Lille, 1990).
Hume, David, *Essays Moral, Political and Literary*, ed. by Eugene F. Miller (Indianapolis: Liberty Fund, 1985).
—— *A Treatise of Human Nature*, ed. by L. A. Selby-Bigge, 3rd edn (Oxford: Clarendon Press, 1978).
Hunter, Alfred C., *J.-B.-A., Suard, un introducteur de la littérature anglaise en France* (Paris: Champion, 1925).
Hunter, J. Paul, *Before Novels: The Cultural Contexts of Eighteenth-Century English Fiction* (London: Norton, 1990).
—— 'Response as Reformation: *Tristram Shandy* and the Art of Interruption', *Novel* 4 (1971), 132–46.
Hutcheson, Francis, *Recherches sur l'origine des idées que nous avons de la beauté et de la vertu*, 2 vols (Amsterdam: [n. pub.], 1749).
Hutton, Ulrich Von, Johann Jaeger et al., *Epistolae Obscurorum Virorum*, ed. and trans. by Francis Griffin Stokes (London: Chatto & Windus, 1925).
Iser, Wolfgang, *The Act of Reading: A Theory of Aesthetic Response* (Baltimore: Johns Hopkins University Press, 1978).
—— *Laurence Sterne, Tristram Shandy*, Landmarks of World Literature (Cambridge: Cambridge University Press, 1988).
Ishii, Shigemitsu, 'Rorensu Sutahn: Sterne in Japan', *The Shandean* 8 (1996), 9–40.
Jackson, H. J., 'Sterne, Burton, and Ferriar: Allusions to *The Anatomy of Melancholy* in Volumes Five to Nine of *Tristram Shandy*', *PQ* 54 (1975), 457–70.
Jacquin, Armand-Pierre, *Entretiens sur les romans: ouvrage moral et critique, dans lequel on traite de l'origine des romans & de leurs différentes espéces, tant par rapport à l'esprit, que par rapport au cœur* (Paris: Duchesne, 1755).
Jauss, Hans Robert, *Question and Answer: Forms of Dialogic Understanding*, ed. and trans. by Michael Hays (Minneapolis: University of Minnesota Press, 1989).
—— *Toward an Aesthetic of Reception*, trans. by Timothy Bahti (Sussex: Harvester Press and Minnesota: University of Minnesota Press, 1982).
Jefferson, D. W, '*Tristram Shandy* and the Tradition of Learned Wit', *Essays in Criticism* 1 (1951), 225–48; rpt in *Tristram Shandy*, New Casebooks, ed. by Melvyn New (Basingstoke: Macmillan, 1992), pp. 17–35.
Johnston, Charles, *Chrisal, ou Les Aventures d'une guinée*, trans. by J.-P. Frénais [?] (London [?] and Paris: Grangé, 1767).
—— *Supplément à Chrisal, ou Les Nouvelles aventures d'une guinée* (Amsterdam: Rey, Lyon: Cellier and Paris: Dufour, 1759).

Jones, Chris, *Radical Sensibility: Literature and Ideas in the 1790s* (London: Routledge, 1993).
Jones, Richard Foster, *Ancients and Moderns: A Study of the Background of the Battle of the Books*, Washington University Studies: Language and Literature, 6 (St Louis, 1936).
Josipovici, Gabriel, *The World and the Book: A Study of Modern Fiction* (London: Macmillan, 1971).
Juliard, Pierre, *Philosophies of Language in Eighteenth-Century France* (The Hague: Mouton, 1970).
Jump, John Davies, *Burlesque* (London: Methuen, 1972).
Kavanagh, Thomas M., *Enlightenment and the Shadows of Chance: The Novel and the Culture of Gambling in Eighteenth-Century France* (Baltimore: Johns Hopkins University Press, 1993).
—— '*Jacques le fataliste*: An Encyclopedia of the Novel', in *Diderot, Digression and Dispersion, A Bicentennial Tribute*, ed. by Jack Undank and Herbert Josephs (Lexington: French Forum, 1984), pp. 150–65.
—— *The Vacant Mirror: A Study of Mimesis through Diderot's* Jacques le fataliste, SVEC 104 (Oxford: Voltaire Foundation, 1973).
Kay, Carol, *Political Constructions: Defoe, Richardson, and Sterne in Relation to Hobbes, Hume, and Burke* (Ithaca: Cornell University Press, 1988).
Keener, Frederick M., *The Chain of Becoming: The Philosophical Tale, the Novel, and a Neglected Realism of the Enlightenment: Swift, Montesquieu, Voltaire, Johnson, and Austen* (New York: Columbia University Press, 1983).
Kempf, Roger, *Diderot et le roman, ou le démon de la présence* (Paris: Seuil, 1964).
Keymer, Thomas, ed., *Laurence Sterne's Tristram Shandy: A Casebook* (Oxford: Oxford University Press, 2006).
—— *Sterne, the Moderns and the Novel* (Oxford: Oxford University Press, 2002).
Kirk, Eugene P., *Menippean Satire: An Annotated Catalogue of Texts and Criticism* (New York: Garland, 1980).
Knight, Douglas, 'Translation: the Augustan Mode', in *On Translation*, ed. by Reuben A. Brower (Cambridge: Harvard University Press, 1959), pp. 196–204.
Korkowski, Eugene, '*Tristram Shandy*, Digression, and the Menippean Tradition', *Scholia Satyrica* I:4 (1975), 3–15.
Kors, Alan Charles, *D'Holbach's Coterie: An Enlightenment in Paris* (Princeton: Princeton University Press, 1976).
Kovola, Urpo, 'Sterne's Long Journey into Finland', *The Shandean* 13 (2002), 29–45.
Kreitman, Lenore, R., 'Diderot's Aesthetic Paradox and Created Reality', SVEC 102 (1973), 157-72.
Kundera, Milan, *L'Art du roman, essai* (Paris: Gallimard, 1986).
—— *Jacques et son maître: hommage à Denis Diderot en trois actes, precédé de Introduction à une variation* (Paris: Gallimard, 1981).
La Fayette, Marie-Madeleine Pioche de la Vergne, Madame de, *La Princesse de Clèves* (1672; Paris: Barbin, 1678).
Lamb, Jonathan, 'Sterne and irregular oratory', in *The Cambridge Companion to the Eighteenth-Century Novel*, ed. by John Richetti (Cambridge: Cambridge University Press, 1996).
—— *Sterne's Fiction and the Double Principle* (Cambridge: Cambridge University Press, 1989).
——'Sterne's System of Imitation', *Modern Language Review* 76 (1981), 794–810.

Lambert, José and Rik Van Gorp, eds, *The Manipulation of Literature* (London: Croom Helm, 1985).
Land, Stephen K., 'Universalism and Relativism: A Philosophical Problem of Translation in the Eighteenth Century', *JHI* 35 (1974), 597–610.
Landy-Houillon, Isabelle and Maurice Menard, eds, *Burlesque et formes parodiques*, Actes du Colloque (Paris: Papers on Seventeenth Century Literature, 1987).
Langford, Paul, *Englishness Identified: Manners and Characters, 1650–1850* (Oxford: Oxford University Press, 2000).
'Langue', *Encyclopédie*, IX, p. 256.
Lanham, Richard A., 'Pastoral War in *Tristram Shandy*', in *Modern Essays on Eighteenth-Century Literature*, ed. by Leopold Damrosch, Jr (Oxford: Oxford University Press, 1988).
Laurens, Henri-Joseph Du, Abbé, *Le Compère Mathieu, ou les Bigarrures de l'esprit humain*, 3 vols (London: Aux dépens de la Compagnie, 1732).
Lefevere, André, 'Translation: Its History in the West', in *Translation, History and Culture*, ed. by Lefevere and Bassnett (London: Routledge, 1991).
—— *Translation, Rewriting, and the Manipulation of Literary Fame* (London: Routledge, 1992).
Lambert, Anne Thérèse, Marquise de, *Avis d'une mère à sa fille* (London: Dulau, 1799).
Lenglet-Dufresnoy, Nicolas, Abbé [Gordon de Percel, pseud.], *De l'usage des romans, où l'on fait voir leur utilité & leurs differens caractères, avec une bibliothèque des romans, accompagnée de remarques critiques sur leur choix & leurs editions*, 2 vols (Amsterdam: De Poilras, 1734).
—— *Histoire justifiée contre les romans* (Amsterdam: J.-F. Bernard, 1735).
Le Roy, Pierre and Nicholas Rapin, Jean Passerat, Florent Chrestien, *Satyre ménippée de la vertu du catholicon d'Espagne et de la tenue des estats de Paris* (Paris: Charpentier, 1841; facsimile rpt Cœuvres and Valsery: Ressouvenances, 1997).
Lespinasse, Julie de, *Deux chapitres dans le genre du Voyage sentimental de Sterne*, in *Lettres de Mademoiselle de Lespinasse, écrites depuis l'année 1773, jusqu'à l'année 1776*, 2 vols (Paris: Colin, 1809), II, pp. 305–22.
Le Tourneur, Pierre, *Voyage à Érmenonville*, in Rousseau, *Œuvres complètes*, 36 vols (Paris: Valade, 1788–93; facsimile rpt Reims: À l'Écart, 1990).
Levi, A. H. T., 'The Reception of Greek Sources in Late Seventeenth-Century France', *French Studies* 42 (1988), 408–23.
Levine, Joseph M., *The Battle of the Books: History and Literature in the Augustan Age* (Ithaca: Cornell University Press, 1991).
Locke, John, *An Essay concerning Human Understanding*, ed. by Peter H. Nidditch (Oxford: Clarendon Press, 1975).
Loveridge, Mark, *Laurence Sterne and the Argument about Design* (London: Macmillan Press, 1982).
Loy, J. Robert, *Diderot's Determined Fatalist: A Critical Appreciation of Jacques le fataliste* (New York: King's Crown Press, 1950).
—— '*Jacques* Reconsidered: Digression as Form and Theme', in *Diderot: Digression and Dispersion, a Bicentennial Tribute*, ed. by Jack Undank and Herbert Josephs (Lexington: French Forum, 1984), pp. 166–79.
MacKenzie, Henry, *The Man of Feeling* (Oxford: Oxford University Press, 1987).
MacLean, Kenneth, *John Locke and English Literature of the Eighteenth Century* (New Haven: Yale University Press, 1936).
McDermott, M., *Novel and Romance* (New Haven: Yale University Press, 1936).

McFarland, Thomas, *Romanticism and the Heritage of Rousseau* (Oxford: Clarendon Press, 1995).
McKeon, Michael, *The Origins of the English Novel, 1600–1740* (Baltimore: Johns Hopkins University Press, 1987).
McMorran, William, *The Inn and the Traveller: Digressive Topographies in the Early Modern European Novel* (Oxford: Legenda, 2002).
McVeagh, John, ed., *All Before Them: English Literature and the Wider World, 1660–1780* (London: Ashfield Press, 1990).
Maistre, Xavier de, *Expédition nocturne autour de ma chambre*, ed. by Michel Covin (France: Le Castor Astral, 1990).
—— *Voyage autour de ma chambre* (Paris: Dufart, An VII/1798–9).
—— *Voyage autour de ma chambre* (Paris: José Corti, 1984).
—— *Voyage autour de ma chambre, suivi de Le Lépreux de la cité d'Aoste* (Paris: Dondey-Dupré père et fils, 1825).
Maixent, Jocelyn, *Le XVIIIe siècle de Milan Kundera, ou Diderot investi par le roman contemporain* (Paris: Presses Universitaires de France, 1998).
Marivaux, Pierre Carlet de Chamblain de, *Pharsamon, ou les Nouvelles folies romanesques*, 2 vols (The Hague: Aux dépens de la Compagnie, 1737).
—— *La Vie de Marianne, ou les Avantures de Mme la comtesse de ****, 11 vols (Paris: Prault, 1731–41).
Marmontel, Jean-François, 'Traduction', *Supplément*, 4 vols (Paris: Panckoucke, Stoupe, Brunet and Amsterdam: Rey, 1776–7), IV, pp. 952–4.
Martin, Angus, Vivienne Mylne and Richard Frautschi, eds, *Bibliographie du genre romanesque français, 1751–1800* (London: Mansell and Paris: France Expansion, 1977).
Marzys, Zygmunt, 'Le Burlesque et les fondateurs de la langue classique', in *Burlesque et formes parodiques*, Actes du Colloque, ed. by Isabelle Landy-Houillon and Maurice Menard (Paris: Papers on Seventeenth Century Literature, 1987), pp. 115–23.
Mat-Hasquin, Michèle, 'Les Influences anglaises en Europe occidentale au siècle des lumières', *Études sur le XVIIIe siècle* (1981), 191–9.
May, Georges, *Le Dilemme du roman au XVIIIe siècle: Etude sur les rapports du roman et de la critique, 1715–1761* (New Haven, CT: Yale University Press and Paris: Presses Universitaires de France, 1963).
Menant, Sylvain, *L'Ésthétique de Voltaire* (Paris: Sedes, 1995).
Merry, Barbara, *Menippean Elements in Paul Scarron's Roman comique* (New York: Peter Lang, 1991).
Miller, John Richardson, *Boileau en France au dix-huitième siècle* (Baltimore: Johns Hopkins Press, London: Oxford University Press, Paris: Société d'Édition 'Les Belles Lettres', 1942).
Montandon, Alain, *La Réception de Sterne en Allemagne* (Clermond-Ferrand: Association des Publications de la Faculté des Lettres et Sciences Humaines, 1985).
Montesquieu, Charles-Louis de Secondat, *De l'Esprit des loix*, 2 vols (Geneva: Barrillot et fils, 1748).
—— *Ésprit des Lois*, in *Œuvres complètes*, ed. by Daniel Oster (Paris: Seuil, 1964).
Mornet, Daniel, *Le Sentiment de la nature en France de J.-J. Rousseau à Bernardin de Saint-Pierre: Essai sur les rapports de la literature et des mœurs* (Paris: Hachette, 1907).
Mortier, Roland, 'L'Idée de décadence littéraire au XVIIIe siècle', *SVEC* 57 (1967), 1013–29.
—— 'Julie de Lespinasse: femme savante et âme sensible', in *La Sensibilité dans la*

littérature française au XVIIIe siècle, Actes du Colloque International de Verona, 8–10 mai 1997, ed. by Franco Piva (Fasano: Schena and Paris: Didier Erudition, 1998), pp. 235–45.

—— *L'Originalité: une nouvelle catégorie esthétique au siècle des Lumières* (Geneva: Droz, 1982).

Mullan, John, *Sentiment and Sociability: The Language of Feeling in the Eighteenth Century* (Oxford: Clarendon Press, 1988).

Myer, Valerie Grosvenor, ed., *Laurence Sterne: Riddles and Mysteries* (London: Vision and Totowa, NJ: Barnes & Noble, 1984).

Mylne, Vivienne, *The Eighteenth-Century French Novel: Techniques of Illusion* (Manchester: Manchester University Press, 1965).

New, Melvyn, ed., *Critical Essays on Laurence Sterne* (New York: G. K. Hall & Co., 1998).

—— *Laurence Sterne as Satirist: A Reading of Tristram Shandy* (Gainesville: University of Florida Press, 1969).

—— *Tristram Shandy*, New Casebooks (Basingstoke: Macmillan, 1992).

—— *Tristram Shandy: A Book for Free Spirits* (New York: Twayne, 1994).

Nisbet, H. B. and Claude Rawson, *Cambridge History of Literary Criticism IV: The Eighteenth Century* (Cambridge: Cambridge University Press, 1997).

Nodier, Charles, *Miscellanées, variétés de philosophie, d'histoire et de littérature*, in *Œuvres complètes*, (1832), V, pp. 16–21; trans. and rpt in *Sterne: The Critical Heritage*, ed. by Alan B. Howes (London: Routledge & Kegan Paul, 1971; rpt 1995), pp. 419–21.

Nordmann, Claude, 'Anglomanie et anglophobie en France au dix-huitième siècle', *Revue du Nord* 66 (1984), 787–803.

Nuttall, A. D., *A Common Sky: Philosophy and the Literary Imagination* (London: Chatto and Windus, 1974).

—— *Openings: Narrative Beginnings from the Epic to the Novel* (Oxford: Clarendon Press, 1992).

—— *The Stoic in Love* (New York: Harvester Wheatsheaf, 1989).

Oates, John Claud Trewinard, *Shandyism and Sentiment, 1760–1800* (Cambridge: Cambridge University Press, 1968).

Ogée, Frédéric, 'Channelling Emotions: Travel and Literary Creation in Smollett and Sterne', *SVEC* 292 (1991), 27–42.

'Originalité', *Dictionnaire comique, satyrique, critique, burlesque, libre et proverbial*, ed. by Le Roux (Amsterdam: [n. pub.], 1718).

'Originalité', *Dictionnaire critique de la langue française*, 3 vols (1787).

'Originalité', *Dictionnaire de l'Académie françoise*, new edn, 2 vols (Avignon: Garrigan, 1777).

'Originalité', *Dictionnaire du français classique* (Paris: Larousse, 1998).

'Originalité', *Dictionnaire historique de la langue française* (Paris: Robert, 1992).

Parnell, J. T., 'Swift, Sterne, and the Skeptical Tradition', *Studies in Eighteenth-Century Culture* 23 (1994), 220–42; rpt in *Laurence Sterne's Tristram Shandy: A Casebook*, ed. by Thomas Keymer (Oxford: Oxford University Press, 2006), pp. 23–49.

Patterson, Diana, 'Tristram's Marblings and Marblers', *The Shandean* 3 (1991), 70–97.

Paulson, Ronald, *Don Quixote in England: The Aesthetics of Laughter* (Baltimore: Johns Hopkins University Press, 1998).

—— *The Fictions of Satire* (Baltimore: Johns Hopkins University Press, 1967).

—— 'Life as Journey and as Theatre: Two Eighteenth-Century Narrative Structures', *New Literary History* 8 (1976), 43–58.

—— *Satire and the Novel in Eighteenth-Century England* (New Haven: Yale University Press, 1967).
Pellan, Françoise, 'Laurence Sterne's Indebtedness to Charron', *MLR* 67 (1972), 752-5.
Penegaute, Luis, 'The Unfortunate Journey of Laurence Sterne through Spain: The Translations of his Works into Spanish', *The Shandean* 5 (1993), 25–53.
Petrakis, Byron, 'Jester in the Pulpit: Sterne and Pulpit Eloquence', *PQ* 51 (1972), 430–47.
Pfister, Manfred, *Laurence Sterne* (Horndon, Devon: Northcote House Publishers, 2001).
Pope, Alexander, *Poems*, ed. by John Butt (London: Routledge, 1963).
Porter, Dennis, *Haunted Journeys: Desire and Transgression in European Travel Writing* (Princeton: Princeton University Press, 1991).
Prévost d'Exiles, Antoine-François, Abbé, *Les Avantures du Chevalier des Grieux et de Manon Lescaut* (Amsterdam: aux dépens de la Compagnie, 1733).
—— *Le Pour et Contre* (Paris: Didot, 1733–40).
Probyn, Clive, *English Fiction of the Eighteenth Century, 1700–1789* (London: Longman, 1987).
Pruner, Francis, *L'Unité secrète de Jacques le fataliste* (Paris: Minard, 1970).
Quérard, J.-M., *La France littéraire, ou Dictionnaire bibliographique*, 12 vols (Paris: Maisonneuve & Larose, 1700–1827; Paris: Firmin Didot père et fils, 1827–35).
Rabelais, François, *Œuvres complètes*, ed. by Pierre Jourda, 2 vols (Paris: Garnier, 1962).
Rawson, Claude, *Satire and Sentiment, 1660–1830* (Cambridge: Cambridge University Press, 1994).
Ray, William, *Story and History: Narrative Authority and Social Identity in the Eighteenth-Century French and English Novel* (Oxford: Blackwell, 1990).
Raynal, Guillaume Thomas, Abbé, *Éloge d'Eliza Draper*, in *Histoire philosophique et politique des établissemens and du commerce des Européens dans les deux Indes*, 4 vols (Geneva: Pellet, 1780); I, pp. 318–20; rpt in *Sterne, A Eliza, ou Quatre-vingt-quinze variations sur un thème sentimental* (Paris: José Corti, 1987), pp. 139–44.
—— *Lettre à l'Assemblée nationale*, 31 May 1790 (Paris: Cussac, 1791).
Relihan, Joel C., *Ancient Menippean Satire* (Baltimore: Johns Hopkins University Press, 1993).
Rex, Walter E., *Diderot's Counterpoints: The Dynamics of Contrariety in his Major Works*, SVEC 363 (Oxford: Voltaire Foundation, 1998).
Richardson, Samuel, *Clarissa, or The History of a Young Lady*, ed. by Angus Ross (Harmondsworth: Penguin, 1985).
—— *Clarisse Harlowe*, trans. by Pierre Le Tourneur, 10 vols (Geneva: Barde and Paris: Moutard and Merigot, 1785–6).
—— *Lettres angloises, ou Histoire de Miss Clarisse Harlove*, trans. by Antoine–François Prévost, 6 vols (London [i.e. Paris]: Nourse, 1751).
—— *Nouvelles lettres angloises, ou Histoire du Chevalier Grandisson*, trans. by Prévost, 8 vols (Amsterdam: [n. pub.], 1755–6)
—— *Pamela, or Virtue Rewarded*, 2 vols (London: Rivington & Osborne, 1741).
—— *Paméla, ou la Vertu récompensée*, trans. by Prévost or Aubert de La Chesnay, 2 vols (London [i.e. Paris (?)]: J. Osborn, 1742).
Richetti, John, *The English Novel in History 1700–1780* (London: Routledge, 1999).
Ricken, Ulrich, *Grammaire et philosophie au siècle des lumières* (Villeneuve d'Ascq: Publications de l'Université de Lille III, 1978).
—— *Linguistics, Anthropology and Philosophy in the French Enlightenment* (London: Routledge, 1994).

Riikonen, H. K., *Menippean Satire as a Literary Genre*, Commentationes Humanarum Litterarum, 83 (Helsinki: Societas Scientiarum Fennica, 1987).

Robert, Marthe, *Roman des origines et origines du roman* (Paris: Bernard Grasset, 1972).

Roelens, Maurice, '*Jacques le fataliste* et la critique contemporaine', *Dix-huitième siècle* 5 (1973), 119–37.

Rosenblum, Michael, 'The Sermon, the King of Bohemia, and the Art of Interpolation in *Tristram Shandy*', *Studies in Philology* 75 (1978), 472–91.

Rousseau, Jean-Jacques, *Entretien sur les romans*, in *Julie, ou La Nouvelle Héloïse* (Paris: Garnier-Flammarion, 1967), pp. 572–86.

—— *Julie, ou La Nouvelle Héloïse: Lettres de deux amans, habitans d'une petite ville au pied des Alpes, recueillies et publiées par J.-J. Rousseau*, 3 vols (Amsterdam: Rey, 1761).

—— *Lettre à M. d'Alembert sur son article Genève dans le VIIe volume de l'Encyclopédie, et particulièrement sur le projet d'établir un théâtre de comédie en cette ville* (Amsterdam: Rey, 1758).

—— *Œuvres complètes*, 36 vols (Paris: Valade, 1788–93).

—— *Œuvres complètes*, ed. by Michel Launay, 3 vols (Paris: Seuil, 1967).

Rousseau, Pierre, *JE* (1 January 1756), 'Avis', pp. 1–9.

—— *JE* (1 May 1776), p. 42.

Roussel, Jean, *Jean-Jacques Rousseau en France après la Révolution, 1795–1830* (Paris: Armand Colin, 1972).

Rowson, Martin, 'Hyperboling Gravity's Ravelin: A Comic Book Version of *Tristram Shandy*', *The Shandean* 7 (1995), 63–76.

—— *The Life and Opinions of Tristram Shandy, Gentleman* (London: Picador, 1996).

Rush, Jane, 'La tradition comique et son renouveau dans les historiettes de *Jacques le fataliste et son maître*', *Recherches sur Diderot et sur l'Encyclopédie* 15 (1973), 41–53.

Saint-Amans, Jean Florimond Boudon de, *Fragmens d'un voyage sentimental et pittoresque dans les Pyrénées, ou Lettres écrites de ces montagnes* (Metz: Devilly, 1789).

Saint-Simon, Louis de Rouvroy, Duc de, 'Essai de traduction littérale et énergique', in Pope, *Essai sur l'homme*, trans. by Saint-Simon (Amsterdam: Changuion, 1787).

Sangsue, Daniel, *Le Récit excentrique: Gautier, de Maistre, Nerval et Nodier: Essai sur la postérité de l'anti-roman à l'époque romantique* (Paris: José Corti, 1987).

Santovetti, Olivia, 'The Adventurous Journey of Lorenzo Sterne in Italy', *The Shandean* 8 (1996), 79–97.

Scarron, Paul, *Le Roman comique* (Paris: Quinet, 1651; Paris: Luyne, 1657).

—— *Le Roman comique*, ed. by Jean Serroy (Paris: Gallimard, 1985).

—— *Virgile travesti*, ed. by Jean Serroy, Classiques Garnier (Paris: Bordas, 1988).

Seidel, Michael, *Satiric Inheritance: Rabelais to Sterne* (Princeton: Princeton University Press, 1979).

Serroy, Jean, *Roman et réalité: les histoires comiques au XVIIIè siècle* (Paris: Minard, 1980).

Sgard, Jean, ed., *Dictionnaire des journaux, 1600–1789* (Paris: Universitas, 1991).

—— 'La Multiplication des périodiques', in *Histoire de l'édition française: le livre triomphant 1660–1830*, ed. by Roger Chartier and Henri-Jean Martin (Paris: Promodis, 1984; rpt Paris: Fayard/Promodis, 1990), pp. 247–55.

Shaftesbury, Anthony Ashley Cooper, Earl of, *Oeuvres*, 3 vols (Geneva, 1769).

—— *Principes de la philosophie morale, ou Essai sur le mérite de la vertu* (Amsterdam: Chatelain, 1745).

Shakespeare, William, *The Complete Works*, ed. by Stanley Wells and Gary Taylor (Oxford: Clarendon, 1986).

—— *Shakespeare*, trans. by Pierre Le Tourneur, 20 vols (Paris: Duchesne & others, 1776–83).

Sherman, Carol, *Diderot and the Art of Dialogue* (Geneva: Droz, 1976).

Shklovsky, Viktor, 'Sterne's Tristram Shandy: Stylistic Commentary', in *Russian Formalist Criticism*, trans. and ed. by Lee T. Lemon and Marion J. Reis (Lincoln: University of Nebraska Press, 1965), pp. 25–57.

Showalter, English, *The Evolution of the French Novel, 1641–1782* (Princeton: Princeton University Press, 1972).

Simon, Ernest, 'Fatalism, the Hobby-Horse and the Esthetics of the Novel', *Diderot Studies* 16 (1973), 253–74.

Smietanski, Jacques, *Le Réalisme dans Jacques le fataliste* (Paris: Nizet, 1965).

Smith, Adam, *Theory of Moral Sentiments* (London: Millar and Edinburgh: Kincaid & Bell, 1759).

Smith, K. E., 'Ordering Things in France: the Travels of Sterne, Tristram and Yorick', *SVEC* 292 (1991), 15–25.

Smollett, Tobias, *Travels through France and Italy* (London: Baldwin, 1766).

Sorel, Charles, *Le Berger extravagant* (Paris: Du Bray, 1627–8).

—— *La Vraie histoire comique de Francion* (1633; Paris: Jacquin, 1641).

Soupel, Serge, 'Crassous, Sterne, and Translation Theory', *The Shandean* 11 (1999–2000), 112–14.

—— 'Laurence Sterne, ses traducteurs et ses interprètes', *SVEC* 4 (2001), 291–8.

—— 'Lavieille, Hédouin, Leloir and the *Voyage sentimental*', *The Shandean* 2 (1990), 202–13.

Staël-Holstein, Anne-Louise-Germaine Necker, *De la Littérature considérée dans ses rapports avec les institutions sociales*, 2 vols (2nd edn; Paris: Maradan, An IX/1800), pp. 367–8.

—— *Lettres inédites de Madame de Staël à Meister* (Paris: Hachette, 1903).

Starobinski, Jean, '"Chaque balle a son billet": destin et répétition dans *Jacques le fataliste*', *Nouvelle Revue de Psychanalyse* 30 (1984), 17–38.

Steiner, George, *After Babel: Aspects of Language and Translation*, 2nd edn (Oxford: Oxford University Press, 1992).

Stendhal, Marie-Henri Beyle, *Racine et Shakespeare* (Paris: Bossange, 1823).

Sterne, Laurence, *Letters*, ed. by Lewis Perry Curtis (Oxford: Clarendon Press, 1935).

—— *Œuvres*, trans. by Frénais and La Beaume, 6 vols (Paris: Libraires Associés, 1797).

—— *A Sentimental Journey and Other Writings*, ed. by Thomas Keymer (London: Everyman, 1994).

—— *A Sentimental Journey through France and Italy*, ed. by Gardner D. Stout Jr (Berkeley: University of California Press, 1967).

—— *The Sermons of Mr. Yorick* (London: Dodsley, 1760).

—— *Suite de la vie et des opinions de Tristram Shandy*, trans. by Charles-François de Bonnay, 2 vols (York: Volland, 1785).

—— *Suite de la vie et des opinions de Tristram Shandy*, trans. by Bonnay, 2 vols (London [i.e. Paris: Cazin], 1785).

—— *Suite et fin de la vie et des opinions de Tristram Shandy, suivies de mélanges, lettres, pensées, bons-mots, & mémoires*, trans. by La Beaume, 2 vols (London [i.e. Paris: (?)]: [n. pub.], 1785).

—— *La Vie et les opinions de Tristram Shandy*, trans. by Frénais, 2 vols (York: Ruault, 1776).

—— *La Vie et les opinions de Tristram Shandy*, trans. by Frénais, 2 vols in 1 (York: Ruault, 1777).

—— *La Vie et les opinions de Tristram Shandy*, trans. by Frénais, 2 vols (London [i.e. Paris]: Cazin, 1784).
—— *Voyage sentimental*, trans. by Frénais, 2 vols (Amsterdam: Rey, and Paris: Gaugéry, 1769).
—— *Voyage sentimental*, trans. by Frénais and others (Paris: Didot le jeune, An VII/ 1799).
—— *Works*, ed. by Melvyn New (Gainesville: University Presses of Florida, 1978–).
Sterneiana, 21 vols (New York: Garland, 1974–5).
Stewart, Neil, *'Glimmerings of Wit': Laurence Sterne und die russische Literatur von 1790 bis 1840* (Heidelburg: Universitätsverlag Winter, 2005).
Streeter, Harold Wade, *The Eighteenth-Century English Novel in French Translation: A Bibliographical Study* (New York: Publications of the Institute of French Studies, 1963; rpt New York: Benjamin Blom, 1970).
Swift, Jonathan, *La Conte du tonneau*, trans. by Van Effen, 2 vols (The Hague: Scheurleer, 1721).
—— *A Tale of a Tub... to which is added An account of a battle between the antient and modern books in St. James's Library* (1704; Dublin: W. Smith, 1726).
—— *Voyages de Gulliver*, trans. by Desfontaines, 2 vols (The Hague: Gosse & Neaulme, 1727).
Szenczi, Miklós J., 'The Mimetic Principle in Later Eighteenth-Century Criticism', in *Studies in Eighteenth-Century Literature*, ed. by Miklós Szenczi and László Ferenczi (Budapest: Akadémiai Kiadó, 1974), pp. 9–54.
Tableau sentimental de la France depuis la Revolution, par Yoryck sous le nom de Sterne; pour servir de suite au Voyage sentimental, du même auteur (London [i.e. Paris (?)]: [n. pub.], 1792).
Texte, Joseph, *Jean-Jacques Rousseau et les origines du cosmopolitisme littéraire: Étude sur les relations littéraires de la France et de l'Angleterre au XVIIIe siècle* (Paris: Hachette, 1895).
Thiébaut de Berneaud, Arsenne, *Voyage à l'isle des peupliers* (Paris: Lepetit, An VII/1798–9).
Todd, Janet, *Sensibility: An Introduction* (London: Methuen, 1986).
Todorov, Tzvetan, *Introduction à la littérature fantastique* (Paris: Seuil, 1970).
Trahard, Pierre, *La Sensibilité révolutionnaire, 1789–1794* (Geneva: Slatkine Reprints, 1967).
Traugott, John, ed., *Laurence Sterne: A Collection of Critical Essays* (New Jersey: Prentice Hall, 1968).
—— *Tristram Shandy's World: Sterne's Philosophical Rhetoric* (Berkeley: University of California Press, 1954).
Trousson, Raymond, *Rousseau et sa fortune littéraire* (Paris: Nizet, 1977).
Van Sant, Ann Jessie, *Eighteenth-Century Sensibility and the Novel: The Senses in Social Context* (Cambridge: Cambridge University Press, 1993).
Van Teighem, Paul, *L'Année littéraire comme intermédiaire en France des littératures étrangères* (1914; rpt Geneva: Slatkine, 1966).
—— *Ossian en France* (Paris: Rieder, 1917).
Van Tieghem, Philippe, *Les Influences étrangères sur la littérature française, 1550–1880* (1961); 2nd edn (Paris: Presses Universitaires de France, 1967).
Vernes, François, *Le Voyageur sentimental en France sous Robespierre* (Geneva: Paschoud and Paris: Maradan: AnVII/1798–9).
—— *Le Voyageur sentimental, ou ma promenade à Yverdun* (London [i.e. Paris]: Cazin and Neufchâtel: Mourer, 1786; Paris: [n. pub.], 1792).

Vernière, Paul, *Lumières ou clair-obscur? Trente essais sur Diderot et quelques autres* (Paris: Presses Universitaires de France, 1987).
Voltaire, François-Marie Arouet, *Candide, ou l'Optimisme* (London [?]: [n. pub.], 1759).
—— 'Conscience', in *Questions sur l'Encyclopédie*, 3 vols ([n. pub.], 1770), II, pp. 71–80.
—— *Dictionnaire philosophique*, in *Œuvres complètes*, 52 vols (Paris: Garnier frères, 1877–85), XVIII (1878), pp. 234–40.
—— *Discours sur la tragedie*, in *Brutus* (1730; Amsterdam: Ledet & Co & Desbordes, 1731).
—— *Letters concerning the English Nation* (London: Davis & Lyon, 1733).
—— *Lettres philosophiques* (Amsterdam: Lucas, 1734).
—— *Œuvres complètes*, ed. by Theodore Besterman and others (Geneva: Institut et Musée Voltaire, and Oxford: Voltaire Foundation, 1970–).
Voogd, Peter de, 'Laurence Sterne in Dutch', *The Shandean* 5 (1993), 150–9.
—— 'Laurence Sterne, the Marbled Page, and the "Use of Accidents"', *Word and Image* I.3 (1985), 279–87.
Voogd, Peter de and John Neubauer, eds, *The Reception of Laurence Sterne in Europe*, Athlone Critical Traditions Series: The Reception of British and Irish Authors in Europe, ed. by Elinor Shaffer (London: Continuum, 2004).
Voogd, Peter de and David Pierce, eds, *Laurence Sterne in Modernism and Post Modernism*, Postmodern Studies, 15 (Amsterdam: Rodopi, 1996).
Wagner, J., 'L'Écriture du temps: une difficulté pour la presse périodique ancienne', in *Le Journalisme d'ancien régime* (Lyons: Presses Universitaires de Lyons, 1982).
Walsh, Marcus, ed., *Laurence Sterne*, Longman Critical Readers (London: Longman, 2002).
Warner, William B., *Licensing Entertainment: The Elevation of Novel Reading in Britain, 1684–1750* (Berkeley: University of California Press, 1998).
Warning, Rainer, *Illusion und Wirklichkeit in Tristram Shandy und Jacques le fataliste* (Munich: Fink Verlag, 1965).
Warton, Joseph, *Essay on the Writings and Genius of Pope* (London: Cooper, 1756).
Watt, Ian, *The Rise of the Novel: Studies in Defoe, Richardson and Fielding* (London: Chatto and Windus, 1957; London: Hogarth Press, 1987).
Weinbrot, Howard D., *Menippean Satire Reconsidered: From Antiquity to the Eighteenth Century* (Baltimore: Johns Hopkins University Press, 2005).
Weisz, Pierre, 'Le Réel et son double: la création romanesque dans *Jacques le fataliste*', *Diderot Studies* 19 (1978), 175–87.
Werner, Stephen, *Diderot's Great Scroll: Narrative Art in Jacques le fataliste*, SVEC 128 (Oxford: Voltaire Foundation, 1975).
West, C. B., 'La théorie de la traduction au XVIIIe siècle par rapport surtout aux traductions françaises d'ouvrages anglais', *Revue de littérature comparée* XII (1932), 330–55.
Wieland, Christoph Martin, *Histoire d'Agathon, ou Tableau philosphique des mœurs de la Grèce* (Lausanne: Grasset and Paris: De Hansy, 1768).
Wilcox, Frank Howard, *Prévost's Translations of Richardson's Novels* (Berkeley: University of California Press and London: Cambridge University Press, 1927).
Willey, Basil, *The Eighteenth Century Background: Studies in the Idea of Nature in the Thought of the Period* (1940; rpt London: Ark, 1986).
Williams, Ioan, ed., *Novel and Romance, 1700–1800: A Documentary Record* (London: Routledge & Kegan Paul, 1970).

Woolf, Virginia, 'Introduction', in *A Sentimental Journey*, The World's Classics (London: Oxford University Press, 1928).

Young, Edward, *Conjectures on Original Composition in a Letter to the Author of Sir Charles Grandison* (London: Millar and Dodsley, 1759).

—— *Conjectures sur la composition originale*, in *Œuvres diverses du Docteur Young*, trans. by Pierre Le Tourneur, 6 vols (Paris: Le Jay, 1770), III.

—— *Les Nuits d'Young*, trans. by Le Tourneur, 2 vols (Paris: Le Jay, 1769).

Zuber, Roger, *Les Belles Infidèles et la formation du goût classique: Perrot d'Ablancourt et Guez de Balzac* (Paris: Armand Colin, 1968).

Zwanenveld, Agnes, 'Laurens Sterne in Holland: The Eighteenth-Century', *The Shandean* 5 (1993), 125–49.

Index

abridgement of text 76, 79, 84
Addison, Joseph 42
D'Alembert, Jean le Rond 54–7, 97
Andrieux, J. S. 109
anglomanie 27, 57–8
Année littéraire 13–14, 33–9, 57–8
Aristotle 11, 14, 124
Arnaud, Abbé 13
Auroux, Sylvain 52

Bakhtin, Mikhail 3, 4, 24, 109, 117
Balzac, Guez de 20, 21, 58
Bandry, Anne 5
Barton, Francis Brown 5
Battestin, Martin C. 91
Batteux, Charles 15–16
Beauzée, Nicolas 53, 56, 59–60
Becket, Thomas 115
Beebee, Thomas 59–60
Bell, Michael 87, 89, 92
belles infidèles tradition 58, 62
Bissy, Comte de 31–2
Blanchard, Pierre 89, 94–7, 103, 107
Boileau, Despréaux 14, 15–16, 21, 37–8
Bonnay, Charles François de 36, 63, 70, 74–84, 89, 131
Booth, Wayne C. 3, 23
Bray, René 14
Brewer, Daniel 120, 121
Brissenden, R.F. 87
Brooke, Frances Moore 64–5
Brune, Guillaume 88
Buffon, Comte de 31
burlesque writing 12, 20–2, 23, 26, 113
Burton, Robert 3, 24, 60, 112, 113

Cash, Arthur 111

Corneille, 27
Censer, Jack 12
censorship 38, 66, 68
Cervantes, Miguel de 23, 73, 94, 110
  Don Quixote 3, 23, 109, 110, 112, 116
  La Galatea 60
Chambers's *Cyclopædia* 113
Chapelain 20
chapter divisions 68–9, 73, 76
chapter titles 73, 76–7
Chaucer, Geoffrey 115
classicism 2, 11–12, 14–17, 18–21, 26, 27, 41, 64–6, 83, 115
  classical gardens 105
  classical views of translation 64–6, 83
  classical works 51, 52
Coleridge, Samuel Taylor 2
Conti, Prince de 31–2
Coudreuse, Anne 87
Craddock, Joseph 111
Crébillon, Claude-Prosper Jolyot 2, 31, 39
  Les Égarements du cœur et de l'esprit 39
Croft, Stephen 89

Damin, Louis 103, 104–7
Deffand, Madame du 97
Defoe, Daniel 3
Denby, David 87, 89–90
Desfontaines, Abbé 37–8
Desmarets de Saint Sorlin, Jean 20, 37
Diderot, Denis 7, 31, 46, 61–2, 97, 107, 109–25
  Ceci n'est pas un conte 116
  Eloge de Richardson 46, 61–2, 116
  Jacques le fataliste xi, 7–8, 107, 109–26
  Le Fils naturel 116

Le Neveu de Rameau 35, 142 n.32
Le Rêve de d'Alembert 97, 121
Paradoxe sur le comédien 142 n.32
Draper, Eliza 31

eccentricity 29–35, 70, 72, 73, 77, 105, 112, 118
Encyclopédie, the 18–19, 25, 52–6
encyclopédistes, 12, 56
Ermenonville 105–7
Eustace, John 2
expectations of readers 6–7, 11, 21, 46, 51, 60, 63, 66, 70, 73, 81, 83, 120, 123, 126

fatalism 110, 121–2
Feraud, Abbé 33
Ferriar, John 80, 112, 113
fideism 3, 11
Fielding, Henry 3, 23, 56, 59, 62, 73
  Tom Jones 116
Florian, Jean-Pierre Claris de 60
Florida edition 3, 112
footnotes, use of 75, 84
Francis I 68
Fredman, Alice Green 5, 109–10
Frénais, Joseph-Pierre 13, 26, 29, 31, 33, 40, 63–73, 74, 75, 76, 81, 83, 84
Fréron, Elie-Catherine 13
Frye, Northrop 23–4
Furetière, Antoine 20, 23
  Le Roman bourgeois 116

Garat, Dominique-Joseph 29, 32, 34, 35
Garrick, David 32
Gazette de France 13
Gazette littéraire de l'Europe 13
Genette, Gérard 12
Geoffroy, Julien-Louis 60–1
gesture 35, 39, 81, 82
Girardin, René-Louis, Marquis de 105
Gomberville, Marin Le Roy de 20, 37
Gorjy, Jean-Claude 101–3, 107
gothicism 102, 106–7
grammar, universality of 52–6, 64
Grand Tour 29, 70, 81, 111, 118

Green, F. C. 5
Grimm, Frédéric-Melchior 57
Guibert, Comte de 97

Hall, Joseph 115
Henri IV 35, 79
Hertford, Lord 31
Hogarth, William 113
d'Holbach, Baron 31
Homer 1, 18, 22, 117
Horace 11, 14–17, 22, 26, 38, 117–18, 124
Howes, Alan B. 4
Huet, Daniel 38

imagination 4, 7, 15–20, 22, 29, 37–8, 40–4, 45, 46, 94–7, 99, 103, 107
imitation 4–5, 7, 8, 14, 15, 18, 19, 36, 40–1, 56, 58, 60, 64, 72, 82, 88–9, 90, 97, 100, 102, 107, 109–10, 111–15, 116

Jaeger, Johann 26
Jaquin, Armand-Pierre 61
Jauss, Hans Robert 5–7, 126
Jefferson, D.W. 3, 23
Johnson, Samuel 2
Journal anglais 12–13, 17
Journal de Paris 12, 17, 36
Journal encyclopédique 13, 14, 17, 20, 21, 25, 30, 33, 34, 36–7, 43, 76

Kavanagh, Thomas 109
Keymer, Thomas 3
Kirk, Eugene 23
Kundera, Milan 109

La Beaume, Antoine-Gilbert Griffet de 36, 63, 70, 74–80, 83–4
La Calprenède 20, 37
La Place, Pierre-Antoine de 2, 56, 59–60, 83
Lafayette, Madame de 4
Lamb, Jonathan 113
language, science of 52–6, 59
Latitudinarianism 91–2, 113

Le Tourneur, Pierre 27, 40–4, 62, 105–6
'learned wit' tradition 3–4, 23–6
Lefevere, André 51
Lenglet-Dufresnoy, Nicolas 38
Lespinasse, Julie de 6, 97–100, 101, 102, 107
Locke, John 3, 23, 55, 72, 112, 115, 118–19
Longinus 113
Louis XIV 2

McMorran, William 110, 125
Mallet du Pan, Jacques 39, 81, 82–3
Marivaux, Pierre Carlet de Chamblain de 2, 23, 38–9
  La Vie de Marianne 38–9
  Pharsamon 116
Marmontel, Jean-François 54–6
Mauzi, Robert 109, 123
May, Georges 37–8, 62
Mercure de France 13, 17, 31, 36–9, 82–3
Montaigne, Michel Eyquem de 1, 3, 110, 112, 113
Montandon, Alain 4–5
Montesquieu, Charles-Louis de Secondat 34
Morellet, Abbé 31
Mortier, Roland 41–2
Mullan, John 87–8, 92, 96
Mylne, Vivienne 123

narrator, 3, 23, 30, 36, 45, 81, 82, 89, 90, 93, 94, 98, 116, 119–25
New, Melvyn 3, 91–2
Nietzsche, Friedrich 2
nouvelle form 4
Norris, John 115
novels as a genre 2, 3–6, 11–12, 15, 23–4, 27, 29, 31, 34, 36–40, 45–6, 51, 56–60, 62, 87, 109–10 115–26
Nuttall, A. D. 117

Oates, J. C. T. 4
originality 4, 7, 11, 12, 14, 17–22, 25, 30, 32–5, 36–7, 40–7, 66, 70–3, 74, 75, 83, 93, 110, 111–15, 120
Orléans, Duc d' 31–2

Panckoucke, Charles-Joseph 13
Parisot, Jules-Octave-Frédéric 63
Parisot, Valentin 63–4
Parnell, J.T. 3, 11
Pascal, Blaise 18
pathos 87–90
Pellisson 20
periodicals, 11, 12–14, 17, 19, 31, 32, 35, 36, 83
philosophes 11–14, 29, 31, 46, 52, 54, 91, 126
Pitt, George 31
Pitt, William 76
plagiarism 111–15
Pope, Alexander 21, 56, 110, 113, 115
Port-Royal grammarians 52, 53
Praslin, Duc de 13
pre-understanding of literature 6–7
Prévost d'Exiles, Antoine-François 2, 56–62, 83, 110
  translations of Richardson 56
Puisieux, Philippe-Florent de 62

Rabelais, François 3, 18, 22–7, 36, 65, 73, 77, 91, 109, 110, 112, 113, 116
Racine 27
Raynal, Guillaume Thomas 31, 75, 92
Reuchlin, Johannes 26
rêveries 90, 94, 96, 103, 105, 106
Rex, Walter E. 110
Riccoboni, Madame 62
Richardson, Samuel 3, 46–7, 56, 58–9, 60–2, 116, 122
Robinet, Jean Baptiste René 65
Roelens, Maurice 109
Rousseau, Jean-Jacques 1, 7, 44–5, 62, 88, 93, 94, 103–7
Rousseau, Pierre 14
Rutledge, James 88

Saint-Amans, Florimond Boudon de 88
Saint-Simon, Louis de Rouvroy 56

salon 31, 35, 97, 99, 100, 107
satire 3, 4, 20, 21, 22–25, 43, 67, 68, 89, 102, 112, 116
 Menippean satire 3, 22–5, 26 *see also Satyre ménippée*
Satyre ménippée 22–5
Scarron, Paul 20, 21, 22, 22, 23, 26, 73, 110
 Le Roman comique 24, 116
scepticism 3, 11
Scudéry, George de 20, 37
Scudéry, Madelaine de 20, 37
Seidel, Michael 3
A Sentimental Journey through France and Italy 1–8, 11–13, 17, 29, 30, 31, 32–4, 43–7, 63, 64, 75, 81, 87–90, 91, 93, 94, 95, 98–101, 107, 111–12, 126
sentimentalism 2, 3, 7, 12, 29, 30, 31, 44–5, 47, 82, 87, 88, 90, 92, 94, 96, 97, 100, 102, 107, 113, 116
Sermons (Sterne) 12, 17, 25, 36, 113–15
Shaftesbury, Earl of 91
Shakespeare, William 27, 112–13
The Shandean 4
Sharp, John 115
Shklovsky, Viktor 2–3, 119
Simon, Ernest 110, 125
slang, use of 66
Smith, Adam 96
Smollett, Tobias 30, 31
Sommery, Mademoiselle de 45, 91
Sorel, Charles 20, 23
Spencer, Viscount 76
spurious text 4, 26, 57, 81, 82–3
Stewart, Neil 4–5
Streeter, Harold Wade 5
Suard, Amélie 44–7, 87
Suard, Antoine Jean-Baptiste 6, 13, 22, 25, 31, 34–5
Swift, Jonathan 3, 11, 22, 23, 24, 26, 36, 112

Tableau sentimental 88, 89, 90–3, 94, 107
Thackeray, William Makepeace 2
Tillotson, John 115
translation 7, 13, 29–31, 36, 40–1, 51–6; of English literature 56–60; new conception of 60–2; of *Tristram Shandy* 63–84
Traugott, John 3, 119
Tristram Shandy 1–7, 12–22, 25–7, 29–30, 36–9, 43, 51, 87–91, 97, 109–20, 126; translation of 63–84
typography 70–3, 75, 76–8, 83

Van Sant, Ann Jessie 87
Van Tieghem, Philippe 5
Vaugelas 20
Vernes, François 89, 93–4, 103, 107
Vincent-Buffault, Anne 87
Volland, Sophie 115
Voltaire, François-Marie Arouet 2, 6, 12, 13, 21, 24, 25–7, 29, 65, 110
 Candide 157 n.32
 Lettres philosophiques 2, 27
 Questions sur l'Encyclopédie 25
volumes, divisions between 69–70, 73, 76, 81
von Hutton, Ulrich 26
voyages sentimentaux 87, 89–90, 104–7, 109

Walker, Obadiah 112–13
Walpole, Horace 140 n.77
Warburton, Bishop 140 n.77
Warning, Rainer 110
Wellek, René 11
Wharton, Joseph 110
Wilcox, F. H. 60
Woolf, Virginia 2

Xenophon 113

Young, Edward 40–3, 65